African civilizations

By the same author

The archaeology of Benin: excavations and other researches in and around Benin City, Nigeria (Oxford University Press, 1975)

Three thousand years in Africa: Man and his environment in the Lake Chad region of Nigeria (Cambridge University Press, 1981)

African civilizations

*Precolonial cities and states
in tropical Africa:
an archaeological perspective*

Graham Connah

*University of New England
Armidale, N.S.W., Australia*

Drawings by Douglas Hobbs

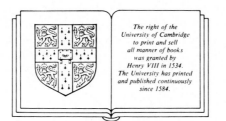

The right of the
University of Cambridge
to print and sell
all manner of books
was granted by
Henry VIII in 1534.
The University has printed
and published continuously
since 1584.

Cambridge University Press

Cambridge
London   New York   New Rochelle
Melbourne   Sydney

Published by the Press Syndicate of the University of Cambridge
The Pitt Building, Trumpington Street, Cambridge CB2 1RP
32 East 57th Street, New York, NY 10022, USA
10 Stamford Road, Oakleigh, Melbourne 3166, Australia

First published 1987

Printed in Great Britain at
the University Press, Cambridge

British Library cataloguing in publication data
Connah, Graham
African civilizations: precolonial cities
and states in tropical Africa: an
archaeological perspective.
1. Africa – Antiquities
I. Title
960'.1   DT13
Library of Congress cataloguing in publication data

Connah, Graham.
African civilizations.
Bibliography: p.
Includes index.
1. Man, Prehistoric – Africa, Sub-Saharan.   2. Africa,
Sub-Saharan – Antiquities.   3. Africa, Sub-Saharan –
Civilization.   I. Title.
GN865.S87C66   1987   967   86-32745

National Library of Australia cataloguing in publication data
Connah, Graham.
African civilizations.
Bibliography.
Includes index.
1. Africa – Civilization. 2. Africa – Antiquities.
3. Africa, Eastern – Civilization. 4. Africa, Eastern
– Antiquities. 5. Africa, Sub-Saharan – Civilization.
6. Africa, Sub-Saharan – Antiquities. I. Hobbs,
Douglas. II. Title.
960

ISBN 0 521 26666 1 hardcovers
ISBN 0 521 31992 7 paperback

SE

Contents

Figures

Preface and acknowledgements

In the last quarter of a century there has been a great number of publications concerned with the archaeology of tropical Africa over the last 3000 years or so. Most of these publications have been highly specialized, however, and it has been apparent to me, as a researcher and teacher in archaeology, that a large part of the reading public of the English-speaking world still has little understanding of the achievements of precolonial tropical African societies. One of the longest-lived and most inaccurate stereotypes has been the vague general notion that such societies consisted only of scattered groups of people living in small villages of grass or mud 'huts'. This book has been written as a synthesis of some of the main archaeological evidence that shows that this was not the case. The much debated word 'civilization' is used in its title as a reminder that tropical Africa *also* attained cultural complexity of a high order. The book is about the material evidence for cities and states, because it is on these that discussion can be most readily focussed. Its aim is to reach a wide range of readers and yet also to be of help to students and teachers of later African archaeology. With these intentions in mind, this book has been substantially illustrated and it is also fully referenced. Working from a base in Australia, my main difficulty has been obtaining the more recently published research results but everything possible has been done to ensure that the book was up to date at the time of going to press.

The book was written between June 1983 and March 1985 and revised in November 1985. It was written on the suggestion of Dr Jeremy Mynott and Dr Robin Derricourt of Cambridge University Press and I am particularly grateful to the latter for his encouragement and help throughout its preparation. I am also grateful to Dr David Phillipson of the University of Cambridge who read and commented on the first draft of the book and to the following scholars who were similarly helpful with respect to the chapters indicated: Professor Bill Adams of the University of Kentucky (Chapter 3); Professor J.W. Michels of Pennsylvania State University (Chapter 4); Drs R.J. and S.K. McIntosh of Rice University, Houston, Texas (Chapter 5); Professor Nicholas David of the University of Calgary (Chapter 6); Dr John Sutton of The British Institute in Eastern Africa, Nairobi (Chapter 7); Professor T.N. Huffman of the University of the Witwatersrand, Johannesburg (Chapter 8); Dr Pierre de Maret of the

Musée Royal de l'Afrique Centrale, Tervuren, Belgium (Chapter 9); Professor Thurstan Shaw of Cambridge, England (Chapter 10). To all these people I owe an enormous debt of gratitude for their assistance in correcting errors and filling in gaps. Any shortcomings which remain in the book are entirely my responsibility.

There are many others whose help has been essential. Douglas Hobbs of the Department of Prehistory and Archaeology, University of New England, prepared the line drawings and Rudi Boskovic and Steve Clarke of the Department of Geography of the same University did the photography of those drawings. Mrs Gibbons of Cambridge typed the first draft of the book and Noelene Kachel, of the University of New England, put the whole thing onto a word processor to allow for its subsequent revision. Di Watson, Secretary to the Department of Prehistory and Archaeology, University of New England, did more things to help than I can remember. Sue Pearson of Tamworth, N.S.W., assisted with the checking of the typescript.

Acknowledgement is also due to Dr A.T. Grove of the African Studies Centre, University of Cambridge, for providing working space when I was on study leave in Cambridge in 1983. My time as a Research Associate of that Centre was most important for the early stages of the writing of this book. During that same period I was also greatly helped by Dr John Alexander of the Department of Archaeology, University of Cambridge, to whom I am indebted for many discussions and for numerous loans of relevant publications.

Similarly, I am grateful to Professor Francis Van Noten of the Musée Royal de l'Afrique Centrale, Tervuren, Belgium, who made me welcome during a brief visit I made to Tervuren in search of reference material. His hospitality and that of Dr Pierre de Maret and his wife is remembered with great pleasure.

I would like to add a special word here for the Interlibrary Loan Service of the Dixson Library in the University of New England. Without the consistent efforts of its staff, I could not have obtained much of the published material that was used. They got it from all over Australia, from Britain, from Germany, from America, from Zimbabwe, and from quite a few places that I have forgotten. In particular, Luise Wissman of that service earned my gratitude many times over.

As stated above, the line illustrations were drawn by Douglas Hobbs but in a book of this nature such illustrations have had to be based in the main on material already published. The sources of each line drawing are given in the captions. Some were heavily based on one source only, others on several sources, but almost all of them are modified by additions or simplifications or changes in lettering to render them more suitable for the purposes of this book. I acknowledge the original authors and artists concerned, for providing such a rich resource of illustration material. The photographs in the book come from a variety of sources. The Cambridge University Library provided Figures 3.4, 6.1, 6.2, 7.9, 9.1, and 9.2. The British Museum provided Figures 4.6 and 6.8. Dr Pierre de Maret of the Musée Royal de l'Afrique Centrale, Belgium, provided Figures

9.4 and 9.5. Professor T.N. Huffman, of the University of the Witwatersrand provided Figures 8.3 and 8.7. Professor Frank Willett of the Hunterian Museum, Glasgow, provided Figure 6.3. The Department of Photography of The University of New England provided Figure 5.6, which was rephotographed from *Man*, Volume 43, 1943. The same Department also provided Figure 5.7, which is rephotographed from *National Geographic*, September 1982. All these photographs are reproduced with permission and details are given in the captions.

I would also like to record the fact that I dedicate this book to Nora Fisher McMillan of the Merseyside County Museums, Liverpool, England, who many years ago introduced me to the world of scientific research.

Finally, to my wife Beryl I owe an enormous debt of gratitude that cannot be measured but must be recorded.

Graham Connah
Department of Prehistory and Archaeology,
University of New England,
Armidale, N.S.W., Australia

March, 1986

To Nora Fisher McMillan

Chapter 1
Introduction

Take out your atlas and find a map of the African continent, preferably one devoted to physical geography. If you are fortunate, your atlas may also contain a good map of African vegetation: find that also. Coded into those two maps is important information that you will need to understand before reading this book. To begin with, Africa is huge; it is so big that you can put the United States of America and the Australian continent into it and still have a bit of space left over. It extends from about 37° North to about 35° South, and has an altitudinal range from depressions that are below sea level to mountain peaks that exceed 5000 metres. As a result it has an incredible diversity of environments. It contains some of the driest deserts in the world, and yet has three of the world's major rivers: the Nile, the Niger and the Congo. Some of the hottest places on earth are in Africa, and yet there are glaciers on its highest mountains. There are steaming rainforests and dry savanna grasslands, low-lying river valleys and high plateaus, extensive deserts and gigantic lakes, mangrove coasts and surf-pounded beaches. This is to give only an impressionistic picture of the very large number of differing environments to be found in the African continent. In reality the major zones merge into one another, so that there is an even greater variety of conditions. Add to this the effects of climatic variation through time and you have an infinitely complex environmental situation.

Into this environmental kaleidoscope introduce human beings and remember that they have been in Africa probably longer than in any other part of the world. For perhaps two million years, or more (depending on how humanity is defined), people have been learning how to get the best out of African environments. Those environments have not determined what men and women could do, nor have the latter been able to ignore the environments in which they have lived. Instead there has been a dynamic relationship between the two, in which human beings have sought to turn to their advantage the opportunities offered by each environment and to come to terms with its constraints. This relationship can be traced throughout the long course of human history in Africa. First as scavengers and gatherers; then as hunters, gatherers and fishers who gradually intensified their exploitation of available resources; then as pastoralists and cultivators; eventually as city dwellers, artisans and traders: men and women have continued to interact with their environment. Geographical location; seasonality of climate; water availability; soil fertility; grass species; access to resources such as timber, stone, clay, minerals, and animal products; and disease vectors. These are merely some of the factors that have helped to shape human culture and which in many cases have themselves been affected by human activity. If you seek to study the history of Africa, you must understand human ecology.

Without doubt, you must also understand archaeology, which is a major source of information about Africa's past. Documentary sources for African history are limited: their coverage is often chronologically patchy and tends to be geographically peripheral. For large areas of Africa, particularly tropical Africa, their time-depth is restricted to the last century or two. In addition, many of the documentary sources that we do have are based on the observations of outsiders; such people as explorers, traders, missionaries, colonial officers and others, who did not always understand what they observed. Such documentary evidence that does exist is often invaluable but Africanist historians themselves have acknowledged its shortcomings for many areas, by giving considerable attention to oral sources of history. Extensive research has been conducted into oral traditions in many parts of the continent and our knowledge of African history has been greatly enriched by these endeavours. However, although it is a matter of some dispute, it seems unlikely that oral sources can throw much light on periods more than say 500 years ago. In these circumstances, scholars interested in Africa's past have turned to a variety of other information sources. Thus, art history and linguistics have contributed useful information, as have ethnographic and anthropological investigations. In addition, a number of other disciplines have been of assistance, such as blood group studies, plant genetics, and faunal research of one sort or another. It is in these circumstances that the archaeological evidence for Africa's past has assumed the very greatest importance.

Many people who are not archaeologists are uncertain about what archaeology is. As for archaeologists themselves, they have spent a lot of time over the last few decades arguing about it. Basically, however, the subject is concerned with the study of the material remains of past human activities, in their original context, in order to reconstruct those activities. Such a reconstruction, it is hoped, will enable us to understand the undocumented past or to increase our understanding of inadequately documented periods of the past. Archaeological evidence, however, has its own strengths and weaknesses and we are still learning ways of gaining the maximum reliable information from it. Perhaps its greatest advantage is that it enables us to examine things that were actually made by the people of the past that we seek to study and to investigate the impact that those people had on their environment. We can discover what human beings actually did, not merely what they or others said that they did. The main disadvantage of archaeological evidence is that it is almost always partial evidence, reflecting only part of the activities of past men and women.

The differential effects of human behaviour, of climate and soil chemistry, and of subsequent disturbance by either natural or human agencies, cause most archaeological evidence to be rather like a jigsaw puzzle from which two-thirds of the pieces are lost, whilst the rest have the picture worn off or corners missing. These strengths and weaknesses of archaeological evidence can be seen in this book. On the middle Nile and in the Ethiopian Highlands we have the remains of stone-built cities and clear indications of centralized authority and we would not know much about this if we were dependent on historical sources alone. In Central Africa, on the other hand, archaeology has been able to contribute little information on urban settlements that were constructed in grass, wood and other organic materials and occupied by people who did not express their sense of nationhood in a material fashion that could leave us evidence. Unfortunately, however, archaeological evidence has another drawback: it results from human endeavour, and archaeologists (just like other human beings) tend to vary in the amount of effort that they expend on different problems. Thus it is easy to search for settlement sites in the open grasslands of the African savanna but extremely difficult to do so in the tangled undergrowth of the rainforest, where in places one has to chop out a path even to walk through it. Similarly, it is easier to locate the sites of stone ruins than it is those of timber buildings and it is easier to excavate mud-brick structures than those of pisé. As a result, archaeological distribution maps of Africa tend to show the distribution and intensity of archaeological research, rather than the distribution of archaeological evidence. Indeed, for extensive areas of the continent one might just as well write the word 'unexplored' across such archaeological maps, just as was done a century and a half ago with so many maps of Africa.

Despite these problems, archaeology is very good for certain things. No longer merely concerned with putting artefacts in museum cases, archaeologists have turned their attention to the study of human behaviour and its change through time. This is as it should be, for over a long time-scale it is probably only they who can throw much light on when and how and why human societies changed in the way that they did. In this book, for instance, an attempt has been made to assess how much archaeology can tell us about the growth of cities and the development of states in tropical Africa. The purpose is not to dispute with historians or social anthropologists or sociologists or geographers, who already have their own ideas, but to evaluate the archaeological data and to determine what it has to contribute to the debates on these issues. In the process of doing this, it will also become apparent that archaeologists have not always asked the right questions and that future archaeological fieldwork will need more carefully thought-out research designs.

As has already been stated, human beings have been in Africa for perhaps two million years but for most of that time they scavenged, collected, hunted and fished for their food and there were probably few of them, widely scattered across the landscape. The outlines of African prehistory (Phillipson 1985) are still far from clear but it appears to have been only about 100 000 years ago that human societies began to diversify in ways that allowed them to adapt to virtually all of the varied African environments. As a result, it is likely that the size of some individual groups increased and that overall population levels rose. This led to increasing pressure on food resources, which during the period between about 18 000 and about 7000 years ago resulted in an intensification of exploitation strategies, such as the harvesting of grass seed, the manufacture of specialized fishing equipment, and possibly the development of management techniques over herds of wild animals. These changes did not take place everywhere, nor did they all take place at the same time but they are known to have occurred at various dates during this overall period, in parts of what is now the Sahara, in parts of the Nile Valley, and in some areas of the high savanna lands of East Africa. It seems likely that it was these changes that then led to the development of food production, which was well under way in the northern half of Africa by about the sixth millennium BC. Thus Africans have been farmers for less than half of one per cent of their history but the development of farming has had a major accelerating effect on the evolution of human culture and particularly on social organization. The domestication of sorghum, millet, *tef*, African rice, wheat, barley, yam, and a host of plants of lesser importance, plus the domestication of cattle, sheep and goats has had the most profound effect on the growth of human populations, on the densities of population that could be maintained and on the growth of human sedentism. This is not the place to discuss the extent to which the development of food production in Africa resulted from local experimentation and the extent to which it was stimulated by influences from South-West Asia. However, the evidence available at the present time seems to indicate that plant domestication was generally an indigenous achievement but that most animal domestication, at least of sheep and goats, resulted from Asiatic initiatives. Whatever the truth of the matter, it is in the context of the development of African farming that all subsequent changes in the continent must be seen.

One of the most important of these changes, in the opinion of many archaeologists, was the adoption of iron metallurgy, which in Africa was taking place from about the middle of the first millennium BC onwards. So great was the impact of this development on both the means of production and the means of destruction during later African prehistory, that archaeologists have tended to emphasize it almost to the exclusion of other considerations. Thus has come into use the phrase: 'the African Iron Age', terminology that is difficult to apply chronologically and which distracts attention from more important changes that were occurring in some African societies. We still do not know anything like enough about these but it would seem that over the last 3000–4000 years or more there was a rapid growth of intergroup dependence. This was probably brought about by a combination of increasing sedentism, ecological diversity, and an uneven distribution of resources. Certain animal and plant products, salt, copper, iron and other commodities began to be exchanged between different population centres and it was into such exchange networks that long-distance trade, both within and outside of Africa, was eventually able to tap. At the local level, such intergroup dependence encouraged a complex interaction between individual settlements, so that some became larger and more important than others and in time came to control all the other settlements in their immediate region. At the same time there was increasing specialization and social stratification amongst the people living in the larger settlements. It was in some such manner that there emerged in certain parts of Africa the cities and states that are the subject of this book. For such there were in tropical Africa before the advent of nineteenth-century colonialism. Neither urbanization nor nationhood were ideas grafted onto Africa from modern Europe, as some might prefer to think. Particularly was this not so for tropical Africa and this book is an archaeologist's attempt to explain how and why this came to be the case.

Chapter 2
Concepts and questions

There were cities and states in tropical Africa long before the colonial ambitions of European peoples transformed that continent. The appearance of such cities and states was one of the most significant developments of tropical Africa's history prior to the colonial experience. It is also a development that has had relatively little attention from world-wide scholarship, although there does exist a substantial *specialist* academic literature on the subject. Outside Africa itself there persists, amongst people in general, a deeply ingrained conviction that precolonial tropical Africa consisted only of scattered villages of mud or grass huts, their inhabitants subsisting on shifting cultivation or semi-nomadic pastoralism. What is more surprising, and more disturbing, is that this sort of stereotype seems also to have had some effect upon scholars considering the emergence of cities and states as global phenomena. For example, in 1978 the Wolfson Lectures at the University of Oxford were devoted to the subject 'The origins of civilization' but in their published version at least (Moorey 1979) they contained no discussion of African developments other than those in Egypt. At a more popular level, a recent book entitled *The encyclopedia of ancient civilizations* (Cotterell 1983) similarly excludes Africa (except, of course, for Egypt) although it does include West Asia, India, Europe, China, and America. Yet such a coverage is liberal indeed compared with what would have been acceptable thirty or forty years ago. Gordon Childe was perhaps the most important exponent of an academic tradition that saw the origins of civilization as the origins of European culture. Glyn Daniel has described how he once asked Childe why he did not give more attention to the American civilizations. Childe's answer was characteristically terse and to the point: 'Never been there – peripheral and highly suspect' (Daniel 1968: 142–3). Could it be that the continued exclusion of tropical Africa from general discussions of world civilization represents a survival of this sort of attitude?

Definitions of 'civilization' and 'city'

Certainly, many of those who omit tropical African civilizations from their discussions have never been there, either in reality or in the literature, and the probability that they feel African examples to be peripheral and suspect can be understood, if not condoned, when one considers some of the definitions that have been given to the word 'civilization'. It is clear that Childe and many of his generation thought that one of the essential elements in any definition of 'civilization' was the existence of writing (Childe 1951: 161) and an interesting discussion developed in the pages of the archaeological journal *Antiquity* in the 1950s, when Kathleen Kenyon, Sir Mortimer Wheeler and O.G.S. Crawford, writing separately, described the evidence from preliterate levels at Jericho in Jordan as throwing new light on the beginnings of civilization (Kenyon 1956; Wheeler 1956; Crawford 1956). Childe speedily objected to their use of the word 'civilization', claiming that there was no alternative to the choosing of writing 'as marking the critical point' (Childe 1957: 37). Wheeler, it may be noticed, was more flexible in his definition and preferred to regard writing 'as a secondary consequence of civic life'. He went on to suggest a definition consisting of 'the two inherent elements of civilization':

1) A settled community of a size sufficient to support specialists outside the normal range of food-production.
2) Public works and needs implying an organized and durable administration. (Wheeler 1956: 132)

It is apparent that these writers thought that 'civilization' implied cities, and vice versa. The problem was: just how could they define a 'city' and how could they tell it apart from a 'town'. After remarking that: 'The concept of "city" is notoriously hard to define', Childe had gone on to do just that, producing in the process a list of conditions that must be met before a city could be said to exist (Childe 1950: 3, 9–16). For long known to university students as 'Childe's ten points', these criteria were clearly influenced by the circumstances of city development and state formation in South-West Asia, and, like Childe's definition of 'civilization', they were as a result of only limited value in other parts of the world.

It seems to have been an increasing interest in those other parts of the world, including Africa, which necessitated the subsequent abandonment of some of the more Eurocentric views of the 1950s. On the one hand, less prescriptive definitions of the terms 'civilization' and 'city' were suggested; and, on the other hand, there developed a greater sophistication in the discussion of the historical processes which had produced these phenomena that were so difficult to define. A tendency towards less prescriptive definitions can already be seen in that of Wheeler quoted above, but Clyde Kluckhohn's definition of 1960 achieved far more attention. Kluckhohn implied that a society could be said to be civilized if it had at least two of the following: towns of upward of, say, 5000 inhabitants, a written language, and monumental ceremonial centres (Kluckhohn 1960: 400). It would be inappropriate, if not impossible, to examine here all of the attempts to define 'civilization' that have been made in recent decades. Nevertheless, one that is perhaps the least prescriptive, the furthest removed from the narrow rigour of Childe's definition, is that of Colin Renfrew. 'Civilization', he wrote, 'is the self-made environment of man, which he has fashioned to insulate himself from the primaeval environment of nature alone' (Renfrew 1972: 11). This definition is so generalized that some readers found themselves wondering if it might just as well stand as a definition of 'culture' but Renfrew did qualify his definition by adding that it was 'not an operational one' and that 'defining criteria such as Kluckhohn's' had to be added to it (Renfrew 1972: 13).

As with the term 'civilization', so also the term 'city' has come to be less prescriptively defined since the 1950s. Thus, Gideon Sjoberg attempted to distinguish between 'preindustrial' and 'industrial' cities, seeing 'preindustrial' cities as ones to which, for instance, both agriculture and kinship ties were still of importance (Sjoberg 1960). Thus also Lewis Mumford, as traditionalist in his association of 'cities' with 'civilization' as was Sjoberg, questioned the 'overparticularized definition of the city' (Mumford 1961: 85). Indeed, some definitions had moved so far away from prescriptive criteria that they were in danger of being overgeneralized. For example, Beaujeu-Garnier and Chabot (1967: 30) could write that: 'In each country a town can be said to exist if the people of the district feel themselves to be in a town'; and E. Jones (1966:5) could claim that: 'A town is what is implied by the local people when they call a locality a town'. So generalized are these definitions that it seems pointless to discuss their use of the word 'town' rather than 'city', and Alexander (1972: 843–4), in citing these statements, declined to comment on that aspect.

Scholars from a variety of disciplines have attempted to define 'civilization' and 'city'. To mention only the more obvious, there have been historians, geographers, anthropologists, sociologists, archaeologists and political theorists. This concern with definition has not been merely a matter of semantics: implicit in the definitions suggested there has often been a real concern with process, that is to say: how did 'civilization' emerge, how did 'cities' develop? Gradually, this concern with process has come to occupy more attention than the problems of definition, and discussion of this whole subject has become increasingly sophisticated. The term 'civilization' has been quietly abandoned by many writers, it is too vague a concept and too subjective to be useful. It also has unpleasant connotations that are at best ethnocentric and at worst egocentric. It implies an 'us' and 'them' situation: we are 'civilized', they are 'uncivilized' or (to use a word that were best dead and buried) they are 'primitive'. Instead, there has been an increasing tendency to investigate what is often called 'the rise of complex society' and to study as virtually separate entities the processes of urbanization and of state formation. Indeed, the rise of the state has come to be seen as central to the emergence of 'complex societies', although some anthropologists would object to the use of the word 'complex' and prefer instead to speak of 'stratified societies' or even, perhaps, of 'pluralistic societies' (the latter term as defined by Kuper and Smith 1969: 3–4).

8

In recent years there has been much discussion of what has been called 'the anthropology of political evolution', to which the volumes by Cohen and Service (1978) and Claessen and Skalník (1978) provide a substantial introduction. The general tendency in such discussion, however, has been towards theoretical considerations and much of the evidence that has been considered has been drawn either from historical sources or from ethnographic observations in the recent past. It has been difficult to relate such theories to archaeological evidence, which makes the book by Jonathan Haas (1982) particularly important, because this is one of the things that he has tried to do.

State-formation theories

Haas has entitled his book: *The evolution of the prehistoric state*, and in it he provides a useful resumé of the literature of state-formation theory, a modified theory of his own, and a discussion of how his modified theory might be used in the interpretation of archaeological data. At the beginning of the book he defines the word 'state' as meaning 'a society in which there is a centralized and specialized institution of government' (Haas 1982: 3) and he then proceeds to examine the various ways in which scholars have attempted to explain the emergence of such societies. He groups these explanations into two general schools of thought: what he calls the 'conflict' school and the 'integration' school (p. 15). Theories which belong to the conflict school argue that 'the state evolved in response to conflict between unequal social classes' and that 'the state is [a] physically repressive governing institution, which serves a basic function of protecting the privileged position of a propertied ruling class' (p. 34). The ideas of Karl Marx and Friedrich Engels are clearly relevant here but it is Morton Fried in his *The evolution of political society* (1967) who has provided the most detailed recent statement of the 'conflict position'. Theories which belong to the integration school, on the other hand, argue that the state evolved when 'social groups voluntarily came together and submitted to a governing authority in order to gain the military and economic benefits of centralization' (p. 61). In this case the ideas of Herbert Spencer are relevant but it is Elman Service in his *Origins of the state and civilization* (1975) who has provided the most detailed recent statement of the 'integration position'. Haas compares these two schools of thought and attempts to test some of their basic propositions with archaeological data. He concludes that a more useful theory can be produced by 'introducing major integration elements directly into a broadened conflict model' (p. 129). He then examines the main specific theories which have been advanced to explain the emergence of state societies, either as a general process or in particular instances. He separates these theories into three different groups (pp. 132–52): (1) warfare theories, of which that of Robert Carneiro (1970) is probably the best known; (2) trade theories, either (a) inter-regional, for example that of William Rathje (1971; 1972) or (b) intra-regional, for example that of Henry Wright and Gregory Johnson (1975); and (3) a famous irrigation theory, that of Karl Wittfogel (1957). Although he admits that there are many differences between the various theories, Haas argues that: 'All the theories begin with stratification and outline alternate ways by which certain members of a society may gain differential access to basic resources' (Haas 1982: 150). In all the theories, he observes, 'This differential access is based on *control over the production or procurement* of the resources in question' [italics in original] (p. 151). It is that control, according to Haas, that gives rulers power and he proceeds to advance what might be called 'the power theory of state formation'.

Haas understands power to be the capacity to oblige somebody else to do something that they would not otherwise do, through the application, threat, or promise of sanctions (p. 157). He identifies nine variables that can be used to measure power in social relationships and the important thing, from an archaeologist's point of view, is that he is able to demonstrate how each of these variables can be recognized in the archaeological record (pp. 159–71). These variables are: (1) power base (exploitable resources); (2) means of exerting power (sanctions, positive or negative); (3) scope of power (the type of things a power holder can oblige other people to do); (4) amount of power (the extent to which people do what they are told); (5) extension of power (the number of people over whom power is exercised); (6) costs of power (to both the power holder and to the people over whom power is held); (7) compliance costs (what people have to do if they do what they are told); (8) refusal costs (what happens to people if they do not do what they are told); and (9) gains (the benefits people get for doing what they are told). Haas then proceeds to redefine the word 'state' in terms of power. His revised definition is 'a stratified society in which a governing body exercises control over the production or procurement of basic resources, and thus necessarily exercises coercive power over the remainder of the population' (p. 172). Haas sees the 'central feature in all of the major theories of state formation' as 'the development of a new economic power base by the society's leaders', giving them the means of coercing large numbers of people and also giving them 'a reason and the ability to develop and exploit additional physical and ideological bases of power' (p. 181). Haas concludes:

> Instead of proclaiming victory for any one position, it would seem to be more productive to acknowledge that the emergence of the state involved both conflict and integrative elements, and that trade, warfare, irrigation, and perhaps one or more additional factors may have each served as different routes to statehood ... Specifically, the initial centralization of a social system involves a process of integration through trade, warfare, irrigation, or some other means. The integrative process itself, in turn, results in stratification of the system, with a leadership group gaining increased access to basic resources by controlling either their production or procurement. This control then provides that leadership group with an economic base for exerting coercive power over the rest of the population. (p. 209)

Also in his final chapter, Haas considers at some length a question that he has already touched on several times earlier in his book. If you have evidence of monumental architecture does this necessarily mean that you have state-level society? This is a question of the greatest significance to archaeologists because, as Haas realizes, 'archaeologists are constantly looking for markers to tell them what they are working with' although 'they eschew simplistic attempts to equate single phenomena, such as monumental architecture, writing, or cities, with complex political organization of the state' (p. 214). Understandably, Haas is unwilling to answer this question in any categorical way, although he does seem to doubt the suggestion that ranked chiefdoms could also produce monumental architecture, even interpreting that to mean any 'large-scale communal labor projects'. Indeed, in an earlier chapter he cites monumental architecture as one of the ways of identifying some of his power variables in the archaeological record. Monumental architecture is seen as evidence of the scope of power, as well as an indication of whether potential power bases and potential means of exerting power have actually been exploited (p. 164).

The book by Haas (1982) has been examined at some length because it not only provides a recent discussion of anthropological ideas about state formation but it also attempts to relate some of those ideas to archaeological data. However, Haas makes little mention of precolonial African states, indeed he draws all his archaeological evidence from Mesopotamia, China, Mesoamerica, and Peru. This is because, like many anthropologists who have written about state formation theory, Haas is concerned to restrict his discussion to what are called 'pristine' states. These are states which arose so early or in such isolation that there can be no question of their being influenced by other states, as may have been the case with what are called 'secondary' states. Thus, Haas ignores the archaeological evidence from precolonial African states presumably because they are considered to be 'secondary' in origin. Indeed, he specifically excludes the early Egyptian state partly because there is some evidence that its development was influenced by Mesopotamia (Haas 1982: 88). It seems strange that so much sophisticated theoretical work should have gone into attempting to understand 'pristine' state formation when, in fact, the greater number of states were inevitably 'secondary' in their origins. Yet, as Barbara Price has commented: 'there has been almost no systematic theoretical treatment of the secondary state' (Price 1978: 161). Except for states that are the results of historical succession from a pre-existing state, Price argues that 'secondary states are formed as a result of the expansion of other states, themselves either pristine or secondary' (p. 179). This can happen, she thinks, in two different ways: (1) by 'direct pressure in the form of political incorporation or of massive economic takeover and control' and (2) by 'more indirect modification by irrevocable alteration of the socio-economic environment' (p. 161). Clearly, Price's ideas could be usefully applied to the precolonial states of tropical Africa, although Renfrew has referred to the whole idea of a division into 'pristine' and 'secondary' 'civilizations' as 'unacceptably diffusionist', offering, he claims, 'a facile taxonomy in place of serious analysis' (Renfrew 1983: 17). Many archaeologists would agree with Renfrew that: 'to understand the origins and development of any civilization, it is necessary to look at the local conditions of its existence: at its subsistence, at its technology, at the social system, at population pressures, at its ideology, and at its external trade' (p. 17). I will be adopting such an approach in this book because, important though state formation theory and urbanization theory might be, it is also important to examine the actual evidence that we have on and under the ground.

Urbanization and state formation in Africa

In this case, the ground in question is African ground and neither I nor any of the scholars whose work has so far been discussed are Africans. We are fortunate, therefore, in being able to refer to the ideas of the distinguished Nigerian geographer, Akin Mabogunje. In his book *Urbanization in Nigeria* (1968), Mabogunje propounds both a theory of urbanization and an interrelated theory of state formation. He reviews what he calls 'the functional specialization theory of urbanization' but points out that the mere existence of specialists within a community need not give rise to urbanization. For that to happen, anywhere in the world, it is essential that functional specialization should take place under three 'limiting conditions'. According to Mabogunje these conditions are:

(a) For functional specialization to give rise to urban centres, there must be a surplus of food production with which to feed the class of specialists whose activities are now withdrawn from agriculture;

(b) For this surplus to be made available to the group of specialists, there must be a small group of people who are able to exercise some power over the group of food producers. This class also has to ensure stable and peaceful conditions in which both the food producers and the specialists can produce of their best; and

(c) For the work of the specialists to be facilitated and their needs for raw materials satisfied, there must be a class of traders and merchants. (Mabogunje 1968: 35)

To define urbanization, Mabogunje calls it simply 'the process whereby human beings congregate in relatively large number at one particular spot of the earth's surface' (p. 33). Recognizing the vagueness of this definition, he is concerned nevertheless to have a definition that can be applied to the development of towns and cities in any part of the world and at any period. Understandably, he rejects the ethnocentric notions that the presence of writing or the absence of agricultural workers can be used to distinguish between those communities that were urbanized and those that were not. To Mabogunje it is 'difficult to accept writing as an index precisely because the literate group which is likely to invent it represents only one class of specialists whose emergence in an urbanized society may or may not be delayed'. So far as agricultural workers are concerned, he remarks that 'most urban centres began with a substantial proportion of their inhabitants being farmers ... the absence of agricultural workers in cities represents only a very late development in the history of urbanization' (pp. 40–2).

Mabogunje appears to be convinced that it was the development of long-distance trade that led to the growth of cities in both East and West Africa (p. 45). On the other hand, the general process of state formation, in his opinion, originated in the necessity to defend urban centres against external aggression. This led to the organization of what he calls 'a city army'. He goes on to say:

> With time, the city which could develop this institution to a relatively higher level liquidated such institutions in neighbouring cities, provided its own 'pax' and created a nation or an empire. A national army then replaced a number of city armies and the presence or absence of stable conditions over the whole area became related to the vigilance and internal conditions of the conquering city. (Mabogunje 1968: 37)

Explanations of this sort belong to what may be called the 'conquest hypothesis' of state formation in Africa. One of the more interesting attempts to apply such an hypothesis to a set of African historical and anthropological data is Jack Goody's book *Technology, tradition and the state in Africa* (1971). Goody is concerned mainly with West Africa, where he distinguishes between what he calls the 'horse states of the savannahs' and the 'gun states of the forest' (Goody 1971: 55). In the West African savanna, for instance, Goody argues that 'states arose on the backs of horses' (p. 69, quoting from Köhler 1953–4: 93). Overall, his book examines the role of technology in social change and relates technology to the means of destruction as well as to the means of production. To Goody, it would appear that the crucial factor in state emergence is the actual means of destruction and their ownership.

Such an hypothesis is only one of a number that have been advanced by both anthropologists and historians to explain the development of states in Africa. The anthropological literature concerned with such explanation is extensive but is usually limited to the discussion of evidence from the present or from the relatively recent past. For this reason, it is the views of Africanist historians that have more relevance for those of us attempting to interpret the archaeological evidence for cities and states in precolonial tropical Africa. Unfortunately, whereas anthropologists, like most archaeologists in recent years, have sought to understand change in terms of process, historians of Africa have sometimes tended to do so in terms of actors and events. Thus, there was a time when the development of African states was explained in a rather bizarre fashion, as resulting from the imposition of a set of political ideas derived from an alien source (for example Oliver and Fage 1962: 44–52). Such political ideas were said to comprise the notion of 'divine' or 'Sudanic' kingship and a popular place of origin was Egypt (Garlake (1978a: 21) discusses these arguments). John Lonsdale (1981) has reviewed the historiography of states and social processes in Africa, commenting on the range of conventional explanations that historians have had to choose from: 'The point of all these hypotheses was that something rather exceptional was needed to explain any concentration of power in a logically tribal Africa' (Lonsdale 1981: 172). It is worth looking briefly at the various hypotheses that Lonsdale identifies. First, there is the one just referred to, that 'kingdoms' were 'imposed upon society by an autonomous will with a political vision'. Second, there is the conquest hypothesis, which has already been mentioned, and which Lonsdale calls 'a favourite explanation'. Third, is the demographic pressure hypothesis, 'with the appropriation of power growing out of conflict over resources'. Fourth, is the managerial hypothesis, with the 'articulation of two or more forms of subsistence, typically farming and herding' or the existence of 'deposits of scarce but necessary minerals, salt, say, or iron' providing the basis of power. Fifth, is the long-distance trade hypothesis; as Lonsdale says: 'The most popular explanation for the rise of state power was the growth of long-distance trade, the Pirenne thesis of medieval Africa' (pp. 171–2). To all these hypotheses, he adds a more recent one: a sixth hypothesis involving drought. As Lonsdale says: 'Drought seems to be emerging to challenge trade as a major explanation of state formation' (p. 175). It should be stressed that these hypotheses are not seen as necessarily mutually exclusive alternatives, and it appears that Lonsdale accepts it as possible for combinations of them to be used in an explanatory role in particular instances. Nevertheless, he stresses that most of these hypotheses originated at a time when there were far fewer data available on African state formation than is now the case. According to Lonsdale, three things are indicated by the information that has now become available. First, state formation was a very slow process: 'it was frequently botched and started again', so that 'the decay and fall of kingdoms is as important a process as their rise'. Second, a great deal more is now known about the politics of state formation and state collapse. Power seems to have been decentralized in early kingdoms with their kings acting as mediators rather than autocrats. State emergence involved centralization of that power and this was achieved by coercion not by consensus. Third, it is now considered more useful to explain the rise of particular states in terms of local politics, rather than to hypothesize about 'the idea of the state' and the diffusion of political ideas (Lonsdale 1981: 172–3).

The archaeology of African cities and states

This chapter has been concerned so far with theoretical matters, both in general and in particular. That is to say that a selection of theories has been discussed, theories concerning state formation and urbanization at both a world level and within tropical Africa itself. They represent only a sample of the extensive theoretical literature on these complex subjects. Also they have been drawn in the main from the work of anthropologists, historians and geographers. The question that now arises is this: What about the archaeology of precolonial cities and states in tropical Africa, with which this book is supposedly concerned? There is obviously a real need for theory, but what about the 'hard' evidence that could be used to test some of those theories? Two things are immediately apparent: first, that there seems to have been less general writing on the archaeological evidence than on explanatory theories; and, secondly, that such is the basis of our knowledge of the later prehistory and protohistory of tropical Africa that it is unwise, if not impossible, to consider the archaeological evidence without also considering ethnohistorical and historical evidence. Indeed, there are dangers here; so that one of the standard textbooks on the relevant period of Africa's past (Roland Oliver and Brian Fagan, *Africa in the Iron Age* (1975)) has been criticized by some readers as insufficiently archaeological and too historical in its treatment. Yet, if such is really the case, it must surely be at least partly the fault of Africanist archaeologists for not providing sufficient data? It is interesting to recollect the reaction that I once had from a fellow archaeologist in the early 1960s, when I suggested how valuable it would be to excavate some of the cities of the West African savannas. 'What on earth for?' he queried, 'We already know all about the medieval cities of West Africa from historical sources.'

Perhaps the relative dearth of general studies concerned with the archaeology of precolonial cities and states in tropical Africa is part of the legacy of such attitudes. Another part of that legacy is the fact that relatively few archaeological research projects in tropical Africa have ever been designed specifically to throw light on the origins and development of cities and states. Nevertheless, scattered through the archaeological literature of tropical Africa there is much relevant information that can be garnered by the would-be synthesizer. An early attempt to do this was Margaret Shinnie's book *Ancient African kingdoms* (1965), which was so widely used that seventeen years after its publication it was still available in print. The coverage of this book was broad indeed: there were chapters on Kush; Ghana, Mali and Songhai; Kanem-Bornu; the Forest States (Nok, Yoruba, Benin, Akan, Congo, Uganda); the lands of Zanj (the East African coast); and on Zimbabwe. It was an important book but unfortunately it was pitched at too popular and too generalizing a level to achieve the notice from scholars that it probably deserved. A similar fate had overtaken an earlier general study that covered a comparable range of subject matter: Basil Davidson's *Old Africa rediscovered* (1959). Davidson's book was at an even more popular level than Shinnie's but again it was so widely read that over a decade later a second edition was published in the United States, under the title *The lost cities of Africa* (Davidson 1970). In fact, Davidson's book of 1959 probably has had a greater overall influence than has usually been admitted.

Since Margaret Shinnie's book, the most significant contribution to the general archaeological literature on cities and states in tropical Africa has been Peter Garlake's *The kingdoms of Africa* (Garlake 1978a). This has a wide coverage, including, amongst other things, Meroë, Aksum, Zimbabwe, the cities of the East African coast, Ife, Benin, Begho, Igbo-Ukwu, and the kingdoms of the savanna. It also examines the archaeological background of the emergence of African kingdoms. This is a book that no student of this subject can afford to ignore although again an attempt at popularization has weakened its impact. Nevertheless, it provides numerous black-and-white and colour illustrations of relevant archaeological material. It is also noteworthy for Garlake's insistence on the indigenous evolution of African states; claiming, as he does, that: 'A continuity between leadership within village societies, based on family groups, and the monarchical principles of African states is very apparent' (pp. 21–2). However, Garlake also stresses the importance of external trade, whereby a small group could monopolize not the resources but the outlets by which they could be converted into a useful surplus. Thus, in Garlake's view: 'centralized authority grew from a monopoly of foreign trade' (p. 24).

There is only one other general work that has made an important contribution to this subject, although the book ignores archaeological evidence almost totally. This is Richard Hull's book *African cities and towns before the European conquest* (1976a) which has been described by O'Connor, in his useful annotated bibliography of urbanization in tropical Africa, as 'the only book devoted specifically to the history of urbanization and tropical Africa as a whole' (1981: xvii). Hull has also outlined his approach to this subject in a paper published in the same year as his book (Hull 1976b).

Hull's main interest is the history of African settlement planning and architecture, but he touches in addition on a number of other aspects of his subject. His starting point is that: 'Scholars in the past have either neglected or grossly underestimated the urban factor in African history' (Hull 1976a: xix). His conclusion, at the end of his book, is 'that Africans possess an architectural heritage of their own; and that they can profess to preindustrial urban cultures worthy of comparison with any urban civilizations of the world' (p. 126). From the point of view of the present discussion, the most relevant parts of the book concern the origins of cities and towns and their decline and disappearance. Hull identifies five main types of cities and towns, assuming that major function explains origin but emphasizing that most cities and towns served a combination of such functions. The five types are: (1) spiritual and ceremonial centres, like Ife in the south-west of Nigeria; (2) commercial centres of exchange, like the Swahili cities of the East African coast; (3) centres of governance, such as the capitals of Buganda's Kabakas to the north-west of Lake Victoria, settlements whose location could change with each new ruler; (4) centres of refuge, most of which had an equally tenuous existence but some of which, like Bida in northern Nigeria, continued to prosper; (5) 'cities of vision', such as Sokoto also in northern Nigeria (pp. 120–1). Hull also outlines what he sees as the prerequisites for the growth of cities and towns in Africa. These were that: (1) government had to be sufficiently developed to exert control over the agricultural surplus; (2) leaders had to have enough power to demand labour from their people for the construction of public works; (3) specialist craftsmen had to be present; (4) government also had to have an ideological power base (p. 2). So far as decline and disappearance are concerned, Hull suggests four main causative factors. These are: (1) environmental deterioration, such as has been suggested in the case of Great Zimbabwe; (2) collapse of political superstructure, such as affected Old Oyo in the south-west of Nigeria; (3) revolt of peripheral cities against the mother city, as happened for a time with the Asante confederacy and Kumasi in Ghana, towards the end of the nineteenth century; (4) external military invasion, like the Portuguese attack on Sofala on the coast of Mozambique (pp. 114–16).

Overall, Hull's book has filled a serious gap in the literature and deserves more attention than it seems to have had. It has brought together some interesting information and some useful illustrations. In particular it contains a good deal of information about traditional African architecture and building techniques. However, these are topics that have been examined by a number of writers in recent years, for example by Paul Oliver (1971) and by Susan Denyer (1978), and it is a pity that Hull did not use the opportunity to discuss the archaeological evidence as well.

Limitations of the archaeological evidence

When we turn, at last, to this archaeological evidence there is a serious discrepancy that immediately becomes apparent. According to historical sources, there was a substantially greater number of cities and states in precolonial tropical Africa than the currently available archaeological literature would suggest. Many students of archaeology inevitably experience a feeling of unreality as they turn the pages of John Fage and Maureen Verity's second edition of *An atlas of African history* (1978). There are numerous cities and states marked on the maps in that atlas, of which little or nothing is known archaeologically. What about the early second millennium AD state of Kanem east of Lake Chad, for instance, of which the capital Njimi has not even been located by archaeologists? Or what about the sixteenth-century state of Kongo with its capital Mbanza Kongo, that (with its environs) was thought by Leo Africanus to have had a population of about 100 000 people (Africanus 1896: Vol. 1, 73)? Virtually nothing is known about its archaeology either. There are other similar examples that could be cited but these two illustrate well enough the two main reasons for the patchy state of archaeological knowledge on this whole subject. First, there is the problem of the archaeological visibility of the actual sites. There is a very great range of variation in the archaeological evidence that might be expected; at the one extreme, a long-established, partly stone-built, commercial centre like Kilwa (Chittick 1974b) and, at the other extreme, a short-lived, grass-built, centre of governance like the Bugandan capital at Rubaga visited by Henry Morton Stanley in 1875 (Stanley 1878: Vol. 1, 199–202). It is likely that the settlements of Kanem, including Njimi, were even more mobile than those of nineteenth-century Buganda and were, as Hull (1976a: 7) has described them, 'tent-cities' that 'could be moved quite easily'. Given the probable pastoralist/shifting cultivator subsistence base of the inhabitants of Kanem, such mobility and the consequent ephemeral nature of even quite large settlements should not surprise us.

The second of the main reasons for the patchy state of our archaeological knowledge, is the problem of the uneven distribution of archaeological field research in Africa, unevenly distributed both in space and time. A relatively large amount of excavation and fieldwork has been carried out, for instance, on settlement sites belonging to the last three millennia along the Sudanese Nile but, in contrast, relatively little such work has been done, for example, on the Mozambique coast. Thus Mbanza Kongo is archaeologically unknown probably because it is situated in northern Angola, where very little work has been done on any later archaeological sites. In this particular case it is possible that this situation will change, however, as the Belgian archaeologist Pierre de Maret hopes to commence excavations at Mbanza Kongo (later known as São Salvador) in the near future. Of course, these two problems (of archaeological visibility and uneven field research) should not only be viewed in isolation, they frequently compound one another. Quite clearly, only the most intensive field investigations will reveal sites of low archaeological visibility and in tropical Africa such investigations have been rare.

An obvious consequence of the patchy state of archaeological knowledge concerning precolonial cities and states in tropical Africa is that any discussion of the relevant archaeological evidence is in danger of giving a distorted picture or at least an incomplete one. Thus the overall picture presented by such books as Shinnie (1965) and Garlake (1978a) could be an artefact of the available archaeological evidence rather than an indication of the processes of state formation and urbanization. Some indication that this is probably not the case may be gained from Chandler and Fox (1974) who have made a world-wide study of the statistics of urbanization over the last 3000 years. They have produced a series of maps of African cities in AD 1000, 1200, 1300, 1400, 1500, 1600, 1700, 1800, and 1850. These maps are mainly based on historical sources and, although the distribution of cities is not necessarily a reliable indicator of the distribution of states, it is interesting that they reflect very generally the geographical pattern indicated by the archaeological evidence. Thus they show (Fig. 2.1) that the main areas of urban development in tropical Africa were: in West Africa along the southern edge of the Sahara; in the West African forest west of the lower Niger River; on the middle Nile in the Sudan; and in the Ethiopian mountains. They also record urban centres on the East African coast; on the Zimbabwe Plateau; around the lower Congo; and in the Lake Victoria

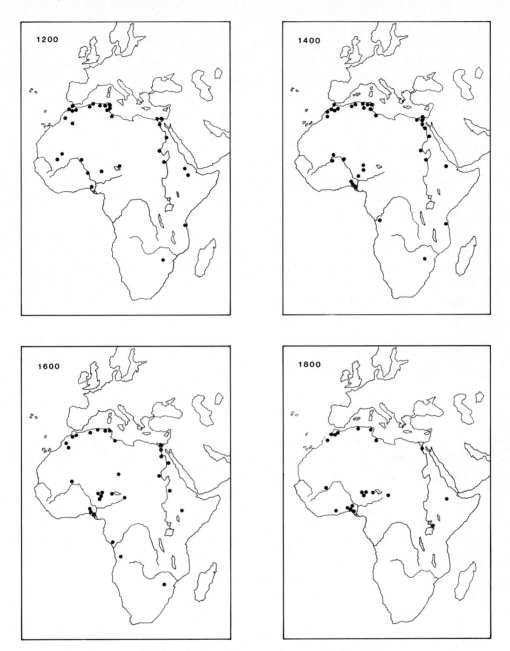

Fig. 2.1 Distribution of African cities with 20 000 or more inhabitants in AD 1200, 1400, 1600, and 1800. After Chandler and Fox (1974: 50, 52, 54, 56).

area. Little or no archaeological evidence is available from the last two of these areas, but it does seem that however deficient the archaeological evidence might be in *quantity* (both in particular cases and in general) it does produce nevertheless a crude geographical *pattern* comparable to that derived from historical and ethnohistorical evidence. It is this impression that has prompted my choice of subject matter for the substantive chapters of this book.

Coverage of this book

The chapters in this book might be regarded as a series of case studies, whose choice has been dictated by the availability of archaeological evidence. In reality, they are probably something more than this and it is hoped that they provide an overall picture, however crude and incomplete, of the processes of state formation and urbanization in tropical Africa. In order to assist in this aim, I have also included a chapter concerned specifically with examples of tropical African precolonial cities and states for which there is little or no available archaeological data (Chapter 9). The other substantive chapters examine the main areas of archaeological evidence by grouping that evidence both geographically and chronologically (Fig. 2.2). Thus, Chapter 3 discusses the

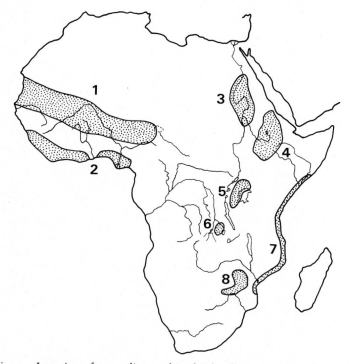

Fig. 2.2 Location of areas discussed in this book.
1: West African savanna (Ch. 5). *2:* West African forest (Ch. 6). *3:* Middle Nile (Ch. 3). *4:* Ethiopian Highlands (Ch. 4). *5:* Interlacustrine area (Ch. 9). *6:* Upemba Depression (Ch. 9). *7:* East African Coast (Ch. 7). *8:* Zimbabwe Plateau (Ch. 8).

evidence from the middle Nile for the cities and states of Kerma, Napata, and Meroë, perhaps the first of such developments in tropical Africa, and also considers the evidence for the successor states of Christian Nubia. This is followed by Chapter 4 with an examination of the evidence for Axum and Christian Ethiopia, in an adjacent part of the continent. The scene is then changed to West Africa and Chapters 5 and 6, respectively, look at what archaeology has to tell us of the cities and states of the West African savanna and of the West African forest and its fringes. Chapter 7 takes us across the continent again to examine the archaeological evidence available from the cities of the East African coast. Chapter 8, in contrast, considers the evidence from the Zimbabwe Plateau of the interior, evidence that has been the subject of so much debate by archaeologists, historians and others.

An obvious problem with this choice of subject matter is that it excludes North Africa and most of Egypt; areas where the processes of state formation and urbanization pre-date those of tropical Africa, and which are thought to have influenced to varying extents the developments that took place in the West African savanna, the Sudanese Nile Valley and the Ethiopian Plateau. This might seem an unfortunate example of that practice of beheading the African continent, which has in recent years become identified by the use of the phrase 'sub-Saharan Africa'. However, there are often good reasons for such treatment of African geography. In the case of this book, the intention has been to look at the cities and states of *black* Africa, because they have not had the attention that they deserve. In addition, North Africa and Egypt have long had such diverse connections with the Mediterranean and South-West Asian world, that it seems legitimate to exclude them from this study. Therefore, the area considered in this book is defined as 'tropical Africa', because in the most literal sense of that term the book is concerned with Africa between the Tropic of Cancer and the Tropic of Capricorn. The former passes through the centre of the Sahara Desert and the latter through the Kalahari Desert, so that none of the areas that it is proposed to consider are excluded.

The subject matter of this book is limited in time as well as in space. The term 'precolonial' has been used to define chronological coverage purely for convenience and without any other intention. The aim has been to find a suitable descriptive term for that complex intermixture of prehistory, protohistory and history constituted by the last three and a half millennia of Africa's past (Fig. 2.3), but prior to the colonial take-over and period of decolonization of the last one hundred years or so. This is a period of time that has often been referred to as 'the African Iron Age' but such techno-epochal terminology has little explanatory value and obstructs rather than aids understanding (Connah 1981: 4). Certainly the period concerned was one of substantial technological change but there were also profound economic and social changes, which it is the purpose of this book to investigate.

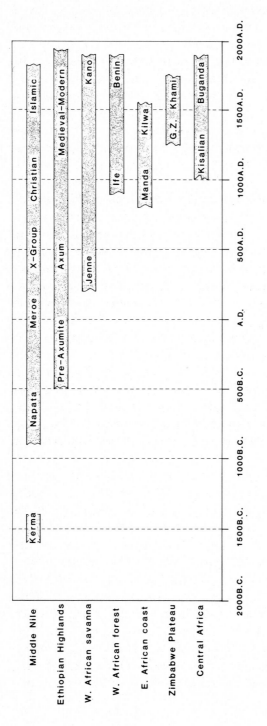

Fig. 2.3 Chronology of urban and state developments discussed in this book. 'G.Z.' indicates Great Zimbabwe.

The basic questions

This investigation will be carried out principally by examining the relevant archaeological evidence for African cities and states. That evidence consists of the material remains of urban settlements and of the culture of their occupants, together with inferences about the relationship of such settlements to the populations of their hinterlands and to the resources available in those hinterlands. In assessing this evidence, it will be instructive to test against it some of the theoretical ideas that have been discussed in this chapter. It will be important, for instance, to ask how we know that a particular archaeological site represents the remains of a city and how we are able to assume that the area around it constituted a state controlled either from that or from some other city. We shall also be able to compare the picture that emerges from the archaeological evidence with the picture that can be reconstructed from any ethnohistorical or historical evidence that is available. At the very roots of our enquiry, however, will be a number of basic questions around which the whole discussion will revolve. When, how and why did cities and states emerge in tropical Africa? In particular, what factors led to their development in some parts of the continent but not in others? Perhaps it is premature to attempt to answer such difficult questions in our present state of knowledge but each of the substantive chapters of this book has been written with these questions in mind. The final chapter, Chapter 10, seeks to identify any 'common denominators' in the different examples of urbanization and state emergence that have been examined. Such common denominators may not answer our questions as satisfactorily as could be wished but they do begin to provide some sort of an answer. They also allow us to assess, principally using archaeological evidence, both the general theoretical explanations of anthropologists like Haas (1982) and Price (1978) and the range of explanatory hypotheses advanced by Africanist historians that Lonsdale (1981) has reviewed. In attempting such an assessment, the approach will be based on that advocated by Renfrew (1983: 17) that has been discussed above (p. 12). Each set of archaeological evidence for African cities and states will be investigated from the point of view of geographical location, environmental conditions, basic subsistence, prevailing technology, social system, population pressures, ideology, and external trade. Whatever the many weaknesses of the archaeological evidence, either in general or in particular, for the emergence of cities and states in Africa, that evidence does have the capacity to increase the time-depth of our understanding of these processes and to test and flesh out our knowledge derived from historical sources, where such sources exist. Haas is more doctrinaire on the matter. 'Archaeology', he claims, 'is the only discipline that can tell us how government began' (Haas 1982: 216). It is to be hoped that some day he may be proved right. In the meantime, we shall see what African archaeology can tell us of the matter at the present time.

Chapter 3
Corridor or cul-de-sac: the middle Nile

The earliest known cities and states of tropical Africa were situated along the middle Nile. One of the best known of these, Meroë, located about 200 kilometres north-east of the modern city of Khartoum, was mentioned as early as the fifth century BC by Herodotus. Drawing on stories from travellers in Upper Egypt, he could record that: '... when thou hast passed through this part in forty days, thou enterest again into another ship and sailest twelve days; and thereafter thou comest to a great city, the name whereof is Meroë. And this city is said to be the mother city of the other Ethiopians.' (Powell 1949: Vol. 1, 121–2) Meroë, however, was neither the first nor the last example of developing social complexity in this part of Africa. Its antecedents lay in Napata and Kerma, the latter dating back to before 1500 BC; its successors lay in the kingdoms of Christian Nubia, that survived until the early centuries of the second millennium AD (Adams 1977). Such continuity may be more apparent than real but at least one city was seemingly occupied throughout this time, and indeed down to the early nineteenth century AD: this was the city of Qasr Ibrim, situated in Lower Nubia, in what is now southern Egypt.

Why should urbanization and state formation have commenced so early in this area and why should they have lasted for so long? In the earlier part of this century, scholars answered these questions by attributing all such developments to the direct influence of Pharaonic, Ptolemaic, Roman and Byzantine Egypt, which is located immediately to the north of the area. Increasing social complexity along the middle Nile was seen as a secondary development, resulting from migrations of people from the more advanced cultures of the north (Trigger 1982). In recent times the emphasis has changed to one that stresses the indigenous character of these achievements but acknowledges the substantial contributions made to them by northern cultural influences. William Adams, the author of a currently standard work on the archaeology of this area, has described Nubia as '*the* transition zone, between the civilized world and Africa'. Entitling his book: *Nubia: Corridor to Africa*, the following passage epitomizes his view of the matter:

> The narrow green strip of the middle Nile Valley, from Khartoum to Aswan, was the corridor through which men, things and ideas passed from the one

world to the other, and within which they met and mingled. The dwellers in this corridor became in every sense middle men – racially and culturally as well as economically. Their unique position between the black and the white worlds has persisted down to modern times. (Adams 1977: 20)

According to Adams, the importance of this narrow corridor through the hot, dry and barren land of Nubia, arose from the fact that it was for long the only dependable route across the great barrier of the Sahara Desert. For the ancient world of South-West Asia and the Mediterranean, it was, therefore, the only road that led into the heart of Africa. The African interior contained resources much coveted by this outside world: gold, ivory and slaves, but also a long list of other mineral, animal, and vegetable products (Adams 1984: 40). All these could be tapped via the Nubian corridor and only with the development of trans-Saharan camel caravans during the first millennium AD did the middle Nile Valley begin to lose its significance as a major world trade route. That role was finally destroyed by the growth of maritime trade around Africa's coasts in the sixteenth and seventeenth centuries AD.

Both archaeological and documentary evidence support the idea of Adams' trade corridor and the growth of cities and states in this area was restricted to this corridor, or at least centred on it. This would suggest that this part of Africa can provide us with a very persuasive example of trade as a major stimulus towards the development of social complexity. Perhaps so, but there seems to be more to it than that. These developments took place at the interface of considerable cultural contact, of which trade was only one element, as Adams indeed stresses. Egyptian culture had a profound effect on the inhabitants of the middle Nile. People are very likely to meet one another in corridors.

Corridors, however, usually lead somewhere and archaeologists have long debated the extent to which the achievements of the inhabitants of the middle Nile Valley might have influenced the rest of Africa. At one extreme, for example, Sayce thought that 'Meroë, in fact, must have been the Birmingham of ancient Africa; ... and the whole of northern Africa might have been supplied by it with implements of iron' (Sayce 1911: 55). At the other extreme, Trigger (1969a) wrote about what he called 'the myth of Meroë' and Shinnie (1967: 167) pointed out that 'not a single object of certain Meroitic origin has been found away from the Nile to the west'. On the basis of present evidence, it does indeed seem that the Nubian corridor, in spite of its impressive social developments, was a cultural cul-de-sac.

Geographical location and environmental factors

The Nile is a very long river that runs from the Lake Region of East Africa to the Mediterranean Sea, passing in the course of this journey through a number of contrasting environments, some of which are amongst the driest in Africa, if not indeed in the world. It is because it flows through so much arid country that, for much of its length, the river and its narrow valley have played such an important role in human history. Ancient Egypt was, as Herodotus called it, 'the gift of the river' (Powell 1949: Vol. 1, 111) but if this was true of the lower Nile, it was also true of the middle Nile which is our subject here. This is the land of the Nile Cataracts, a series of rocky swift rapids, conventionally numbered from one to six, that impede or prevent navigation and are set in a landscape of rocky outcrops and narrow canyons. The First Cataract is just south of Aswan, in southern Egypt; the Sixth Cataract is a little way north of Khartoum in the Sudan. It is this very long and very narrow strip that became known as 'Nubia', although, as Adams (1977: 20–21) points out, its southern limits have varied in location over the centuries. For the purposes of this discussion, the 'middle Nile' will be considered to be that part of the Nile Valley between the confluence of the Blue and White Niles at Khartoum, in the south, and the First Cataract at Aswan, in the north (Fig. 3.1). It is impossible to consider the valley without some reference to the lands to its east and west but because of the extreme environment of much of those areas, the emphasis must remain on the valley itself. As already discussed, this was not only a corridor between the Mediterranean and Africa, it was also a narrow corridor.

It is no exaggeration to say that the climate of much of the middle Nile is one of the most extreme on earth. At Wadi Halfa, in the northern Sudan, the mean daily temperature between May and September is about 32°C but the temperature nearly always exceeds 38°C during the day and may reach above 49°C. However, the period from November to March is comparatively mild, with temperatures that can occasionally drop almost to freezing, and the real problem with this climate is that between Aswan and Dongola, that is to say in the northern half of the middle Nile region, it almost never rains. Sporadic, short showers can occur but sometimes a generation elapses before it rains again in the same place. Humidity is usually as low as 15–20 per cent. In the southern half of the region there is, however, a well-defined wet season of eight to ten weeks, in July and August, but the actual rainfall is very limited, increasing from north to south from about 25 millimetres at Dongola to about 180 millimetres at Khartoum. Another climatic factor of environmental importance is wind, which blows steadily out of the north for the whole year, varying little in direction but rising at times to gale force. This has led to considerable accumulation of desert sand, particularly on the west bank of the Nile, where it has constantly encroached on both settlements and fields. However, with the exception of the reverse bend between Abu Hamed and Debba, it has also made upstream navigation possible on the river, just as the direction of the current has facilitated downstream navigation (Adams 1977: 33–5).

As a result of the climate, the vegetation of the middle Nile region varies from total desert in the north to acacia desert scrub in the south (Andrews 1948: 34). It might be argued, however, that neither the climate nor the general vegetation of this region are the most relevant factor in the history of its settlement. The most important element of the environment is, without doubt, the River Nile itself, rising over 3000 kilometres to the south and bringing to Nubia both the water and the soil which are necessary to sustain human settlement. As Adams (1977: 35) has written: 'Nothing is demanded of the local environment except a growing season long enough to take advantage of these exotic resources. Neither Nubia nor Egypt contributes a drop of water to the Nile, nor an acre of their own soil to its banks.' It is paradoxical, therefore, that most published vegetation maps are of too small a scale to show the most important vegetation type of the middle Nile: that of the long, narrow river littoral. So narrow is this strip, that in places it is a mere few hundred metres wide or does not exist at all, but wherever it is present it supports much the same sort of vegetation. One of the most common features of this vegetation is the date palm (*Phoenix dactylifera*). This is really a domesticated tree but date palms are so numerous, fringing the river, separating cultivated fields and in actual groves, that they look like part of the natural vegetation. Other trees also grow along the river littoral, the most important being the *dom* palm (*Hyphaena thebaica*), various acacias, and the tamarisk. Most of the rest of the vegetation consists of cultivated plants but halfa grass grows wherever it can find moisture, and when the river is low, a fringe of papyrus reed can be found in some places at the water's edge (Adams 1977: 37–8).

There is, however, a variety of environments to be found along the narrow littoral of the Nubian Nile. This is because of topographic diversity resulting from differences in geology. From Khartoum to Aswan, the Nile flows alternately over Nubian sandstone and basement complex (which is mostly granite), changing from one to the other a number of times. As a result, it is possible to identify six geographic subdivisions of the middle Nile (Adams 1977: 21–33). In most cases, the boundaries of these subdivisions consist of the main cataracts of the river, the majority of which have been formed where the river crosses from one geological formation to the other. The most southerly of these physiographic subdivisions is the Shendi Reach, extending from the confluence of the Blue and White Niles to about the mouth of the River Atbara (Fig. 3.1). This is an area of Nubian sandstone, although there are also numerous outcrops of granite. Alluvium is found in most places on both banks of the river and there are many farming villages. Beyond the river littoral there is semi-desert grassland and therefore nomadic pastoralism is important. Within this reach lay the heartland of the Meroitic state, including the city of Meroë itself. To the north of the Shendi Reach lies the Abu Hamed Reach, a region of barren granite with low productivity. This reach extends as far as the Fourth Cataract and judging from archaeological evidence seems never to have been an important area for settlement. Downstream of the Fourth Cataract lies the Dongola Reach, extending as far as the Third Cataract. Again the surface geology is Nubian sandstone, providing an almost featureless landscape that in many places has

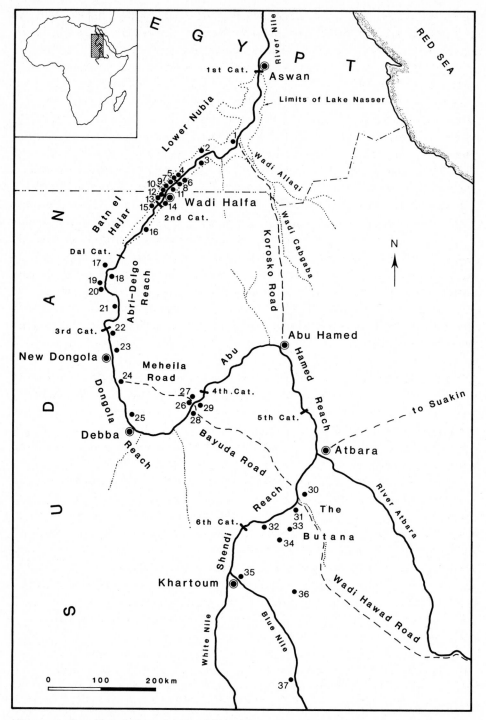

Fig. 3.1 Archaeological sites of the middle Nile.
  1: Maharraqa. *2:* Karanog. *3:* Qasr Ibrim. *4:* Arminna West. *5:* Tamit. *6:* Gebel

potentially cultivable land on both sides of the river, as well as in overflow basins that were at one time parts of the bed of the river. This is the most productive of all the subdivisions of the middle Nile, being the only part of it that enjoys an annual Nile flood similar to that which has been so important for human settlement in Lower Egypt. It is hardly surprising that it was the Dongola Reach that was the scene of the earliest developments of complex society on the middle Nile, for both Kerma and Napata were situated in this region.

From the Third Cataract to the Dal Cataract is the Abri-Delgo Reach, a region of granite and clay plains. There is a wide floodplain in many places and much of it is intensively cultivated. This reach was particularly important during the period of Egyptian (New Kingdom) colonial expansion, in the second half of the second millennium BC. North of the Abri-Delgo Reach is the *Batn el Hajar*, a name that means 'belly of rock' and is most appropriate for this barren landscape of bare granite, that extends from the Dal Cataract to the Second Cataract. This is a wild and rugged region with only occasional riverside pockets of alluvium that can be irrigated and cultivated, and human settlements seem always to have been limited. Its most important role in the past seems to have been to act as something of a barrier to upstream movement.

Last of the geographic subdivisions of the middle Nile is Lower Nubia, that stretches from the Second Cataract to the First Cataract. This region is now almost totally submerged beneath Lake Nasser, which has created a waste of water amidst a desert of land. Formerly, however, it was a moderately prosperous region, where the river cut mainly through Nubian sandstone and provided discontinuous alluvial deposits, particularly at the mouths of the larger wadis. Archaeological evidence suggests that it was a relatively important area of settlement during some periods in the past, and that its proximity to Egypt gave it a particularly important role as a cultural contact zone.

Overall, the hot, dry and often barren land of the middle Nile had few resources. Nevertheless, traditionally its agriculture could support the limited population of the region. Cultivation of seasonally inundated land or of land that could be irrigated by one means or another, *in recent times* produced sorghum, barley, beans, tobacco, lentils, peas, watermelons, maize and some wheat. Lucerne, dates, mangoes and citrus fruits were also grown. In addition, animal husbandry was important: involving cattle, sheep, goats, donkeys, and – rarely – camels and water buffalo. Chickens, pigeons, ducks and dogs were also kept but horses and pigs were very rare (Trigger 1965: 19–22; Adams 1977: 54).

Fig. 3.1. contd.
Adda. *7:* Abu Simbel. *8:* Qustul. *9:* Ballana. *10:* Faras. *11:* Debeira East. *12:* Debeira West. *13:* Buhen. *14:* Meinarti. *15:* Kasanarti. *16:* Duweishat. *17:* Amara. *18:* Sai. *19:* Seddenga. *20:* Soleb. *21:* Sesebi. *22:* Kerma. *23:* Argo. *24:* Kawa. *25:* Old Dongola. *26:* El Kurru. *27:* Jebel Barkal. *28:* Sanam. *29:* Nuri. (Note: Sites *26–29* constitute Napata.) *30:* Meroë. *31:* Shendi. *32:* Wad ben Naqa. *33:* Musawwarat es-Sufra. *34:* Naqa. *35:* Soba. *36:* Jebel Qeili. *37:* Sennar. After Adams (1977).

Little of the native fauna seems to have survived to later historical times, and the only part that constituted a continuing important resource was fish, of which there are more than forty species in the Nile, most of which can be eaten. It seems likely, however, that the disappearance of wild game from Nubia resulted from its early exploitation for animal products by the Egyptian trade. At first a primary source of such commodities as ivory, ostrich eggs and feathers, skins and even live animals, Nubia gradually became merely a funnel through which these things passed on their way north.

A longer-lasting Nubian resource consisted of various minerals, including copper, fine-grained igneous rocks and, most important, gold. Gold was scarce but occurred widely, particularly in the desert to the east of the Nile Valley. The most important of the gold mines were situated along the Wadi Allaqi, between Lower Nubia and the Red Sea. A final resource, of considerable importance throughout most of the history of the region, was slaves. Even with this commodity, however, as time went on Nubia became the pipeline rather than the source. One is left with the overall impression that the indigenous resources of Nubia were less important than those which it obtained from further south. Nubia was, it appears, a classic example of an entrepôt: a commercial centre of import, export, collection and distribution. With only modest resources of its own, its unique location allowed Nubia to grow rich handling those that belonged to others (Adams 1977: 41–3).

The constraints on human settlement in the middle Nile were numerous and some of them could at times assume a determinative role. Most important of these, in an area with the sort of climate that has been described (p. 26), was the level of the Nile itself, whose height in the flood season could in some years be too low for irrigation to be possible in particular places and in other years be so high that floodwater swept away both settlements and cultivable alluvium. It also seems likely that there were long-term fluctuations in the average level of the river, such as Adams (1977: 242) has hypothesized, to explain the virtual abandonment of Lower Nubia during the first millennium BC. This region was only re-occupied at the beginning of the first millennium AD, with the advent of the *saqia*, the ox-driven waterwheel, that made it possible to raise irrigation water to greater heights than were possible with the man-powered *shaduf*. Given suitable technology to lift water to the required level, there still needed to be alluvium suitable for irrigation, and its distribution varied considerably in the six geographic subdivisions of the middle Nile which have been discussed (p. 27). The second constraining factor was, therefore, the availability of alluvium that could be both irrigated and cultivated. There were, in practice, three sorts of arable land: *seluka* land, *saqia* and *shaduf* land, and basin land (Trigger 1965: 19–21). *Seluka* land was situated on the floodplain and was inundated each year when the river was high. When the level of the river fell, the land could produce a crop without further watering and was therefore a type of land that was highly valued. Its exploitation was an example of 'recessional cultivation', that is discussed in Chapter 5 (p. 101). In contrast, *saqia* and *shaduf* land consisted of relatively small areas that had to be watered mechanically but could be cropped almost continuously. *Shaduf* land was land to which water had to be lifted to a height of three metres or less, whereas *saqia* land could be situated as much as eight metres above the source of water. The amount of land that could be irrigated with either of these devices varied according to the height to which the water had to be lifted: the greater the height, the smaller the irrigated area. This area was further reduced during the hotter period of the year, when the evaporation rate was high. Basin land, although of importance in Egypt, was more limited in Nubia, and only along the Dongola Reach could it be exploited to any great extent. It consisted of land lying in natural depressions, adjacent to the river, into which floodwater overflowed, or was channelled by a canal. Basin agriculture could be highly productive but it required co-operation between large numbers of farmers. The availability of these different forms of land, at any point along the middle Nile, was an important factor influencing the location and extent of human settlement.

The life-giving waters of the Nile brought suffering to the inhabitants of Nubia also. Schistosomiasis, a water-borne disease that is common to all of tropical Africa and is caused by a blood fluke that lives in freshwater snails found in stagnant water, is particularly prevalent in the Nile Valley. Free-swimming at one stage in its life cycle, the fluke gains entry to the human bloodstream usually through breaks in the skin and then attacks the liver and other organs. A gradual deterioration in condition follows and this may continue for over twenty years. Another affliction in parts of the middle Nile region that is associated with water is onchocerciasis, or river blindness, caused by filarial worms transmitted by the minute fly *Simulium damnosum*, found chiefly between the Third and Fourth Cataracts (Manson-Bahr and Apted 1982: 166). Malaria, tuberculosis, and trachoma are other diseases which are to be found along the middle Nile and which may have been there for a long time (Adams 1977: 40–1).

A further constraint on human settlement that perhaps deserves mention, is the infestation of cultivated fields by large numbers of crows and sparrows, that extensively damage grain crops (Adams 1977: 39). During substantial periods of the past, however, it has been the depredations of human beings that have been a really major limiting factor. Not only has the middle Nile Valley suffered numerous military invasions from the technologically more sophisticated lands to its north, but also the sedentary farmers of the narrow riverine strip have been repeatedly terrorized by the nomadic pastoralists of the vast adjacent deserts. Particularly the latter was the case after the desert nomads adopted the camel, probably during the last century BC (Trigger 1965: 131). Circumstances such as these must have been a strong incentive to more powerful political organization and to greater social complexity. It is now appropriate to consider the evidence for these developments.

Sources of information

Present understanding of early cities and states in the middle Nile region is based on two types of evidence: historical documentation and archaeological data (Fig. 3.2). Except for the Islamic period of the second millennium AD, with which this chapter has little concern, the time-span is too great for oral tradition to be able to contribute. Adams (1977: 66) has identified six groups of historical sources and it is worth examining these in order to show both their strengths and their weaknesses.

The first group consists of Egyptian texts in hieroglyphic and hieratic. These cover the period from the first half of the third millennium BC to near the end of the second millennium BC, but there are relatively few which contain more than a passing reference to Nubia and they are primarily intended to record Egyptian exploits. Most commonly, they refer to Nubia as 'Kush', and the tone of these sources is indicated by the fact that they usually refer to it as 'miserable Kush'. Overall, these Egyptian sources provide us with an Egyptian version of Egyptian trading, military and colonial enterprise in the middle Nile region. In short, they give a one-sided view of economic and political history and tell us relatively little about Nubia itself (Adams 1977: 66–7; Adams 1984: 36).

The second group of historical sources comprises Nubian hieroglyphic texts of the Napatan period, from the eighth to about the fourth century BC (Adams 1977: 67–8). These sources date from after the Nubian conquest of Egypt, where Nubians ruled as pharaohs of the Twenty-Fifth Dynasty, during the latter part of the eighth century and the earlier part of the seventh century BC. At that time and even after they lost control of Egypt, the Nubian rulers had their view of things written down by Egyptian scribes in the Egyptian language and in hieroglyphics. It also appears that these texts were mainly intended for an Egyptian audience, and Adams (1977: 68) has claimed that: 'Many of them are not "Nubian" documents at all, but the annals of Nubian rulers and would-be rulers of Egypt.' Like the Egyptian texts, these sources have little to tell us about Nubia itself but they do shed valuable light on the political history of the Nubian and Egyptian region as a whole. Because they were written in Egyptian, however, they throw no light on the contemporary Nubian language or languages; so that when in later times Nubians developed their own indigenous 'Meroitic' alphabet, they left texts which remain unintelligible, largely (it appears) because the language in which they were written bears no recognizable relationship to any other language at present known to scholars. Used for texts from about the second century BC to about the fourth century AD, Meroitic writing can be read but the language of the writing cannot be really understood. In spite of extensive study of this problem (e.g. Trigger 1973) it is still true, as Peter Shinnie said in 1967, that: '. . . until this language has been successfully read and the inscriptions translated, much of the story of Meroë will remain unknown' (Shinnie 1967: 132).

The third group of historical sources is made up of historical and geographical writings by classical authors (Adams 1977: 68–9). One of the earliest and one of the most important of these was Herodotus, who visited Egypt in the fifth century BC and pieced together an account of the lands immediately to its south that still makes an important contribution to our knowledge of the Meroitic state. Other classical writers who contributed information on Nubia were Strabo, Diodorus Siculus, Pliny, Priscus, Olympiodorus, and Procopius. Collectively, these Greek and Latin texts are useful but they are essentially the view of the outsider looking in, and (so far as Nubia is concerned) they were written from hearsay evidence.

The fourth group of historical sources, that of medieval ecclesiastical histories, is comparatively limited in its value (Adams 1977: 69). A number of church historians, including John of Ephesus, wrote about the conversion in the sixth century AD of Nubia to Christianity but their accounts conflict with one another depending on their doctrinal background. Also, the information that they give is mainly concerned with the first century of Christian Nubia, because after that the Arab conquest of Egypt cut off Nubia's contact with the rest of Christendom until the end of the medieval period.

The fifth group of historical sources consists of medieval Arab histories and geographies (Adams 1977: 70). The most important of these is the fourteenth-century geographer al-Maqrizi, whose writing also preserves part of a tenth-century first-hand account of Nubia. Other sources of this type include works by al-Masudi, al-Umari, Abu Salih, and ibn Khaldun. Again, these represent the views of outsiders and they are confined to the first half of the second millennium AD, coming to a halt with the Ottoman conquest of Egypt and northern Nubia in the early sixteenth century.

The sixth and last group of historical sources takes over where the medieval Arabic sources leave off. This group consists of works by European travellers in the early modern period (Adams 1977: 70). Their value is very limited for the sixteenth and seventeenth centuries but the eighteenth-century travellers, Poncet, Krump, and Bruce each recorded some information on Nubia. It is to the nineteenth century, however, that the bulk of this type of source material belongs. Most important of the nineteenth-century travellers who have left accounts of the region are Burckhardt, Waddington and Hanbury, Cailliaud, Linant de Bellefonds, Hoskins, and Lepsius. Yet again, these are accounts by outsiders but they are an extremely important source of information for modern scholars.

Thus there are nearly 5000 years of some sort of historical documentation for the middle Nile. This documentation has three characteristics, however, that considerably weaken its value as a source of information. First, generally speaking the further up the Nile one goes, the less informative are the historical texts. Second, in total these texts provide only an intermittent recorded history, which is frequently broken by periods of which little is known. Third, and

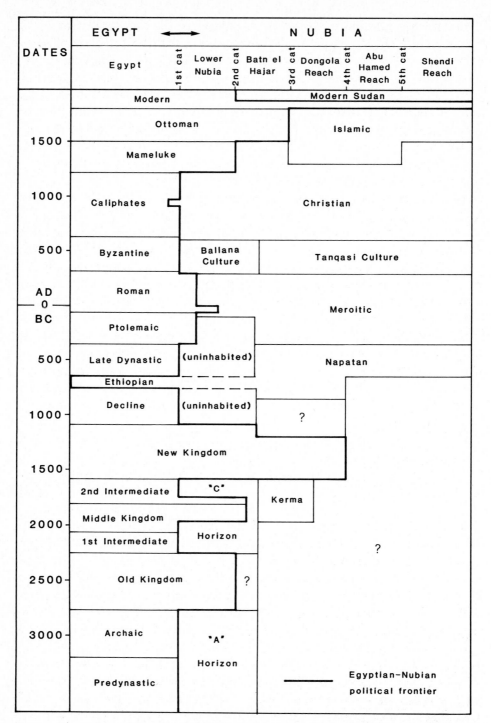

Fig. 3.2 Chronology of Egyptian and Nubian cultural periods. Read time from bottom to top and space from left (north) to right (south). After Adams (1977: Fig. 2).

perhaps most important, most of the documentation that exists was written by foreigners to Nubia, who were, at best, visitors to the region attempting to understand what they saw and, at worst, distant scholars using information that had already passed through several hands. The situation would be different for part of the time if the numerous Meroitic inscriptions could be properly understood but they cannot. During the periods with which this chapter is concerned, Nubia belongs neither to history nor to prehistory but to that grey zone that some have called protohistory (Hawkes 1951: 1–2).

In such circumstances archaeological evidence has a vital role to play, although neither the historian nor the archaeologist can afford to ignore one another. Nevertheless, studies of ancient Nubia seem to have suffered from something of an historical bias, probably because of the way that archaeological research developed in the area. Although archaeological fieldwork in Nubia commenced at the beginning of the present century with the work of Reisner, Firth, Griffith, Garstang, and Wellcome, to be followed in the years up to 1958 by various others (Adams 1977: 78–80), there was an unfortunate tendency for excavations to be tomb-temple-and-palace oriented and for much of the detailed information never to reach publication. Only with the international archaeological campaign of the 1960s, that was made necessary by the construction of the Aswan High Dam and the creation of Lake Nasser, did there develop both an interest in the excavation of settlement sites and a substantial archaeological literature. It was at that time that Adams, reviewing post-pharaonic Nubia in the light of the available archaeological evidence, complained:

> ... it seems that in Nubia archaeology has suffered at the hands of written history. Any kind of documentary evidence, no matter how fragmentary, ambiguous, or unreliable, has generally been accorded a higher place than archaeological evidence – a priority which it certainly does not invariably deserve. (Adams 1966: 156)

With this quotation in mind, and having already outlined the strengths and weaknesses of the historical evidence, it is now appropriate to review the major areas of the archaeological evidence.

The earliest archaeological sites relevant to the origins of cities and states in the middle Nile region are not Nubian at all but Egyptian. They represent two main periods of colonial expansion, first during the pharaonic Middle Kingdom, and second during the New Kingdom. The first of these expansions belonged mainly to the Egyptian Twelfth Dynasty of the first quarter of the second millennium BC and resulted in the construction of a series of forts in Lower Nubia, most of them clustered around the Second Cataract (Adams 1977: 175–83). Of the at least ten forts in the latter area, Buhen is the most completely published of those that have been excavated and consisted of an elaborate series of mud-brick fortifications built on a massive scale. Its carefully designed defences were of a rectangular plan and enclosed a small town containing houses, barracks, workshops, a temple, and a Governor's palace (Emery 1965: 149). Indeed, it appears that this was not the first Egyptian town at Buhen, for during the Fourth and Fifth Dynasties, around the middle of the third millennium BC, and perhaps even earlier, there was already a sizeable town surrounded by a stone wall (Adams 1977: 170–74). Evidence for Egyptian occupation as far south as this during the Old Kingdom is rare, however, whereas the Middle Kingdom forts are numerous. This has led to an assumption that they were constructed in order to protect Egypt's new southern frontier. Adams has questioned this and has suggested that their locations indicate that they were primarily intended to protect and control the commerce of the Nile Valley. 'In sum, the Second Cataract Forts should probably be regarded as the Adens and Gibraltars of the Nile trade, rather than as territorial defenses of Egypt' (Adams 1984: 47).

During the pharaonic Second Intermediate Period, which lasted from about the end of the first quarter of the second millennium BC to about the middle of that millennium, Egyptian political control of Lower Nubia seems to have weakened and the Second Cataract forts may have been abandoned. However, the New Kingdom, of the second half of the second millennium BC, saw a new colonial initiative by Egypt that extended her dominion further up the Nile than ever before, or indeed ever again until the conquests of Mohammed Ali early in the nineteenth century AD. In addition, the Egyptian New Kingdom seems to have aimed not merely to control Nubian trade but to control Nubia.

Egyptian authority was established as far south as the Fourth Cataract, and perhaps further. The Middle Kingdom forts were restored and enlarged and new fortified towns were built in the Abri-Delgo Reach and in the Dongola Reach. As time went on, the military character of Egyptian settlement diminished and the building of temples replaced the building of fortresses. During the period as a whole, however, colonial settlements of importance grew up particularly in the Abri-Delgo Reach and included such towns as Sai, Amara, Soleb, Seddenga, and Sesebi (Delgo), of which the last has been extensively excavated (Fairman 1938). Further south, in the Dongola Reach, there was less Egyptian colonization but towns developed at both Kawa and Napata, possibly to control the Meheila Road, a desert route that cut across the great bend of the Nile in this region. There are also numerous remains of Egyptian temples, of New Kingdom date, in Nubia. Perhaps the most remarkable of these is the temple of Abu Simbel in Lower Nubia but probably the most important from the point of view of the subsequent history of Nubia was that constructed far to the south at Jebel Barkal, where the Temple of Amon, founded by the Egyptian pharaoh Rameses II, was later to become the ideological centre of the indigenous Nubian Napatan State. New Kingdom colonization of the middle Nile terminated towards the end of the second millennium BC, probably because of growing political problems in Egypt itself but possibly also because the level of the Nile was falling. The colonial domination of Nubia by Egypt was over but its consequences for the people of Nubia were to be far-reaching and long-lasting (Adams 1977: 217–45).

Indeed, Egyptian commercial and colonial involvement in Nubia had already elicited an indigenous Nubian response by the latter part of the Second Intermediate Period. It was at this time, that is to say in about the sixteenth century BC, that the Nubian kingdom of Kerma was at the climax of its development (Adams 1977: 195–216; Adams 1984: 48–53). It seems that this kingdom arose at a time of Egyptian weakness, when the Second Cataract forts may have been abandoned, and that it disappeared at the time of Egypt's colonial expansion during the New Kingdom. This would suggest that Kerma, the earliest example of centralized political authority in Nubia, depended heavily on the control of Nubian commerce.

Most of the relevant archaeological evidence comes from Kerma itself, a complex of sites situated on the east bank of the Nile at the northern end of the Dongola Reach, the most fertile region of the middle Nile. Not only is the floodplain broad at this point but the Kerma Basin, that is flooded each year by the river, permits basin agriculture which is otherwise rare in the Sudan (Adams 1977: 199). Excavations were conducted at Kerma by G.A. Reisner, in 1913–1916, and were concentrated on an extensive cemetery which is thought to have contained several thousand graves (Reisner 1923). A substantial number of these were covered by burial mounds, or 'tumuli' as the excavator called them. Of these tumuli, eight were unusually large, the largest of them being about 91 metres in diameter. Like the smaller examples they contained burial chambers but in the case of the three largest, the body of the mound had an internal structure made up of a series of long, straight, parallel, mud-brick walls that seem to have provided a kind of framework for the mound. Part of this internal structure consisted of a corridor which ran right across the mound and the other walls were oriented at right angles to this corridor. In the main chamber, the principal burial lay upon a bed, accompanied by weapons and personal possessions. The rest of the space, however, was taken up by other human bodies, whose attitudes suggested to the excavator that they had been sacrificed. A far larger number of sacrifices lay in the transverse corridor, and later subsidiary burials, some also accompanied by human sacrifices, had been inserted in many places between the walls that ran at right angles to the 'sacrificial corridor', as Reisner called it. In Tumulus X, where the main chamber had been long ago robbed, Reisner found 322 sacrifices in the sacrificial corridor (Fig. 3.3), and estimated that there had originally been as many as 400 before disturbance by tomb robbers (Reisner 1923: Parts I–III, 312). Adams (1977: 203) has claimed that this is a larger number of human sacrifices 'than in any other known tomb of any civilization'. He could well be right. Such evidence surely suggests a highly centralized political authority and, if such did exist at Kerma, might it not be justifiable to claim this place as the earliest state in black Africa? Reisner thought that the burials were those of Nubianized Egyptians of

Middle Kingdom date, and that Kerma had been the headquarters of the Egyptian official known as the 'Viceroy of Kush' but subsequently both Reisner's dating and his Egyptocentric interpretation have been rejected (Adams 1977: 208–10). Although Kerma is now seen as an indigenous development, whose origins can be traced back to the third millennium BC (Bonnet 1984), there is nevertheless substantial evidence of Egyptian influence during its period of greatest attainment and it is possible that a small number of Egyptians were actually living there at that time in order to supervise the Nubian end of the Nile commerce.

Indications that this may have been so, come particularly from two massive mud-brick structures that Reisner also investigated at Kerma. These very striking archaeological features appear to be the remains of enormous towers of solid mud-brick and are locally known as the *deffufas*. From the manner of their construction it seems that they were designed by Egyptian architects. The smaller of them, the Eastern (Upper) *Deffufa*, is situated in the cemetery already discussed and appears to have been some sort of outsize mortuary chapel (Reisner 1923: Parts I–III, 122–34). It is actually one of two such structures in the cemetery but far less has survived of the other (Reisner 1923: Parts I–III, 255–71). Both contain relatively narrow chambers, the insides of which have been painted in an Egyptian style, but their mud-brick walls are over 9 metres in thickness. The Western (Lower) *Deffufa* is situated some way from the cemetery and is even larger (Reisner 1923: Parts I–III, 21–40). It is a solid rectangular mass of mud-brick, measuring about 27 by 52 metres at the base and originally probably far exceeding the height of 19 metres that has survived to this century. This strange structure has no internal chambers, only the remains of a narrow, winding stair that must have led to its top. Recent excavations by Bonnet, however, have now shown that it was not originally a solid structure but a temple with interior chambers that were later filled in with brickwork (Bonnet 1982a). In this later form it seems probable that the Western *Deffufa* was some sort of watchtower associated with the Nile trade and, indeed, attached to one side of it was a building from which were excavated over five hundred mud sealings of Egyptian type, which had been affixed to various sorts of containers. There were in addition many fragments of items of Egyptian manufacture and various kinds of raw materials, as well as evidence that some manufacturing was taking place on the spot. In short, in its final form, the Western *Deffufa*, in the words of Adams (1984: 51), 'was a factory, in the older sense of the word: a depot where the goods of the south were assembled for shipment to Egypt, and where the manufactures of the north were received (and to some extent produced) in exchange.'

If Kerma *was* the earliest black African state, and Adams has claimed that it was 'a chiefdom rather than a state' (Adams 1984: 50), then was there any associated evidence of urbanization? Until recently, no habitation sites were known at all and therefore this question could only be answered in the negative

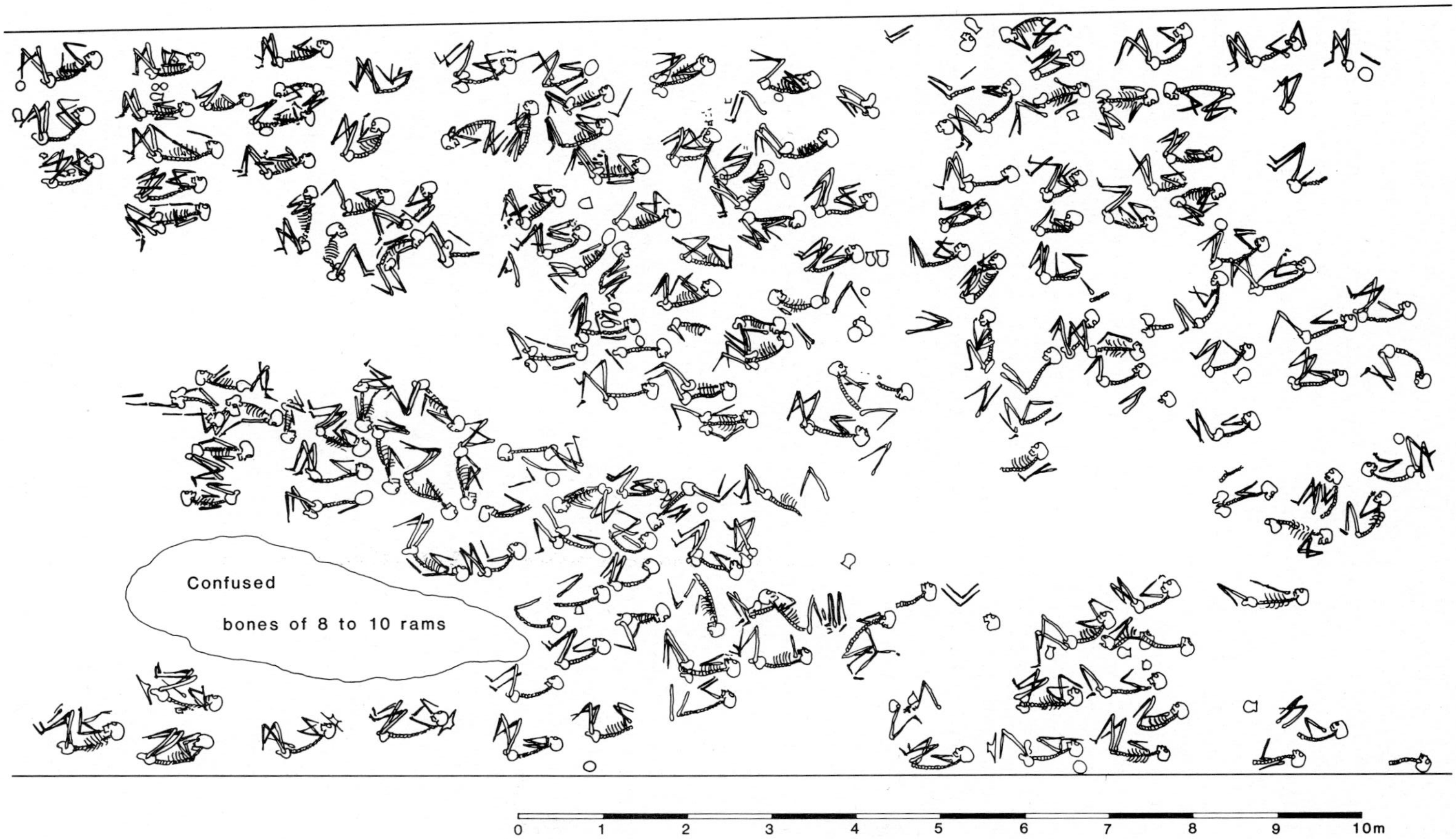

Fig. 3.3 Part of the human sacrifices in Tumulus X at Kerma. After Reisner (1923: Part III, Plan XXIV).

Confused bones of 8 to 10 rams

0 1 2 3 4 5 6 7 8 9 10m

or at best remain an open one. It has now been demonstrated, however, that the site of a city lies adjacent to the Western *Deffufa*. Here Bonnet (1982b; 1984) has excavated part of a large fortified city, whose origins have been dated to the third millennium BC, containing houses built of stone or mud-brick or wood. Whether Kerma was indeed a state could, no doubt, be debated but it is clear that if it had not actually arrived, it was well on its way.

The next indigenous response to Egyptian influences in Nubia was that of Napata, a kingdom that arose on the Dongola Reach of the middle Nile during the ninth century BC (Haycock 1968; Adams 1977: 246–93). This kingdom, usually known as the Kingdom of Kush, was focussed until the fourth century BC on an area extending downstream from the Fourth Cataract for a distance of 24 kilometres or so. It is the whole of this district that is usually referred to as Napata, and it includes major cemetery sites at El Kurru (Dunham 1950) and Nuri (Dunham 1955), a cemetery and temple sites at Jebel Barkal, and a cemetery, temple and town site at Sanam (Griffith 1922). After the fourth century BC, the political focus of Kush seems to have moved south to Meroë on the Shendi Reach of the Nile, although the cultural and chronological relationship of Napata and Meroë is still not fully understood. Napata seems to have had its origins in the power vacuum left by the collapse of Egyptian colonial domination towards the end of the second millennium BC. As already mentioned (p. 36), the Egyptian colonization of the New Kingdom period had led to the growth of a town at Napata and to the construction of a temple of Amon at Jebel Barkal. With the end of Egyptian control, it seems that power fell into the hands of local rulers who, with the sanction of the priests of Jebel Barkal, went on to control not only much of Nubia but also, for a brief period in the eighth and seventh centuries BC, Egypt itself which they ruled as the Twenty-Fifth Dynasty. Subsequently, Napata gradually became of less significance but neither its rulers nor those of Meroë, its apparent successor, ever relinquished the style or titles of the Egyptian pharaohs. In particular, the culture of Napata seems to have become little more than a diluted and provincial imitation of that of pharaonic Egypt. Napata remained important to Meroitic rulers, however, who continued to be crowned there, to build temples there, and on occasion even to be buried there long after the transfer of the capital to Meroë.

Archaeological evidence for the Napatan state, if it can be called such, is mainly limited to the sites already mentioned. The cemeteries at El Kurru, Jebel Barkal and Nuri have been interpreted as 'royal' cemeteries, and it is from El Kurru and Nuri, excavated early this century by Reisner, that much of our information comes. All three cemeteries are characterized by tombs covered by small pyramids and even mummification was practised but at El Kurru there are also tumuli which on typological grounds are thought to be of earlier date. Temples at Jebel Barkal and Sanam have also been excavated and in a number of other places there are the remains of temples constructed by Taharqa, one of the Nubian rulers of Egypt. Nevertheless, there is little known about Napatan settlement sites, in spite of the fact that there appears to have been a very large town at Sanam, which may have been the principal population centre of Napata. Thus, although hieroglyphic inscriptions from excavated tombs have enabled a substantial reconstruction to be undertaken of the Napatan dynastic sequence (Dunham and Macadam 1949), we have relatively little information about the social and economic organization of the people that these rulers governed. Adams (1977: 293) is of the opinion that this was not a 'complex, urbanized society' or one with an 'extensive commerce'. Instead, he sees it as 'a primitive, largely agrarian state with a small middle class, whose rulers derived their excessive wealth primarily from a monopoly of gold production'. Be this as it may, the achievements of Napata were clearly important for the subsequent development of the Meroitic state. It is also interesting to note that Napata was at both the terminus of the Bayuda Road, the land route to Meroë, and of the Meheila Road, the land route to Kawa and Argo, which possibly, with Seddenga further to the north, were also Napatan settlements of importance. Napata, it would appear, must surely have been a major staging point in the trade of the middle Nile.

As Napata declined, Meroë rose to prominence and in its case there is abundant archaeological evidence that has been widely accepted as indicating both urbanization and state development. Meroë seems to have been of particular importance during the first century AD but its total life-span probably extended from before the fourth century BC to about the fourth century AD. Excavations at the site of Meroë itself have indeed indicated that its earliest building level could have belonged to the seventh century BC (Shinnie and Bradley 1980: 16). Like Napata, Meroë seems to have been an indigenous Nubian response to the classical world to its north. In the case of Napata, it was pharaonic Egypt that was the main cultural influence; in the case of Meroë, it was Ptolemaic Egypt, which was in turn part of the wider Hellenistic world. As Adams (1977: 295) has expressed it: 'Ptolemaic Egypt and Meroitic Kush were provincial expressions of a world civilization'.

Archaeological evidence for the Meroitic period includes the remains of a number of towns or cities, of which Meroë itself is the most important. Situated on the east bank of the Nile, some 200 kilometres downstream from modern Khartoum, Meroë has suffered a chequered archaeological history. Forgotten until its rediscovery at the end of the eighteenth century AD, parts of the site were 'ransacked' by Ferlini in the 1830s (Adams 1977: 295) and early in the present century parts were excavated at various separate times by Budge, Garstang, and Reisner. Only Reisner's work was conducted in an adequate fashion and even his excavations had to be published posthumously by Dows Dunham. The extensive excavations by Garstang were both unscientific and largely unpublished, only the first season's work being described in any detail (Garstang, Sayce and Griffiths 1911). The rather limited excavations by Peter Shinnie during the 1960s and 1970s remain, in fact, the only archaeological investigations at Meroë to have been carried out and published in a proper scientific fashion (Shinnie and Bradley 1980). Fortunately, however, prior to those excavations, Shinnie drew together much of what was then known about Meroë and related sites into a monograph, that although intended to be a popular publication has remained a standard work (Shinnie 1967).

The city of Meroë appears to have covered an area measuring roughly three-quarters of a kilometre by one kilometre (for plans, see Shinnie 1967: 76; Adams 1977: 299, 314; Bradley 1982: 164). Within the city was a large, stone-walled precinct, more or less rectangular in shape, within which lay a labyrinth of buildings, mostly of monumental character. Many of these buildings, which were usually of mud-brick, often with an external facing of fired brick, were excavated by Garstang who interpreted the area as the residence of the rulers of Meroë, calling it the 'Royal City'. Its buildings were believed to include palaces, audience chambers, stores, and domestic quarters for the palace staff (Adams 1977: 314–5). There was also a small temple, in front of which was found a bronze head of Augustus, of Roman manufacture (Shinnie 1967: Plate 28). Perhaps the most remarkable feature of the Royal City, however, was its so-called 'Roman Bath'. This consisted of a large brick-lined tank with water channels leading into it from a nearby well. Its general design and ornate decoration suggested that it had been a place of recreation and it was interpreted as a swimming bath (Shinnie 1967: 79).

Outside of the Royal City, much of the rest of the site is covered by two extensive occupation mounds and it has recently been suggested that the city originated as a settlement split between three separate alluvial islands in a braided channel of the River Nile, the course of the river having since changed (Bradley 1982). The south mound remains unexcavated and the only investigations of the north mound have been test excavations by Shinnie. These revealed remains of mud-brick structures serving industrial, domestic and public functions (Shinnie and Bradley 1980; Bradley 1982). Other than this, little is known of the ordinary buildings of the city, although Shinnie (1967: 77) describes the 'greater part of the town area' as 'consisting of many mounds covered with red [fired] brick fragments' and mentions 'six large mounds of slag and other debris of iron smelting' on the edges of the city. The significance of these mounds of slag has long been discussed but no systematic excavation has been attempted on them. Some idea of their size can be gained from the fact that a railway-cutting has had to be made through one of them to carry the line from Khartoum to Atbara. It is presumed to be this mound into which Arkell excavated an unpublished trial trench in 1940, recording that it consisted of 'solid slag and debris from iron smelting from top to bottom' (Shinnie and Kense 1982: 18).

The site of Meroë is also characterized, however, by the remains of a number of temples and, in contrast with the scant attention given to the residential and industrial areas of the city, the more important of these have been entirely excavated. They include a major temple of Amon, adjacent to the Royal City; a temple of Isis, on the northern edge of the city; the Lion Temple, which stands on top of one of the slag heaps on the eastern edge of the city; and the Sun Temple, which is situated about one kilometre east of the city. There is also the Shrine of

Apis, located about 2.5 kilometres south of the Royal City, and several lesser temples within the city itself. In addition, archaeological attention has been focussed on the cemeteries of Meroë. Just to the east of the city lie three cemeteries which have been entirely excavated and which were found to contain a total of 599 graves, thought to have been occupied by common citizens of Meroë. Some 3–4 kilometres east of the city, however, lie three other cemeteries. The most important of these is the North Cemetery, which was the main burial place of the rulers of Meroë and their immediate relatives, characterized by the best preserved of the small stone pyramids for which Meroë has become famous. The South Cemetery comprises over 200 graves, most of which were found to contain common citizens, but it also includes a number of mastabas and pyramids belonging both to rulers and (it is thought) to members of the ruling family. In contrast the West Cemetery, which contains about 500 graves, including a number of pyramids, seems to have been intended for less important members of the royal family and also for commoners (Shinnie 1967: 75–87).

In many ways it is most regrettable that the attention of archaeologists who have worked at Meroë has been concentrated so often on the tomb-temple-and-palace aspect of the place, rather than on the city itself. Nevertheless, such an emphasis has resulted in the discovery of both inscriptions and artistic representations that have made substantial contributions to our knowledge of Meroitic society and history. In particular, we know the names and approximate dates of most of the rulers of Meroë, even though there is still some uncertainty about the details of this dynastic sequence (Shinnie 1967: 58–61; Adams 1977: 251–2). The inscriptions are in Meroitic, however, either rendered in hiero-glyphs or in the distinctive Meroitic cursive alphabet, and because this language cannot be fully understood (p. 32) they can only be read in part. Luckily, the temple and Pyramid-chapel reliefs and the small number of pieces of sculpture in-the-round, are more informative: depicting gods, rulers (male and female) and vanquished enemies and generally throwing light on royal dress and regalia and on iconography and religion (Shinnie 1967: 101–9).

There are many other sites along the middle Nile which both culturally and chronologically can be described as 'Meroitic'. Perhaps the most important of these are situated in the western part of the 'Island of Meroë', a name usually applied to the area known as the Butana, in the triangle formed by the confluence of the rivers Atbara and Nile. Two of these sites are particularly significant: Naqa and Musawwarat es-Sufra (Shinnie 1967: 87–95; Adams 1977: 318–21). No excavations have been carried out at Naqa but there are remains of a town nearly as extensive as those of Meroë itself and there are at least seven stone temples and two large cemeteries. One of the temples, the Lion Temple of Natakamani and Amanitere, has remarkable exterior reliefs depicting the first-century-BC to first-century-AD king and queen (Fig. 3.4) and the lion-god Apedemak. The reliefs on the two pylons of this temple are a particularly explicit statement of autocratic authority, showing both king and queen brandishing weapons whilst grasping their vanquished foes by the hair. The message could

Fig. 3.4 Queen Amanitere depicted on the Lion Temple at Naqa. From Budge (1907: Vol. 2, 133).

not be clearer! In contrast, the site of Musawwarat es-Sufra remains something of a mystery, in spite of fairly recent excavations. This site consists only of a cluster of monumental stone buildings, of which the largest, the Great Enclosure, is a maze of enclosures, corridors, ramps and chambers that has no Nubian or Egyptian parallel. Shinnie has suggested that it was 'a centre for the training of elephants for military and ceremonial purposes' (Shinnie 1967: 94) and Adams, although commenting that this 'sounds somehow far-fetched', admits that 'it is difficult to propose a more logical explanation' (Adams 1977: 320). Whatever the correct explanation, it would seem that the purpose of this site was at least partly religious.

One other site in the Meroë area deserves a mention here. This is Wad ben Naqa on the east bank of the Nile, where there is evidence of a considerable town. Excavations here have revealed the remains of an enormous square building of at least two storeys, that has been interpreted as a Meroitic palace. It was built of mud-brick, its exterior walls faced with fired brick and plastered over with white stucco. Only the lower floor was preserved and this consisted mainly of long, narrow rooms that were probably vaulted storerooms, supporting more important rooms in the storey above. Nevertheless, the plan (Fig. 3.5) is an impressive indication of the development of centralized authority in the Meroitic state (Vercoutter 1962; Adams 1977: 322–3).

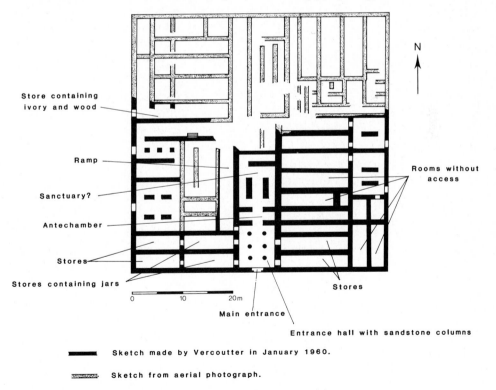

Fig. 3.5 Plan of Meroitic palace, Wad ben Naqa. After Vercoutter (1962: Fig. 8).

Other evidence of Meroitic occupation has been found as far south as Sennar, far up the Blue Nile, and as far north as Maharraqa, in Lower Nubia, a distance of over 1100 kilometres as the crow flies. The distance along the river itself is very much greater, of course, but Meroitic settlement on the middle Nile was discontinuous, being concentrated along those stretches of the river that were economically more viable. Adams (1977: 302) has identified three main areas of Meroitic culture: the Southern Province, containing Meroë itself; the Napatan Province; and the Lower Nubian Province. The Southern Province, which may be regarded as the Meroitic homeland, was connected to the Napatan Province not by the barren Abu Hamed Reach of the Nile (p. 27) but by the Bayuda Road, a most important desert road that bypassed both the Fifth and Fourth Cataracts and the contrary winds of this part of the Nile. In the Napatan Province there was Meroitic activity at Jebel Barkal, Sanam, Kawa and Argo and (further north) at Seddenga, but the development of the Korosko Road – a desert route leaving the Nile at Abu Hamed that rejoined it far downstream in Lower Nubia – cut this area off from the mainstream of commerce, so that the Napatan Province became something of a cultural and economic backwater. It seems quite likely that the introduction of the camel, probably in the last century BC, was one of the main factors in bringing about this change (Adams 1977: 304–5). North of the Napatan Province lay the barren and empty *Batn el Hajar* (p. 29) but beyond that was the Lower Nubian Province where there is evidence of almost continuous Meroitic settlement (Adams 1977: 345–81). Because of the extensive excavations carried out in this area during the 1960s, in connection with the construction of the Aswan High Dam, we probably know more about Meroitic life in Lower Nubia than in either of the other two provinces. This was no mere frontier zone adjacent to Ptolemaic and Roman Egypt but a most important part of the Meroitic state. As already explained (p. 30), it was an area that had been virtually uninhabited for some centuries but was resettled in the second and third centuries AD as a result of the introduction of the *saqia*, the ox-driven waterwheel, that made it possible to cultivate land along this section of the river that previously could not be utilized. The evidence of both cemeteries and occupation sites indicates that Meroitic settlement in Lower Nubia was characterized not by large urban centres with monumental buildings, as in the southern provinces, but by a nearly continuous line of prosperous farming villages along the Nile, together with a few relatively small administrative centres. The latter included Qasr Ibrim, Gebel Adda, and Faras, all of them walled cities. Qasr Ibrim and Gebel Adda, indeed, stood on high promontories overlooking the east bank of the Nile and were heavily fortified. Karanog appears to have been another important centre but it consisted of a rather scattered collection of houses without a surrounding wall. Instead, it was defended by a massive, three-storey castle of mud-brick that seems to have been unique in Nubia at this time. The cultural differences between the Meroitic north and south have prompted Adams to observe that 'the monumental remains of the Meroitic north are suggestive not of divine kingship but of military feudalism' (Adams 1974: 47). He has concluded that in Lower Nubia there had been a secularization of government and that control of trade had passed into private hands, allowing a widespread development of material prosperity (see also Adams 1976).

These developments in Lower Nubia foreshadowed the eventual disintegration of the Meroitic state. This seems to have occurred at some time in the fourth century AD, significantly at a time when substantial changes were taking place in the Mediterranean world to the north. The only indication, in the archaeological record, of the emergence of a successor state to Meroë is in Lower Nubia, where the remains of the 'X-Group', called by Adams the 'Ballana Culture' (1977: 392), suggest the development of an absolute monarchy during the fifth and sixth centuries AD. The X-Group was first recognized on the basis of burial evidence from scattered cemeteries but as time went on a number of village sites were identified and it also became apparent that there had been major settlements at Gebel Adda and at Qasr Ibrim. Excavations at this latter site have, indeed, revealed the remains of well-built stone houses belonging to this period, arranged along straight, intersecting streets, and associated evidence suggests that Qasr Ibrim was a manufacturing centre of some importance at this time (Adams 1982: 27–8).

Nevertheless, the X-Group continues to be best known from the remarkable burials of Ballana and Qustul, situated a little upstream of Gebel Adda. These were excavated by Walter Emery in the early 1930s and produced evidence of an enormous concentration of wealth and autocratic power in the hands of a few individuals, who were interpreted as having been kings (Emery 1938; Emery 1948). There were 122 tombs at Ballana on the west bank of the Nile and 61 at Qustul on the east bank. All 183 of these tombs were excavated, and the size of the structures and richness of contents of perhaps 40 of them might suggest that they contained 'royal' burials. Typically, these larger tombs consisted of a series of brick chambers, constructed at the bottom of a large pit, which was entered by means of a ramp cut into the hard alluvium. The chambers were roofed with barrel-vaulting and in front of them there was often a small open court into which the entrance ramp opened. After the burials and offerings had been placed inside the chambers, in the court and at the bottom of the ramp, both the pit and the ramp were filled with earth and a large earthen mound was raised over them. At Ballana the largest of these mounds measured 77 metres in diameter and 12 metres in height. It was the contents of these tombs that were most impressive, however. The 'king' was buried with his 'queen', with his servants, with his horses, camels, donkeys, dogs, sheep and cows. Also included were furniture, food and drink, cooking utensils, jewels, weapons, tools and all manner of personal possessions. Without going into considerable detail, it is impossible to give an adequate impression of the richness of these burials or of their complexity.

Many of these tombs had been ransacked by tomb-robbers in the past but some of them had survived intact. One of the more remarkable of these was Tomb 95 at Ballana, the plan of which is reproduced here (Fig. 3.6). Animal burials lay at the bottom of the entrance ramp, beyond which were three sealed burial chambers. Inside the first chamber was the skeleton of the 'king', who had been laid, wearing his silver crown and other finery, on a wooden bier from which he had been displaced soon after burial by the collapse of the chamber roof. Also in the chamber were the skeletons of his 'queen', wearing a silver crown, and of a male servant and of a cow. Weapons and other personal possessions lay in some other parts of the chamber. In an adjacent chamber were the skeletons of no less than six additional servants, two of them children, accompanied by more weapons and by lamps, iron ingots, pottery wine jars, drinking cups and several other things. Most of the third and final chamber was packed with more pottery wine jars and drinking cups and with them were numerous bronze cups, a bronze flagon and pan, a stone bowl, a large vessel of

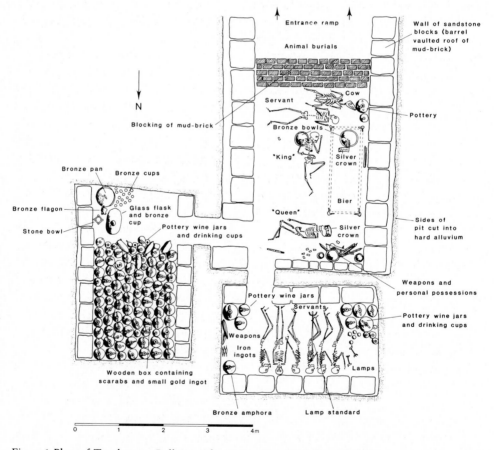

Fig. 3.6 Plan of Tomb 95 at Ballana. After Emery (1938: Vol. 1, Fig. 68).

green glass, several scarabs and a small gold ingot. In all, the excavator listed 295 objects from this tomb, plus the burials themselves (Emery 1938: Vol. I, 135–41).

The animals buried in the tombs at Ballana and Qustul had been pole-axed and it was presumed that the human beings, other than the main burial in each tomb, had met their deaths either by the cutting of their throats or by strangulation. The combination of monumental tomb, of wealth and of human sacrifice, for the burial of crowned individuals, is surely indicative of some form of absolute monarchy in Lower Nubia during the time to which the X-Group belongs?

Reisner, who first identified the X-Group, thought that it represented an invasion of a new people. If one accepted such an interpretation, the burials of Ballana and Qustul might be seen as suggesting a nomadic pastoralist origin for the deceased. There is, however, increasing evidence that the X-Group evolved within the Nile Valley, where both settlement and burial evidence (such as that from Qasr Ibrim) suggest that it was a direct successor culture to the Meroitic state, with similar subsistence strategies. Then, with the conversion of the people of the middle Nile to Christianity in the sixth century AD, a new period of state development and urbanization was inaugurated along these parts of the great river (Adams 1977: 421–2, 429; Trigger 1969b).

The Christian kingdoms of Nubia (Adams 1977: 433–546) existed from the sixth century to about the fourteenth century AD, their last remnant actually disappearing at the end of the fifteenth century. The two major states were Makouria, to the north, and Alwa, to the south, and they have left a large quantity of archaeological evidence. There are, for instance, the remains of a hundred churches built of brick and stone. There is also evidence of great urban centres at Qasr Ibrim, Gebel Adda, Faras, Old Dongola and Soba, as well as evidence elsewhere of many smaller towns and villages, fortresses, monasteries, industrial sites and cemeteries. The churches of medieval Nubia have attracted archaeological interest since early this century (Clarke 1912) but it was not until the 1960s that much work was done on other Christian sites. Study of church architecture has revealed a steady reduction in size and a decline in pretentiousness as time went on, reflecting the gradual decline of Christian Nubia and the concomitant increasingly esoteric character of the Monophysite, Coptic church. Nevertheless, many of the buildings were impressive structures with stone columns, masonry piers and brick vaults. Most important of those studied so far are the episcopal cathedrals at Qasr Ibrim, Faras, and Old Dongola and a possible cathedral at Gebel Adda (Adams 1977: 473–8). The insides of many churches were originally decorated with brightly coloured wall paintings, which achieved artistic expression of a high order. Only fragmentary remains of these were known until the 1960s, when excavations revealed well-preserved paintings in three different churches, of which those discovered in Faras cathedral have been called by Adams (1977: 482) 'the outstanding archaeological find of this generation'. The cathedral at Faras (Vantini 1970) had been abandoned after it had become filled with blown sand during the heyday of Nubian Christianity. Within it were numerous large paintings depicting biblical scenes and individuals, as well as Nubian kings, bishops and eparchs (high-ranking government officials), most of whom were identified by name. The Faras paintings have provided an important insight into Christian Nubia.

The archaeological remnants of the churches of Nubia indicate the existence of organized religion and secular authority as separate but interacting entities, each needing the protection of the other. Under their joint umbrella, the society of the middle Nile developed its commercial activities to a high level and became, at least in the northern part of the region, probably more densely urbanized than in earlier periods. Unfortunately, archaeological excavation of the major urban centres has not been as extensive as could be wished, both Faras and Gebel Adda, for instance, being lost beneath Lake Nasser before much could be done. Work has continued at the remarkable site of Qasr Ibrim, however, which was occupied throughout the Christian period and which has survived as an island at the edge of Lake Nasser. Excavations there have demonstrated that the Early Christian period (c.500–c.800 AD) displayed a remarkable continuity from X-Group times, with many of the same houses remaining in use and manufacturing activities, particularly weaving and woodworking, continuing on a large scale. Only the conversion of Meroitic temples to churches and the building of a cathedral and of a monastery mark the introduction of Christianity. During the Classic Christian period, however, which lasted roughly from c.800 to c.1200 AD, the city seems to have become primarily a religious and pilgrimage centre, with most of its housing being cleared to provide a large open plaza, perhaps to accommodate the large numbers of religious visitors. Nevertheless, during the Late Christian period (c.1200–c.1500 AD) the site was again fortified and once more became crowded with houses, regaining its commercial importance and (according to excavated manuscript material) also becoming an administrative centre (Adams 1982: 28–30).

Excavations have also been proceeding at the site of Old Dongola, far to the south, which was the capital city of the Christian kingdom of Makouria. Some indication of the standard of living in this city during the Classic Christian period, for at least some of its citizens, may be gained from the heated bathroom with piped hot water and painted decorations which has been found in one supposed house (Jakobielski 1982). Even further to the south the site of the city of Soba, the capital of the kingdom of Alwa, has also been subject to excavation and has revealed rectangular buildings of mud-brick and fired brick, as well as a remarkable collection of imported glass of the sixth to twelfth centuries (Shinnie 1955). More recent excavations have added to this evidence and have confirmed the chronology with radiocarbon dating (Welsby 1984). At none of these great urban centres, however, has there yet been sufficient area excavation to reveal the layout and overall characteristics of the settlement. For such details, we must turn to smaller settlements, of which a number have been excavated. These include Arminna West, Debeira West, Meinarti, Tamit and Kasanarti; places that Adams (1977: 488) calls 'villages' but describes as 'densely urbanized'. Both Arminna West (Weeks 1967) and Debeira West (Shinnie and Shinnie 1978) are in fact referred to as 'towns' by their excavators. These were primarily farming communities, that Adams thinks numbered only 200–400 inhabitants. The settlements had no formal plan or nucleus, consisting merely of tightly clustered, irregular blocks of houses usually of mud-brick, which were separated by narrow, winding alleys. Nevertheless, Meinarti, for instance, with its huddle of houses, its market place, its church and its tombs, seems to encapsulate Nubian 'urban' life at this time (Adams 1965; Adams 1977: 490 for plan).

Debeira West is in comparison somewhat dispersed (Shinnie and Shinnie 1978: 4) but the packed houses of Arminna West (Fig. 3.7), surrounded by emptiness, again give an impression of urban living. It should also be noticed that many houses in these settlements attempted to deal with one of the perennial problems of such a life-style by providing 'inside' latrines (Adams 1977: 491). Usually these would have required the services of night-soil carriers but at Debeira West there were some latrines that were designed to discharge into their own, individual, vaulted soakaways that were filled with ash and potsherds (Shinnie and Shinnie 1978: 106). Clearly, if people had to live in a crowded town, it might as well be made as comfortable as possible.

One distinctive feature of these Christian Nubian settlements was that they usually lacked fortifications, suggesting a time of peace and stability. The Late

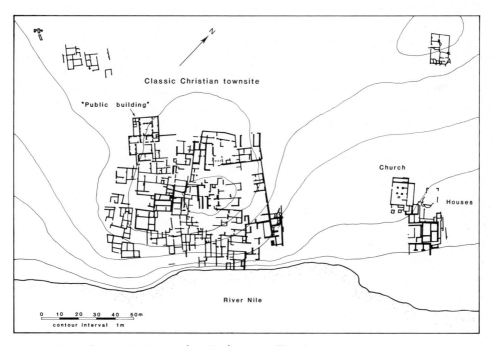

Fig. 3.7 Plan of Arminna West. After Weeks (1967: Fig. 1).

Christian period, however, was typified by fortified settlements, which concentrated particularly in the *Batn el Hajar*, in which poor and isolated region much of the Lower Nubian population seems to have sought refuge. There was also a growing tendency to build fortified houses and castles. Christian Nubian civilization was, in fact, breaking down and disintegrating into a feudal society of peasant farmers gathered around the castles of local rulers. The Christian Church was also in decline and bedouin Arabs from the desert were moving into the region of the middle Nile. With the gradual Arabization and Islamicization that overtook the middle Nile by about the fourteenth century AD, central government was replaced by numerous Arab sheikhdoms based only on the tribe. Eventually a series of loose feudal confederations appeared, the largest and longest-lasting of which was the Fung kingdom of Sennar, which survived from the sixteenth century to the early nineteenth century AD, although in a somewhat run-down condition towards the end (Crawford 1951). There is, however, little published archaeological evidence from post-Christian Nubia that is relevant to our theme. It should be noted, nevertheless, that the remarkable city of Qasr Ibrim, whose occupation dates back to perhaps as early as 1500 BC, was not finally abandoned until the early nineteenth century AD. Indeed this site epitomizes the continuity of the urban tradition in the middle Nile region and contains deposits belonging to many of the episodes of state development along this part of the river (Adams 1977: 508–636).

Subsistence economy

The archaeological evidence that has been reviewed above is more extensive than any available for the other areas of Africa that are considered in this book. It remains to analyse this evidence to see what it tells us about the origins and development of cities and states in the middle Nile region. The first question that must be asked is about the nature of the subsistence base which supported these developments. Information from both pharaonic Egypt and from ethnographic sources would suggest that, throughout the period under consideration, a form of mixed farming was practised, depending on the cultivation of both cereals and vegetables and animal husbandry. The key factor in much of this arid land must have been the availability of suitable soils that either received seasonal floodwater or could be irrigated mechanically (Trigger 1970: 354). It is interesting to observe that all the developments that have been discussed took place in areas which in one way or another were relatively favoured agriculturally. Of the six geographic subdivisions of the middle Nile that were described at the beginning of this chapter, the barren Abu Hamed Reach and *Batn el Hajar* were ignored, while the remainder, particularly the Shendi Reach and the Dongola Reach, were more than once the scenes of great achievements.

Direct archaeological evidence for details of subsistence economy, at various times during the 3500 years that need to be considered, is not as plentiful as could be wished. Many excavators in the past have not given this aspect of their sites the attention that it merited. Prior to the Meroitic period there is little direct evidence that can be cited, although it may be noted that Bonnet (1984) has recently recovered both barley and fish bones from a Napatan context at Kerma. It is also significant that sacrifices of sheep and goats were a consistent feature of Kerma burial and in many cases a row of ox skulls was placed around one side of the burial mounds of Kerma (Adams 1977: 197–8). This would suggest an early importance of animal husbandry in Nubia and further evidence during Meroitic times reinforces this impression. A bronze bowl from Karanog in Lower Nubia, for instance, is decorated with a charming engraved scene showing a cow being milked and another cow suckling a calf, whilst other calves have been tied to a tree to keep them out of the way. A total of ten cows are shown on this bowl, one wears a bell, and milk is being presented to a woman seated nearby before a corn-stalk hut, similar to some that have been made in parts of the African savanna until recent times. The apex of this hut is decorated with an ostrich egg (Shinnie 1967: 18–19). To this informative rural scene can be added the fact that the quantities of cattle bones excavated from Meroë itself indicate that meat as well as milk was an important element in Meroitic subsistence (Adams 1977: 330). Indeed, Ali (1972) has suggested that the archaeological sites of the Butana region near Meroë indicate that it was an important area for semi-nomadic pastoralists and that therefore pastoralism played an important part in the Meroitic subsistence economy. Adams (1981) is unconvinced of this and stresses the role of cultivation, mentioning Strabo's reference (of the first century BC) to what appears to have been *Sorghum vulgare* and inferring the existence of a general pattern of cereal, vegetable and date production. He also admits, however, that there is a lack of direct archaeological evidence for such a conclusion and that the diet must have been supplemented to varying extents with meat and dairy products, depending on local grazing conditions. Nevertheless, in the drier northern Meroitic provinces it is very likely that the cultivation of irrigated land provided the greater part of the subsistence base. Thus the re-occupation of Lower Nubia during the first few centuries AD seems to have been made possible by the introduction of the *saqia*, the ox-driven waterwheel, and it is significant that Meroitic sites in this area 'are never without the remains of distinctive, knobbed pottery vessels (*qadus*) which were and still are made only for use with the *saqia*' (Adams 1977: 346). What the most common staple cereal might have been in Meroitic times is uncertain but sorghum is indeed one of the likely candidates. Thus it is perhaps significant that a relief on a granite boulder at Jebel Qeili, in the southern Butana, depicts the sun god apparently presenting the Meroitic King Sherkarer, of the first century AD, with a number of heads of sorghum (Hintze 1959: Fig. 2; Shinnie 1967: 51, 96).

For the X-Group, however, a nomadic pastoralist bias is suggested by the number of domestic animals buried in the tombs of Ballana and Qustul, amongst which there were both sheep and cows. Nevertheless, the numerous and bulky possessions included in the more important of these tombs look more like the status symbols of sedentarists than the portable equipment of nomads. In addition, grains of primitive cultivated sorghum, *Sorghum bicolor bicolor* race bicolor, have been identified in X-Group deposits at Qasr Ibrim (Adams, Alexander and Allen 1983: 59). This evidence for cereal agriculture is not really a surprise from a city which at that time had a major manufacturing industry and streets of well-built stone houses.

Such archaeological evidence as exists for the subsistence base of Christian Nubia suggests a continuation of this mixture of cultivation and animal husbandry. Debeira West, for instance, had numerous ovens, storage bins, fragments of the flat dishes traditionally used for making unleavened bread, castor oil seeds, date stones, cucumber seeds, groundnuts, and dom-palm nuts. This evidence, together with the numerous knobs of *saqia* pots found in the site, indicated the importance of cultivation. There were also bones of sheep, goats, cattle and pigs as well as copious quantities of goat droppings, that showed the importance of animal husbandry. It is apparent that pigs provided a substantial part of the meat that was eaten and one may surmise that the numerous goats that were kept may have provided milk as well as meat (Shinnie and Shinnie 1978: 107).

Archaeological evidence for the subsistence economy of Islamic Nubia is rather more detailed and may – with some reservations – be used to throw light on earlier times. The site of Qasr Ibrim is again informative, showing sheep, goats and cattle to be common at that time and demonstrating that there was cultivation of sorghum, wheat, barley, beans, peas, and lentils (Adams, Alexander and Allen 1983: 50, 52).

So far as subsistence economy is concerned, therefore, even this arid land had the capacity to support a sedentary population that stretched along the Nile in a thin ribbon and nucleated at points which were particularly favoured with water and fertile silt. Human ingenuity, in the form of mechanical means of irrigation, further increased the agricultural viability of small parts of the region, and far to the south limited rainfed cultivation was a possibility. Thus there was an adequate subsistence base to support a growth of social complexity.

Technology

In contrast with the situation for subsistence economy, there is an abundance of direct archaeological evidence that throws light on the technology of the middle Nile during the periods under review. From this, it is apparent that at times this part of Africa reached a level of technological sophistication seldom if ever matched by the other areas of the continent considered in this book. There is, however, a major problem in interpreting such evidence. The question is: how much of this technological achievement is attributable to indigenous endeavour and how much to exotic sources, be they actual importation or merely the presence of expatriate craftsmen? Because of the repeated cultural contact along the middle Nile, this is a most difficult problem to resolve, indeed some detailed aspects of it may be insoluble. Possibly, it is an irrelevant problem, because it may be argued that it matters little what the origin of a technological base may be, so long as the society concerned benefits from its presence. In this discussion, however, we are concerned with causes for growing social complexity, and when evaluating the role of technology in such causes, it is obviously important to identify the indigenous and the foreign import. In the following discussion an attempt will be made to do this in general terms, whilst recognizing the difficulties in such an approach.

Perhaps the most outstanding aspect of middle Nile technology was the area of building and construction. Ashlar masonry, coarser types of stonework, fired brick, and mud-brick were all handled with skill to produce structures that were often complex in design and sophisticated in execution. The foreign hand is evident in much of this, from the Temple of Amon at Jebel Barkal, which we know to have been built originally by the Egyptians, to the pyramids of Napata and Meroë, or the *deffufas* of Kerma, or the churches of Christian Nubia, all of which are examples of buildings of alien inspiration, if not of actual foreign construction. Nevertheless, most of these structures are not merely foreign buildings far from home: they have characteristics which are distinctively Nubian and it is clear that Nubians played a part in the technological achievements that they represent. The tombs of Kerma or of Ballana and Qustul were, indeed, completely indigenous in both design and execution and both their size and structural complexity demand admiration. So also does the Great Enclosure at Musawwarat es-Sufra which is both unique and mysterious. In addition, it is impossible to deny the enormous expenditure of energy on building that Nubians themselves made. Many of their less important structures were probably of grass and wood, as the Karanog bowl reminds us (p. 53), but such evidence as the Meroitic palace at Wad ben Naqa, or the cities and towns of Meroitic and Christian Nubia, are eloquent of considerable effort as well as of substantial building skills.

Associated with building were a number of other skills that indicate the level of sophistication that Nubian technology reached on occasions. There is evidence of considerable sculptural ability during the Meroitic period and of remarkable painting skills during the time of Christian Nubia. Even the Meroitic art of writing seems to have been partly an adjunct to building decoration. Foreign models and sometimes even foreign execution also played a part in these achievements but, again, the end-products usually had a strong Nubian flavour, suggesting that there was also a very real local input.

The degree to which Nubian building technology was developed is indicated particularly by evidence of a concern to provide domestic buildings with washing facilities and sanitation. Admittedly the swimming bath in the Royal City of Meroë (p. 42) and the heated bathroom of the supposed house at Old

Dongola (p. 50) are exceptional features but there seems to have been little that was exceptional about the numerous latrines of Christian Nubia.

Another important area of Nubian technology lay in the extraction and manufacturing of metal, especially of iron. It is clear that many items of bronze, of silver and of gold were imported but the substantial quantities of iron slag at Meroë would suggest that there at least an extensive, iron-working industry flourished. Further evidence that this was so is provided by the range of iron weapons and tools recovered from Meroitic sites, including spears, arrowheads, hoe blades, adzes, axes, shears and tweezers (Shinnie 1967: 162–5). Mounds of iron slag, probably of a similar date, have also been reported from Kerma, Kawa and Argo (Shinnie 1967: 182), and the iron objects from the Ballana and Qustul tombs indicate that iron-working skills remained at a high level even after the collapse of Meroë.

In addition, manufacturing along the middle Nile produced pottery, textiles, leatherwork, woodwork and basketry. The pottery is particularly deserving of comment. Even during the Kerma period remarkably fine pottery had been made but exceptionally high quality wares were produced during Meroitic, X-Group, and Christian Nubian times. These were wheel-made, well-fired and often had painted decoration. It is apparent that they were fired in specially constructed pottery kilns of brick, of which a number have been excavated at Debeira East which date from late X-Group and Early Christian times (Adams 1977: 402–3). Other kilns have also been uncovered at Faras, dating from the Early and Classic Christian periods (Adams 1961; Adams 1977: 496, 498). Some of these fine quality wares are amongst the best pottery ever produced in tropical Africa.

Textile production seems also to have been important, largely because cotton was grown in the area, at least by Meroitic times if not before. Similarly, leatherworking depended on the widespread animal husbandry, and basketry was based on palm fibres and grasses that were widely available. Only the appearance of woodworking remains difficult to understand in terms of the environment of the region but there is plentiful direct evidence for it in both X-Group and Christian deposits at Qasr Ibrim (Adams 1982: 28–9).

There are many items in Meroitic, X-Group, and Christian sites which suggest even more sophisticated technologies than those that have been discussed. Glassware, lamps, furniture, jewellery of gold or silver set with semi-precious stones: these and other things mostly represent imported status symbols that cannot be considered relevant to the subject of Nubian technology.

Finally, there were several aspects of Nubian technology that were absolutely vital for the development of human societies on the middle Nile. All of them had exotic origins but in all cases their application was in Nubian hands. The most important of these was mechanical irrigation technology. To modern eyes both the *shaduf* and the *saqia* may look simple contrivances but without them it is most unlikely that either states or cities would have appeared in Nubia. Almost as important was transportation technology, enabling the life-giving commerce of the region to exist. The oldest aspect of this was the sailing boat, whose importance on the Nile throughout the period under discussion is so easily forgotten. Nubians have long been skilled boatmen, and still are, as I discovered when I sailed with two of them at Aswan in 1984. It was, however, the development of desert transportation systems, particularly that involving the camel, that seems to have had the greatest impact on the commercial life of this region. These aspects of irrigation and transportation technology emphasize the importance of technology to social development on the middle Nile and, together with the other achievements that have been discussed, would suggest that the technological base was clearly adequate to support such development.

Social system

Archaeological evidence cannot talk to us, yet sometimes its appearance is eloquent enough. There is abundant indication from the middle Nile region, during the period under review, of the development of social complexity. Monumental tombs at Kerma, Napata, Meroë and Ballana and Qustul, in their scale, their sophisticated construction, and their contents show the presence of absolute monarchy at various times. The divinity and/or autocracy of such rulers is demonstrated by the practice of human sacrifice at Kerma, and Ballana and Qustul, and by the sculptured reliefs of some Meroitic buildings. Just in case the beholder should miss the message, some of the latter reinforce their point with inscriptions, which unfortunately we cannot always fully understand. Interestingly, Meroitic monarchy gave women an important role (Fig. 3.4), indeed sometimes they governed in their own right. Absolute monarchy is also suggested by the existence of large and elaborate domestic buildings interpreted as palaces, of which those at Meroë and Wad ben Naqa are perhaps the most convincing. In addition, numerous temples from various periods represent ideologies in which both spiritual and secular power were intertwined. Indeed, not only is the archaeological record eloquent of the emergence of absolute authority but it also chronicles its dissolution, as in the growth of localized feudalism that is indicated by the numerous fortified buildings of Late Christian and Islamic times.

At the other end of the social scale, the archaeological evidence shows us a numerous labouring class that presumably consisted, during most periods, of both free peasants and slaves. Their presence is indicated not only by the clusters of small houses in many settlements and the numerous 'poorer' graves in cemeteries but also by the monumental constructions such as temples, tombs and burial mounds that were as much the achievement of their labour as of the authority of their rulers. The relationship of this lowest level of society, to both the rulers and their associated elite, is on occasion starkly demonstrated by the willing or enforced sacrifice of such lesser human beings at the burial of those to whom they were subservient, as was the case at Kerma and at Ballana and Qustul.

What about a middle class? Archaeological evidence for the development of trade and manufacturing, particularly perhaps in the Meroitic and Christian periods, would suggest that at times such a class did exist. One would expect that its membership would have included merchant-entrepreneurs and some skilled craftsmen, as well as various government officials and holders of temple or church appointments. Direct archaeological evidence for such a class is, however, not easy to find and when found is often ambiguous. However, some burials at Napata and at Meroë, but less certainly at Kerma, seem to belong neither to the elite nor the peasantry. The problem is to know where to draw the line. Settlement evidence is slightly better, with Meroitic houses including both 'de luxe' and 'humbler' structures (Adams 1977: 357–8) in locations where one would not expect to find residences of the elite. The houses of some Christian Nubian settlements also suggest that some residents were better off than others. The evidence is hardly satisfactory but there is enough to suggest that, at least during the Meroitic and Christian periods, there were the beginnings of a third class between the two extremes.

Just as the archaeological evidence suggests the existence of social stratification, so it also indicates the development of functional specialization. Cross-cutting the peasant and middle classes, and indeed contributing to their differentiation, there emerged a host of specialized occupations. A number of the societies on the middle Nile during the periods under consideration did not merely consist of peasant farmers and autocratic rulers. The archaeological evidence indicates that by Meroitic and Christian times, for instance, there were also specialist potters making high quality wheel-formed wares, as distinct from traditional potters who continued to turn out rougher hand-built pottery in their spare time. In addition, there must have been iron-smelters, blacksmiths and perhaps other metalworkers; spinners, weavers and builders, who would have included both masons and brickmakers; leatherworkers, carpenters and joiners, basketmakers and boatmen. At a somewhat higher plane, there would also have been scribes, artists (both sculptors and painters), priests and temple and church officials and merchants.

Thus, it is possible to demonstrate, from the archaeological evidence, the existence of both social stratification and functional specialization. From this, and from other archaeological evidence, it can be shown that both state formation and urbanization were well advanced in the middle Nile region during several periods. The requisite level of social complexity was apparently reached on a number of occasions. It seems likely, however, that the social systems which have been discussed, were as much symptomatic as causative of the development of cities and states. It is necessary to look further if this development is to be explained.

Population pressures

The people of the middle Nile were agriculturalists who lived in a desert and, in the far south, in extremely dry savanna. They were able to do this because of the existence of the river, which provided water for the irrigation of such limited areas of fertile silts as could be reached either by seasonal flooding or by mechanical means. Thus, cultivable land was a limited resource, indeed in some areas it was absent altogether. Yet, where present, it had the potential to yield a surplus and to support population growth. If the population grew, however, there was nowhere to go: there was only a finite amount of land that could be exploited by the means available. As a result, the settlement of the region was restricted to a long, narrow and frequently-broken strip of viable agricultural land, with some isolated more fortunate areas. Theoretically, therefore, the middle Nile constitutes a classic example of environmentally-induced population pressures. The question is: have we any archaeological evidence that such pressures actually existed?

Unsatisfactory though they might be, there are some archaeological indications of population pressure during certain periods. For instance, the distribution of archaeological sites in Lower Nubia, which is still the best studied area, seems particularly dense for later Meroitic and Christian times. This is strongly suggestive of a relatively dense population during those periods. Similarly, the existence of Meroitic sites in the dry western Butana, away from the Nile but along *wadis* that would provide some seasonal cultivation, suggests that the population of that area found it necessary to exploit its available resources to the limit. It is also possible that the tight clustering of Meroitic and Christian settlements was at least partly caused by a desire to conserve potentially cultivable land, again an indication of a population pressing against the limits of its resources. A suitable analysis might even demonstrate that many settlements and cemeteries were sited in such a way as to avoid any waste of valuable farmland.

The most obvious way that the carrying capacity of the region could be improved was by increasing the available cultivable land, and the only way to do this was to introduce better irrigation technology. Two such improvements are known to have taken place during the period under review and perhaps the best archaeological evidence for population pressure concerns the consequences of the second of these. The first was the introduction of the *shaduf*, an idea imported from Egypt probably during the New Kingdom. Quite possibly it helped to encourage the growing population of that time that has been calculated by Trigger (1965: 156–66). The second was the *saqia*, again a foreign idea, that was adopted in Nubia at the beginning of the first millennium AD. The result in Lower Nubia was what Trigger called a 'population explosion' (1965: 163), although as Adams suggests (1977: 346, 420) it is likely that the sudden increase in the number of sites in this area actually resulted from a re-occupation of the long-abandoned region by people from elsewhere. This seems the best explanation, but whether the population merely grew *in situ* or arrived from elsewhere, does not alter the fact that the sudden response to this innovation suggests a desperate land hunger that the *saqia* went some way to assuaging.

There is, therefore, some archaeological evidence that suggests the existence of population pressures on the middle Nile. It seems that cultivable land could indeed have been a scarce resource at times, and control of it might have provided a power-base for an emerging elite. The hot-house conditions which could well have resulted must surely have been at least a contributory factor in the growth of cities and states.

Ideology

The Nubian archaeological record is, in general, highly informative on ideological matters. Tombs, temples and churches have much to tell us about the beliefs of those who built them. Their designs, their sculptural and graphic decorations, sometimes even their inscriptions, indicate that throughout much of the period under review, Nubia was a borrower and adapter of foreign faiths. Until about the middle of the first millennium AD it was the gods of pharaonic Egypt that dominated the Nubian scene, indeed their observance survived longer on the middle Nile than in Egypt itself. The most important of these seem to have been Isis and Amon, the worship of the latter becoming a state cult for both Napata and Meroë, with their rulers often taking the name of Amon as one element of their throne names, for example Tenutamon, Arkamani, Natakamani. From about the middle of the first millennium AD to about the middle of the second millennium, Christianity became the dominant faith, to be replaced, in its turn, by Islam. Nevertheless, all these faiths developed their own peculiar Nubian characteristics and there were also at times separate indigenous beliefs. This would seem to be indicated by the human sacrifices at Kerma and at Ballana and Qustul, and also by the worship of Apedemak, the lion god of Meroë, who seems to have been a consequence of Egyptian–Meroitic syncretism (Zabkar 1975).

The archaeological evidence also suggests that these different ideologies played a significant contributory role in the development of states and cities. Prior to the arrival of Christianity on the middle Nile, the religious beliefs of Nubia were characterized by that close integration of secular and spiritual authority which was common in the ancient world of South-West Asia and the Mediterranean. In such cases, the ruler became the personification of the god, a notion that manifests itself archaeologically in monumental tombs and temples, which were at once both an expression of human and divine authority. Thus was provided a legitimization for the rule of an absolute monarch, who could literally claim a divine mandate. In addition, ideas of this sort considerably strengthened the power-base of such a ruler, who was enabled to exert both physical and spiritual force. The state developments of Kerma, Napata, Meroë, and the X-Group, all betray the importance of this ideological contribution. With the advent of Christianity, the ruler was no longer a god, even though his rule might be strengthened by being divinely sanctioned. Human and divine authority were separated and 'royal' tombs disappeared from the archaeological record. However, this does not necessarily mean that there was any loss of authority by the temporal ruler who, as the Faras paintings show, could still call on ideological support from a Church that he in turn protected. As a result, the Christian states of Nubia were ruled by both the Crown and the Cross: the one claiming authority over people's bodies, the other over their souls (Adams 1977).

The role of ideology in the process of urbanization was rather different. It is apparent that the construction of an important temple or church at a particular place sometimes led to development of a settlement at that place, or led to increased growth of a settlement that already existed. In this way, some cities came into existence as religious ceremonial centres, or became more important because they assumed such a ceremonial role. It seems likely that Qasr Ibrim was an example of both these processes. Adams has also stressed the more general symbolic role of the Nubian city, irrespective of whether religion, administration, or commerce was its main activity. In his view, the Nubian city was 'a symbolic focal point for the civilization that gave it birth', conferring 'political and ideological legitimacy' on the regime that controlled it. As a result, he suggests, the Nubian city endured, in contrast to those in other parts of Africa which have been 'notoriously ephemeral' (Adams, in press). Clearly, ideology could have played an important part in the developments that we are investigating.

External trade

All our sources for the period under review indicate that long-distance trade was the life-blood of Nubia. As was discussed at the beginning of this chapter (p. 25), Adams has described Nubia as the only trade corridor into the heart of Africa, so far as the ancient world of South-West Asia and the Mediterranean was concerned. Moving north seem to have been gold and other minerals, ivory, slaves and a whole range of African exotica; going south in exchange was a variety of manufactured goods, including many best described as luxury goods. It was a classic example of that age-old interchange between developed and underdeveloped world: manufactures for raw materials.

Archaeological evidence for this trade is abundant, although it has little to tell us about some aspects of it. Least well represented in the archaeological record are the commodities that were traded north to Egypt but there are some significant pieces of evidence. Thus, diorite quarries have been discovered in the Nubian desert west of Abu Simbel; they were being exploited during the Egyptian Old Kingdom and Middle Kingdom. This rock was the favoured material for statues and stelae in Egypt at this time and apparently was transported as far as Giza, near modern Cairo, a distance along the Nile of more than 1200 kilometres (Adams 1977: 169–70). Similarly, copper-smelting furnaces have been found in the Old Kingdom town investigated at Buhen (Adams 1977: 170–4) and numerous gold mines, that were producing at least by

New Kingdom times, are known in the desert around the Wadi Allaqi, east of the Second Cataract area, and at Duweishat in the *Batn el Hajar* (Adams 1977: 233–5). There is archaeological evidence that all these activities were at first in Egyptian hands and we may assume that, originally at least, their output was only intended for Egyptian use. Thus, the trade in gold and other minerals can be shown to have developed at an early date. Evidence for the trade in ivory is less easy to find but it is surely significant that in the Napatan town of Sanam, one room of a possible storehouse was found by its excavator to have part of its floor 'covered with tusks of raw ivory injured by fire' (Griffith 1922: 117, Plate LIIIb). Clearly some sort of disaster had overtaken the stock. In addition, a mixture of ivory tusks and pieces of wood were found in one of the storerooms in the palace at Wad ben Naqa (Vercoutter 1962: Plate XXb). Almost invisible in the archaeological record, however, is the trade in slaves, which was probably of substantial importance for much of the time that we are considering. The people sacrificed at Kerma, or Ballana and Qustul, for instance, were not necessarily slaves, as sometimes has been assumed, although they might well have been. It could be significant, nevertheless, that the relief at Jebel Qeili and those on the pylons of the Lion Temple at Naqa, show live rather than dead captives; they were worth more alive. As for the other tropical exotica that were traded north to Egypt, Egyptian documentary and archaeological sources provide details but, amongst other things, they seem to have included ostrich eggs and feathers, various skins from wild animals, live wild animals, ebony and incense. It seems likely that all the commodities sought by Egyptians were collected together at trading stations during earlier times, until their handling came under indigenous control in Napatan and later times. The Second Cataract Forts, for instance, and the building attached to the Western *Deffufa* at Kerma, seem to have had some such role.

There is rather better archaeological evidence for the commodities that were traded south into Nubia, although it is not without its own problems. Outstanding amongst these imports were a whole range of manufactured items that seem often to have been prized as status symbols and therefore buried in the more important graves. Sometimes these objects can be attributed on the basis of their style to their places of origin, although more commonly their foreign manufacture has merely been assumed because of the sophistication of the technology by which they have been produced (p. 56). Perhaps the most impressive, by reasons of its fragility and the distances that it nevertheless travelled, is the glassware that has been found in Meroitic, X-Group, and Christian Nubian contexts. Shinnie (1967: Plates 82–4) illustrates two glass vessels from Meroitic graves at Faras in Lower Nubia and one from Meroë itself which are remarkable enough but the most impressive Meroitic collection of glass is perhaps that excavated from tombs at Seddenga on the Abri-Delgo Reach of the middle Nile (Leclant 1973). In addition to glassware, fine metalwork and jewellery seem also to have figured amongst the imports to

Nubia. Thus, for example, a silver gilt goblet, probably of Roman origin, was found at Meroë (Shinnie 1967: Plates 78–81) and a gold ring, also from Meroë, was inscribed in Greek (Shinnie 1967: Plate 61). From various Meroitic contexts have also come an assortment of bronze lamps, bowls, beakers, bottles and vases, whilst the X-Group tombs of Ballana and Qustul produced a bewildering mass of metal goods and other manufactures which seem to have originated in Byzantine Egypt. However, the most common imports in Meroitic Nubia, according to the archaeological record, were beads of glass or stone, so common indeed that Adams (1977: 373) has suggested that they may have been used as a medium of exchange.

The range of durable manufactures that was traded into Nubia at various times was, in fact, too great to discuss in more detail. It is apparent, however, that the imported goods also included some consumables, and some other commodities that have not usually survived in archaeological deposits. Some of the Meroitic glass vessels, for instance, are of shapes that are known to have been used elsewhere for containing unguents and oils, and it is likely that they were imported for their contents rather than for their own sakes (Shinnie 1967: 130–1). Similarly, some of the imported Graeco–Roman pottery that appears alongside indigenous wares in Meroitic contexts, could also have arrived in Nubia as containers for consumables. An Egyptian Old Kingdom text, for example, mentions the Nubians' fondness for Egyptian honey (Adams 1984: 41) and it should not be supposed that their sweet tooth disappeared in later times. Certainly, the Egyptian amphorae that are found in Nubian sites of Meroitic, X-Group, and Early Christian date, seem to have been imported full of Egyptian wine. It seems, in fact, as if the alcohol trade was at times really big business and in the Meroitic period taverns were built so that the wine could be enjoyed to the full (Adams 1977: 363–4). There must also have been other commodities that have left little or no archaeological evidence of their importance as trade goods. One such was probably fine cloth, which was evidently imported in Islamic times at Qasr Ibrim (Adams, Alexander and Allen 1983: 52) and could well have been imported in far earlier times.

Another form of archaeological evidence that throws light on the organization of Nubian trade is the location of some of the major urban sites. As has been pointed out by Adams (in press) 'all of the enduringly prosperous towns of Nubia were, or became, "points of articulation" in the Nile trade: places where the export products of the Sudan interior were collected at the riverbank, for shipment to Egypt.' As time went on, explains Adams, and trade networks expanded ever further into the interior, so these 'points of articulation' appeared successively further up the Nile: first there was Buhen, then Kerma, then Napata, then Meroë and finally there were Shendi and Sennar. Some of these places, and indeed others also, grew particularly important because they were situated at a point where a major desert route reached the Nile. Thus, Meroë and Napata stood at the southern and northern end respectively of the Bayuda Road, that cut off the great bend of the Nile containing the Fourth and Fifth Cataracts. In turn, Napata and Kawa stood at each end of the Meheila Road, that cut off the next great bend of the river further downstream. These routes were only part, however, of those that seem to have existed by Meroitic times, including the Korosko Road, that cut off the whole of the Nile bend that contained the Second, Third, and Fourth Cataracts; the Wadi Hawad Road that led south-east from Meroë to Axum; and another route that led north-east from the Atbara-Nile confluence to the Red Sea port of Suakin (Adams 1977). The location of the urban centres that have been mentioned and the existence of these important land routes suggest two things: first, that the external trade of the Nile may have played an important role in urban growth; second, that such trade was, in fact, part only of a vast network of regional trading links about which little is known.

Until we do have more archaeological evidence that can throw light on regional trading systems in this part of Africa, it is probably premature to assess the actual contribution that *external* trade made to the development of cities and states on the middle Nile. Nevertheless, it could be argued that trade in general provided the main causative factor for these developments and that if there had been no trade along the Nile, then there would have been very little social development there either. Perhaps the most important point to recognize, however, is that the external trade was only one aspect of a long-continued cultural interaction between the middle Nile region and the world to its north. It was, as it were, merely one symptom of that interaction that happens to be more susceptible to archaeological study than some others.

Conclusion

With such an extreme environment, Nubia would seem to have been an unlikely place for the development of states and the appearance of cities. Yet not only did these things happen, they happened here earlier than anywhere else in tropical Africa. It is little wonder that a common historical explanation has been to regard such developments as 'secondary' in character, resulting directly from contact with Egypt and South-West Asia. An examination of the archaeological evidence reveals a very much more complex situation, in which exotic influences undoubtedly played a continuing although fluctuating role but where important contributions came from within, so that the resultant social complexity had its own quite distinctive Nubian characteristics.

First of all, Nubia was as much a gift of the Nile as was Egypt. Without it, Nubia could not have existed. Its water and its silt allowed the development of a sound subsistence base which in some favoured areas was capable of producing a surplus. It is noticeable that all of the major socio-cultural developments, that have been discussed in this chapter, were located on more favoured parts of the river and not in the less productive areas. Secondly, Nubian technology, although often dependent on foreign ideas and products, was able to extend the cultivated land and to intensify its exploitation, by means of mechanical irrigation. It was also able to provide both land and water transportation systems that could overcome the communication problems of a population strung out along many hundreds of kilometres of river.

It seems likely that cultivable land rapidly became, and remained, a scarce resource; providing a power-base for those who controlled it and creating population pressures that contributed to a tendency for people to gather in urban aggregations. Social stratification followed, with society divided between the rulers and the ruled, and with an increasingly sophisticated technology encouraging the development of functional specialization. Without doubt, however, it was trading and commercial activities, and the general cultural interaction of which they were a part, that became the catalyst of major social development in Nubia. It is quite likely that the middle Nile had long been part of an extensive regional trading system but from Egyptian Old Kingdom times onwards, the demand of the developed world to the north for raw materials and tropical exotica created a major interest in external trade. Nubia became both a pipeline of supply and a successful entrepôt, profiting not so much from its own products but from those that it merely handled on their way north or on their way south. At first, Egypt controlled this trade herself, extending her authority into Nubia in both Middle Kingdom and, more extensively, in New Kingdom times. When her grip weakened, however, indigenous control quickly developed, first of all with the city state of Kerma and eventually with the city states of Napata, Meröe, and of later times. The earlier of these polities were probably only tentative and incompletely formed but by Meroitic times we find evidence of a highly complex society of at least three classes. It is, however, apparent from archaeological evidence that all of these autocratic regimes sought to strengthen and legitimize their control by sheltering behind powerful religious ideologies, the observance of which in turn contributed to the growth of urban centres. The foreign origin of most of those religions indicates the very considerable contribution made to Nubian developments by cultural contacts with the north, but even with religion there was a strong indigenous input that cannot be denied.

The emergence of social complexity on the middle Nile may thus be seen as the result of a complex interaction between local and exotic factors but an interaction in which indigenous people made their own decisions. As Shinnie (1967: 169) wrote of the best known of these polities: 'Meroë was an African civilization, firmly based on African soil, and developed by an African population.' But, was Nubia really a 'corridor to Africa'? At one time scholars thought so and saw ideas of divine kingship spreading from the Nile to as far away as West Africa (for example Arkell 1961: 177). Lack of archaeological evidence, however, suggests that Nubia had very little influence on the rest of Africa. Surely corridors usually lead to a few rooms, but the Nubian corridor, in which so much happened, does not seem to have led anywhere. Developments on the middle Nile did not set off a series of chain reactions across the African continent. Perhaps this raises basic theoretical questions about the nature of cultural diffusion between human groups, or perhaps it merely tells us that the relationship between the urbanized Nubians and their pastoralist/cultivator neighbours of the interior never rose above that of the pillager and the pillaged, the latter providing whatever trade commodities (including human beings) were currently required for the Nile trade. For the Nubians, their valley was perhaps a corridor of exciting cultural interaction but for Africa, as a whole, archaeologists suspect that it was a cul-de-sac.

Chapter 4

The benefits of isolation: the Ethiopian Highlands

'Rugged escarpments overlooking the Sudan, and desert plains in north-east Kenya, separate the highlands of Ethiopia and the Horn of Africa from the rest of the continent.' It is in such words that the geographer A.T. Grove introduces a discussion of this part of Africa (Grove 1978: 222). For many observers, indeed, it has been the isolation of this region, particularly that of the central highlands of Ethiopia, that has made the greatest impression on them. The core of Ethiopia is a great block of mountains, everywhere over 1000 metres in height, that reaches a general level of 2300 metres and in places exceeds 4200 metres above sea-level. At first sight, one could not imagine a less likely setting for state emergence and urbanization. Nevertheless, there is clear evidence of such developments by the first century AD, if not before. Not only is this an early date for the attainment of social complexity in tropical Africa but also the Ethiopian achievement was at a particularly high level of sophistication. The state of Axum, as it became known to the ancient world, boasted urban centres; its own form of writing; coinage in gold, silver and bronze; multi-storeyed masonry buildings of a distinctive architectural style; unique monuments that indicate substantial quarrying and engineering skills; extensive trading contacts both within and outside Africa; and a significant role in the international politics of its period. Indeed, Axum seems to have been one of the first states to accept Christianity (Pankhurst 1961: xi). Far from being isolated, Ethiopia would appear to have formed, at times, a most important zone for cultural integration. Edward Ullendorff sums up the situation eloquently:

> In its long history the country has always formed a bridge between Africa and Asia, and many of its inhabitants were immigrants from South Arabia from which it is separated only by the narrow straits of the Bab-el-Mandeb, a distance of less than twenty miles. With its ancestry astride two continents and its position in the horn of Africa, Ethiopia has always occupied a favoured place at a cross-road of civilizations and a meeting point of many races (Ullendorff 1960: 23).

On the other hand, after the rise of Islam in the seventh century, Ethiopia did become increasingly isolated, leading the eighteenth-century historian Gibbon to make his famous exaggerated remark that: 'Encompassed on all sides by the enemies of their religion, the Aethiopians slept near a thousand years, forgetful of the world by whom they were forgotten' (Gibbon 1952: Vol. 2, 159–60). However, the Ethiopians' struggle to survive through those centuries can hardly be likened to sleep, nor can their success in that struggle. For some form of Ethiopian state did survive down to modern times, albeit one of a feudal and mostly non-urban type. In addition, the Christian Church of Ethiopia also survived, leaving as a legacy of those centuries of sleep some of the most remarkable ecclesiastical architecture in the world. As a result, the Ethiopian Highlands provide one of the most impressive examples of cultural continuity in Africa; indeed, Ethiopia has been claimed to be 'the longest-lived independent Christian kingdom in the world' (Buxton 1970: 56).

It might be argued, therefore, that the apparent isolation of this region is like that of a well-planned fortress. In times of peace, it is so placed that it can take full advantage of all that goes on around it and there will be frequent contact between the garrison and the surrounding population. In times of war, however, the fortress is able not only to withstand a protracted siege, while life continues within it, but also it is so designed that the defenders can sally out to smite the attackers. Isolation of such a kind clearly has benefits.

Geographical location and environmental factors

The mountains of Ethiopia are divided into two parts by the northern end of the East African Rift Valley, here occupied by a string of relatively small lakes and by the Awash River (Fig. 4.1). It is the highlands to the north and to the west of this valley that form the heartland of old Ethiopia, formerly called Abyssinia. This huge area of mountains is roughly triangular in shape and the northern end of this triangle lies close to the western shore of the Red Sea. Compared with the surrounding dry, hot plains, either on the African or on the South Arabian side of the Red Sea, the Ethiopian Highlands offer a range of relatively attractive environments. As a result, cultural contact and even movement of people between the lowlands and the highlands might be expected to have taken place from an early date. Because of the narrowness of the Red Sea at this point, the presence in it of numerous islands, and a comparable range of environments in South Arabia, it might further be expected that such contact and movement would have Asiatic as well as African sources. It is of some interest, therefore, to note that both archaeological and historical evidence indicate that social complexity developed first in the northern extremities of the Ethiopian Highlands and only later gradually moved south in response to changed circumstances in international politics.

The proximity of the northern part of the Ethiopian Highlands to the Red Sea had other more important consequences. For the ancient world, as indeed for the modern world, the Red Sea comprised a major shipping route, that connected

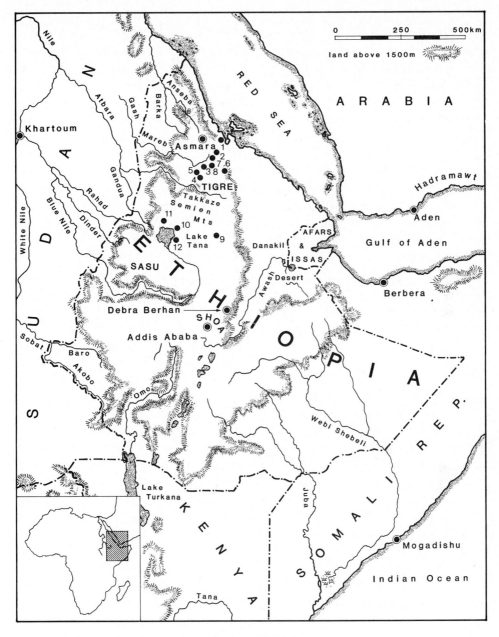

Fig. 4.1 Archaeological sites of the Ethiopian Highlands.
1: Adulis. *2:* Kohaito. *3:* Yeha. *4:* Haoulti-Melazo. *5:* Axum. *6:* Addi Galamo. *7:* Matara. *8:* Debra Damo. *9:* Lalibela. *10:* Gouzara. *11:* Gondar. *12:* Lalibela Cave. Based on Ullendorff (1960).

the Mediterranean with the trade of the Indian Ocean. Ethiopia, able to tap the resources of the African interior, had direct access to this major route, and this was clearly an important contributory element in the rise of the Axumite state.

The Ethiopian Highlands are the result of Tertiary earth movements and associated volcanic activity and typically consist of basalts and other lavas overlying sandstones and limestones. Most of the region is tilted to the west and therefore drains into the Nile, particularly into the upper Blue Nile which issues from Lake Tana. The drainage pattern has cut deeply into the landscape, carving spectacular gorges, often hundreds of metres deep, that break up the otherwise gently undulating surface of the high plateau. In some cases the walls of these gorges descend in steps that provide habitable areas at very different levels. Similarly the highlands fall away sharply to the east, where a great escarpment drops down to the hot plains below. Parts of the original high plateau have been so eroded that very little level country remains, except in the form of flat-topped *ambas*, isolated hills with precipitous sides (Buxton 1970: 18–20).

The most important environmental factor in the Ethiopian Highlands is altitude. Within about 250 kilometres of each other lie the hot dusty salt-flats of the Danakil Desert and the cool heights of the Semien Mountains that sometimes experience heavy falls of snow (Buxton 1970: 18). Altitude is thus a major determinant of both climate and vegetation. Ethiopians themselves recognize three main climatic zones. These are *dega*, which is land above 2400 metres that has a temperate climate with an average temperature of 16°C; *woina dega*, which is land between 1800 and 2400 metres that has a sub-tropical climate with an average temperature of 22°C; and *kwolla*, which is land below 1800 metres that has a tropical climate with average temperatures of 26°C and over. All three zones can sometimes be found within relatively short distances. However, although temperatures vary greatly with altitude, there is little seasonal variation. The major factor determining seasonality is rainfall. The highlands occasion a somewhat greater rainfall than is usual at this latitude in Africa, but because the rain is brought by winds from the south-west, rainfall is heaviest and the wet season longest in the south-western highlands, and the far north has less rain and a shorter wet season. In general, the main wet season lasts from late June to early September and is followed by a long dry season that lasts until February. The average annual rainfall in the central highlands is about 1000 millimetres. The nearby plains of the Red Sea coast have a comparatively slight rainfall but this occurs in January and February when the highlands are dry, and the coastal plains are at their hottest and driest at the time when the heaviest rain is falling in the highlands. There is thus ample scope for some pastoralists and agriculturalists to exploit this seasonal and altitudinal variation in rainfall (Ullendorff 1960: 26–8; Buxton 1970: 20–1).

Given both the height and the open character of much of the Ethiopian Highlands, it is not surprising that exposure to wind is another environmental factor of significance. Much of the high plateau is sufficiently wind-swept for this to affect its utilization. Thus Buxton (1970: 60) recorded that the population of the Debra Berhan area in Shoa tended to cluster in and around the gorges, rather than on the open plateau itself. Furthermore, Doresse (1959: 162, 203) has noted how Menelik II, in the late nineteenth century, first sought to establish his new capital at Entotto but after a few years moved it to a more sheltered site at nearby Addis Ababa because Entotto was so windy.

The wide range of altitude and climate is responsible for a great variety of vegetation. Within the boundaries of the modern state of Ethiopia this extends from desert scrub to rainforest but even within the Highlands there was originally an impressive range. Temperate forests of *Podocarpus* sp. occurred below 2200 metres and of *Juniperus* sp. above that level, with some overlap of their distribution. Both have been extensively destroyed by human activity, however, leaving most of the high plateau bleak and empty, but the successful introduction of Australian Eucalyptus trees, at the end of the nineteenth century has alleviated this situation to some extent. Nevertheless, much of the vegetation cover of the high plateau now consists of short grass, which provides excellent grazing. Finally, at the highest levels of the highlands occurs an 'Afro-Alpine' association, corresponding in general to that of the East African mountains (Buxton 1970: 21–2).

The considerable altitudinal range of the Ethiopian Highlands has thus given rise to very great environmental diversity. Little is known about Ethiopian soils but they are derived from volcanic rocks and seem to be much more fertile than most African soils, although soil erosion has been a problem (Grove 1978: 224). Such a combination – a variety of environments and the availability of fertile soils – has enabled agriculture to provide the most important traditional resources of the region. In many places it is possible to obtain two or three crops in the same year, and in some places it is possible to sow and harvest at any time. This is achieved by growing a very great range of crops. Among cereals, for instance, *tef*, wheat, barley, sorghum and finger millet can all be grown, although it is *tef* that is most commonly grown in areas of middle and higher altitude. Traditional agriculture in Ethiopia also produced a remarkable selection of vegetables; including chickpeas, lentils, peppers, onions, tomatoes, beans, asparagus, lettuce and artichokes. In addition, many types of fruit could be grown; including bananas, mangoes, lemons, grapefruit, oranges, papaws, guavas, pineapples, peaches and prickly pear. Other agricultural products of importance comprised maize and *ensete* (in the high rainfall areas of the south-west), coffee, cotton, *chat* (a narcotic), *nug* (a source of oil), various medicinal plants and sugar-cane. Some of these plants were obviously introduced in later times but this picture of the traditional farming of the second half of the present millennium gives some idea of the likely importance of agricultural resources during earlier times. However, those resources also included very large numbers of livestock, particularly cattle (for milk and meat), sheep (not usually with wool) and goats. Working animals included oxen for pulling ploughs, whose use was unique in tropical Africa, horses, asses and mules, the last of these being very important for carrying loads in the often broken landscape. Additional useful animals were chickens, dogs, and bees, while civet cats were kept in cages in order to collect the civet that was used as a perfume (Ullendorff 1960: 28–30; Pankhurst 1961: 200–19).

The native fauna of the Ethiopian Highlands provided other resources of significance. Not only could fishing and hunting supplement diet but valuable trade goods could be obtained from some of the numerous wild animals which included elephants, rhinoceros, crocodiles, lions, leopards, giraffes, zebras and many others. Further, traditional resources of significance included minerals, of which gold and iron ore seem to have been the most important, but silver, lead and tin could also be found (Pankhurst 1961: 224–9). In addition the region produced plentiful supplies of good building stone, and timber only became difficult to find in more recent centuries. Finally, human life, as so often in tropical Africa, provided an important resource in the form of slaves. It will be noticed that, as with Nubia, the non-agricultural resources consisted in the main of commodities much sought after in the ancient Mediterranean world. The Ethiopian Highlands were thus well placed to develop important trade links with the outside world.

The environment of the Ethiopian Highlands was clearly an attractive one for human settlement, much of the region possessing a kind climate and being rather healthier than most of tropical Africa. Nevertheless, constraints did exist. The first and most obvious of these is that extensive areas of the highlands were too rocky, too exposed or too high to have any great agricultural value. In addition, much of the landscape was so rough and so obstructed by gorges and other natural features, that communication remained difficult down to modern times. A second constraint, surprisingly enough, is that close inspection of historical sources reveals that Ethiopia was not quite as healthy as would at first appear. Thus Pankhurst (1961: 238–47) shows that the highlands have suffered from occasional epidemics of great severity. Some of these cannot now be identified but it is apparent that smallpox, cholera, and influenza were amongst them. Dysentery, leprosy, eye diseases, Guinea worm and elephantiasis are also mentioned amongst diseases found in Ethiopia; and in the lowlands (which do not directly concern us here) malaria and other fevers were a serious problem. In the highlands themselves, tapeworm was prevalent, largely because of the long-established practice of eating raw meat, but this affliction has been customarily treated with indifference because of the existence of the *kosso* tree, whose flowers produce a drug that is highly effective in expelling these intestinal worms. Perhaps the most serious constraint in the Ethiopian Highlands, however, has been the periodic recurrence of famine, recorded as early as the ninth century and still a cause of major concern in modern times (Pankhurst 1961: 230–7). Famines could result from crop failure, brought on by inadequate or even excessive rainfall, or by unusually low temperatures. They could also result from crop destruction, caused by swarms of mice, troops of monkeys, or (most important of all) by massive invasions of locusts. Early European visitors in the sixteenth and seventeenth centuries were astounded by the size of these invasions and by the fearful destruction that these insects could bring. Serious as some of these constraints might appear, however, the greater number of them were episodic, so that overall they seem to have had little inhibiting effect on the growth of social complexity in the Ethiopian Highlands. It is to the evidence for that growth that we must now turn.

Sources of information

Oral traditional, historical and archaeological sources all throw some light on the development of urbanization and the process of state emergence in this region but each of these sources suffers from particular limitations. Least valuable of them appears to be oral tradition, much of it preserved in later documentary sources. It attempts to explain the past with fantastic stories and the Axumite period, which is the main interest of this chapter, is somewhat beyond its range. Nevertheless, the most famous of Ethiopian oral traditions, that concerning the visit of the Queen of Sheba to Solomon and the consequent birth of the founder of the Ethiopian royal house (Buxton 1970: 34), does perhaps provide further corroboration of the Semitic contribution to Ethiopian developments that is indicated by other sources.

Historical sources are considerably more important and may be broken up into four different types. First of these are references to Ethiopia by classical writers. Thus Pliny the Elder (about 60 AD) mentions Adulis, and the *Periplus of the Erythraean Sea*, also of the first century AD, mentions Adulis, Koloè, and 'the city of the people called the Aksumites' (Kobishchanov 1979: 41; Anfray 1981: 363). Other similar sources are Claudius Ptolemy in the second century AD and Cosmas Indicopleustes of the sixth century AD (Kobishchanov 1979: 42). These and further classical sources give us a picture of a powerful Axumite kingdom that was able to conquer parts of South Arabia in the sixth century AD and, before that, was already partly urbanized and exporting ivory, rhinoceros horn, tortoise-shell and obsidian through Adulis (Anfray 1981: 363). To these classical sources may also be added some early Islamic sources, that tell us a little more of Axum's relationship with the outside world.

The second type of historical sources consists of inscriptions on stone found in Axumite contexts, and inscriptions and representations on Axumite coins. These constitute historical documents even though their discovery is the result of archaeological endeavour. They are particularly valuable because they are the only internal historical data that exist for the Axumite period. Unlike Meroitic inscriptions, those from Axumite or pre-Axumite times can be read, being written in Ge'ez (the old Ethiopian language), or in Sabaean (South Arabian) or even sometimes in Greek. These inscriptions provide information about important military exploits, such as King Ezana's destruction of Meroë in the fourth century AD and King Aphilas' conquest of parts of South Arabia in the third century AD (Buxton 1970: 38–9). In addition they tell us the names and titles of some of the rulers of Axum, as do the coins that may record as many as twenty-four different Axumite kings (Pankhurst 1961: 401). The coins are also informative in other ways, recording, for instance, the fourth-century acceptance of Christianity, by replacing the pagan crescent and disc with the cross (Fig. 4.6). Nevertheless, this internal historical source material is very limited in what it can tell us about the Axumite state and cities: so much so that scholars have even disagreed as to whether Ezana, one of the best known of Axumite kings, was actually one king or two different kings (Munro-Hay 1980).

Few of these inscriptions are later than the fourth century and probably none are later than the ninth (Buxton 1970: 119). The Axumite kingdom finally disappeared in the tenth century AD and there followed a period of some centuries for which there is very little historical source material, either internal or external. Occasionally, Arab or Western European authorities have something to say about Ethiopia but there is little of real value. It is not until the end of the fifteenth century that there is again a substantial body of external sources and these constitute the third type of historical data. These writings, this time by European visitors, throw a great deal of light on traditional Ethiopian society from the sixteenth century onwards. Amongst these accounts, those by the Portuguese Francisco Alvares, relating to 1520–1526, and by the Scotsman James Bruce, relating to 1768–1773, stand out as remarkable but there were many other writers who made significant contributions (Pankhurst 1961: 100). Overall, these external sources of the second half of the present millennium provide one of the richest sources of ethnohistory available in any part of Africa. Because they are accounts by outsiders, however, they must always be treated with caution.

The fourth and final type of historical sources consists of writings by Ethiopians themselves. The oldest surviving manuscripts date from the thirteenth century but the greater part of Ethiopian writing was on religious subjects and provides little information on secular matters. However, royal chronicles were also written from the fourteenth century onwards and these form the principal source for later Ethiopian history, although their value is considered to be variable (Buxton 1970: 129; on Ethiopian history in general, see also Sergew 1972, Tamrat 1972).

Rich though the historical sources are, therefore, it is apparent that many of them consist of observations by outsiders and that there are substantial periods and numerous subjects on which both outsiders and insiders have little to say. So far as the development of cities and states is concerned, it is clearly necessary to draw also on such archaeological data as is available.

There is, in fact, no shortage of archaeological evidence in Ethiopia. What is perhaps deficient is its investigation and publication. In particular, excavation has tended to concentrate on sites with Axumite masonry structures and publication has been inclined to be descriptive, rather than concerned with analysis and synthesis. Perhaps the best introduction to the subject of Axumite archaeology is that by Joseph W. Michels, inserted at the beginning of his English edition of Yuri Kobishchanov's book on Axum (Kobishchanov 1979: 1–34). Michels emphasizes the importance of the pioneering work of the German Axum expedition of 1906 and of the research programme of the Ethiopian Institute of Archaeology from the 1950s to the early 1970s. Since the early 1970s, political events in Ethiopia seem to have prevented further work.

Ethiopian archaeological evidence that is relevant to the present discussion can be divided into three main periods: pre-Axumite, Axumite, and medieval-modern Ethiopian. These represent the fifth century BC to the first century AD, the first century AD to the tenth century AD and the tenth century AD to the present. So far as the theme of this chapter is concerned, it is the first two which are of greatest importance and it is indeed these periods that have attracted most archaeological attention. Francis Anfray, who was responsible for much of the excavation in Ethiopia during the 1960s and early 1970s, suggested a further subdivision of these two periods. He divided the pre-Axumite into a South Arabian period, lasting from the fifth to the fourth century BC, and an intermediary period, lasting from the third century BC to the first century AD. He also suggested subdivisions of the Axumite period itself (Anfray 1968: 355–8).

Best known of the pre-Axumite sites is that of Yeha, situated in the northern end of the Ethiopian Highlands, where the Axumite state was to develop. In this place are the remains of a temple built of ashlar masonry set on a stepped base. Parts of this ruin still stand to a height of about 9 metres and the German Axum expedition of 1906 was able to produce a remarkable reconstruction of the building (Buxton 1970: 88), which is thought to date from the fifth or fourth century BC and to have similarities to contemporary South Arabian buildings of a similar date. Yeha has also produced a number of inscriptions which are written in a South Arabian language and in a South Arabian syllabary. There is, in addition, a cemetery of subterranean tombs (which has yielded a large collection of distinctive artefacts, including very fine objects of bronze) and the site of a stone building which excavation has shown to have been destroyed by a violent fire. Anfray, who excavated a part of this latter structure, which is known as the Grat-Be'al-Guebri, is of the opinion that it was a palace. Yeha also seems to have other occupation deposits and it appears reasonable to conclude that it was an early urban centre. It should be noticed that iron was already in use and that amongst the bronze objects recovered from Yeha are some curious 'identification marks', consisting of openwork geometrical or animal designs which often incorporate alphabetical characters. These appear to have been a type of personal seal and their impressions have been found on pottery (Buxton 1970: 36–7; Anfray 1972a; Michels, in Kobishchanov 1979: 10–12; Contenson 1981).

The strong South Arabian influence seen at Yeha is also apparent in the two localities of Haoulti-Melazo, situated in the same general area as Yeha, where several sites have produced pre-Axumite material. There is some dispute over the interpretation of the stratigraphic contexts of this evidence but it includes numerous fragments of dressed stone with South Arabian inscriptions, two limestone statues of seated female figures and a sophisticated limestone throne decorated with low-relief carving. It also includes symbolism associated with the moon-god, Almouqah, who was apparently venerated in the northern part of Ethiopia as well as in South Arabia. The statues are comparable with one of similar date found accidentally at a place on the eastern edge of the Ethiopian Highlands known as Addi Galamo, but formerly referred to as Azbi Dera, or Haouilé Assaraou, or Makalle. This was found with a number of other things, including a broken altar showing the crescent and disc of Almouqah. South Arabian influence has been seen in all of this evidence (Doresse 1959: 42; Contenson 1962; Contenson 1963a; Beek 1967; Pirenne 1970; Michels, in Kobishchanov 1979: 12–13; Contenson 1981).

Pre-Axumite material is also known from other sites, such as Seglamien (near Axum) and Matara, and perhaps from Adulis, although at both of the latter sites most of the artefacts are Axumite proper (Michels, in Kobishchanov 1979). There seems little doubt that the earliest pre-Axumite culture was strongly influenced by South Arabia; this is indicated by both stylistic and linguistic evidence. Nevertheless, from the beginning, pre-Axumite culture showed signs of originality and gradually it developed distinctive characteristics of its own, while those of South Arabia slowly faded. In particular, the language and syllabary used for inscriptions grew less and less like the South Arabian from which it had originated, and more and more like Ge'ez, the ancestor of the Ethiopian languages Tigré, Tigrinya and Amharic. At first a consonantal syllabary, it was not until the fourth century AD that a system of vocalization was introduced and this was clearly an Ethiopian development (Buxton 1970: 30–1, 178).

It seems probable, therefore, that the Axumite culture was a development from the pre-Axumite but in time it came to be characterized by quite unique qualities. Archaeological evidence for the Axumite period is more common than for the pre-Axumite and while pre-Axumite evidence suggests that urbanization and state formation may have been at an early stage, Axumite evidence clearly indicates a society in which these processes had reached a relatively mature stage.

Undoubtedly the most important and most thoroughly researched of the Axumite sites is Axum itself. It is justly famous for its stelae, tall, thin, standing stones of which the largest have been carefully dressed to represent multi-storeyed buildings. Such standing stones are known at other Axumite sites but none of them have such enormous proportions nor such careful finishing and decoration as some of those in the main stelae group at Axum. One of the larger ones of that group still stands and it consists of a single block of granite 21 metres high, carved to represent ten storeys, with a false door at its base (Fig. 4.2). The

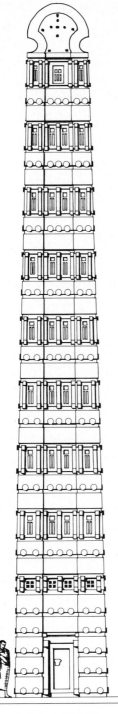

Fig. 4.2 Granite stela still standing at Axum. After Krencker (1913: Tafel VI) as reproduced in van Beek (1967: Pl. 2).

fallen pieces of a taller one were taken to Rome in 1937 and re-erected there. The largest of all, however, lies broken on the ground at Axum and was over 33 metres high, being carved to represent thirteen storeys. Buxton (1970: 89–90) has called it 'probably the largest single block of stone ever quarried, carved and set up in the ancient world'. Beek, indeed, has suggested that perhaps it fell while being erected (Beek 1967: 117). A total of 119 of these curious archaeological phenomena are known from two groups in Axum, although most are far smaller than those just described. Excavations amongst the main stelae group at Axum have revealed extensive, subterranean, multi-chambered Axumite tombs, so that it seems that the area was intended to serve as a cemetery (Chittick 1974a).

Of the archaeological sites known at Axum, tombs do indeed form an important part. Two notable stone tombs, called respectively 'Kaleb's tomb' and 'Menelik's tomb', were investigated by the German Axum expedition at the beginning of this century. In the early 1970s Chittick discovered what he called the 'Tomb of the False Door', a subterranean granite tomb connected to a surface structure which appeared to be intended to represent a temple or palace. The burial chamber within this tomb contained a stone sarcophagus. Also, Chittick's suggested reconstruction of the curious structure known as the Nefas Mawcha, which is situated adjacent to the main stelae group, makes it look as if that structure was originally a tomb. This consisted of a giant granite slab, 17.3 metres long, 6.5 metres wide and 1.1–1.7 metres in thickness, that rested on supporting slabs and walls. This enormous slab is thought to weigh about 200 tonnes (some people think more) and its suppporting structure had collapsed in antiquity due to its being struck by the largest of the stelae when it fell, weighing as it probably did some 750 tonnes (Doresse 1959: 55; Chittick 1974a: 183–6).

In addition to tombs, of which more examples have been investigated at Axum than are discussed here, there are a number of monolithic stone platforms which have been interpreted as the bases of thrones. Such thrones seem to have been important in Axumite culture: one existed also at the site of Matara, they are mentioned in two inscriptions of King Ezana and in the sixth century Cosmas Indicopleustes saw one close to a stela at Adulis. Ezana's inscriptions also say that he erected metal statues and although none of these have been found, a stone slab was discovered in Axum at the beginning of this century that had hollowed-out footprints 92 centimetres long. If this slab really was the plinth for a statue, as has been claimed, then the statue must have been of enormous size (Anfray 1981: 372).

Axum is also notable for the discovery of several stone-cut inscriptions of the fourth-century King Ezana, in whose reign Christianity appears to have been adopted (Pankhurst 1961: 28–30). These inscriptions, already referred to several times, are of very great historical significance. It is rare indeed that African archaeological evidence can speak to us so directly: 'I will rule the people', claims Ezana, 'with righteousness and justice, and will not oppress them, and may they preserve this Throne which I have set up for the Lord of Heaven' (Pankhurst 1961: 30).

Similarly of great interest, Axum has produced some extraordinary residential building evidence, that throws a remarkable light on Axumite society. At the beginning of the present century, the German Axum expedition excavated three multi-roomed structures of monumental scale, that were provisionally identified as palaces. These are known, respectively, by the names: Enda Mika'el, Enda Semon, and Ta'akha Mariam. An attempt was made by the German expedition to produce architectural reconstructions of these buildings, using both the excavated archaeological evidence and evidence from ancient church construction still observable in the area. The result for the central part of Enda Mika'el was a castle-like structure of four square towers, standing four storeys high on a stepped base (Fig. 4.3). In the case of Ta'akha Mariam the reconstruction was even more impressive, producing a huge complex of courtyards and towers and connecting buildings, that measured overall 80 by 120 metres and was of two storeys and, in places, three storeys in height (Buxton 1970: 93; Michels, in Kobishchanov 1979: 6).

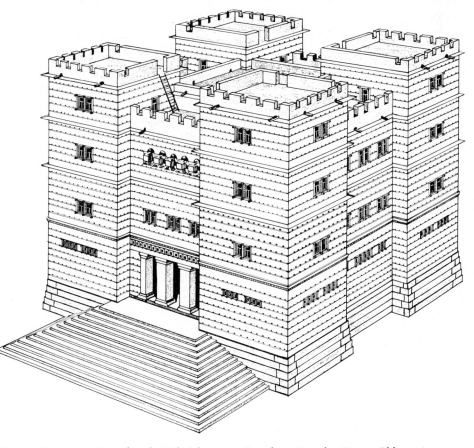

Fig. 4.3 Reconstruction of Enda Mika'el, Axum. Based on Krencker (1913: Abb. 245) as reproduced in Doresse (1959: 84).

These buildings, in common with other major Axumite buildings now known, were of a quite distinctive architectural style (Buxton 1970: 91–102). They were built on a massive masonry podium or base with stepped sides, a feature of pre-Axumite and South Arabian origin that must have increased a building's apparent height. They were also built with a characteristic 'indented' plan, that is to say both the podium and the wall surfaces above were alternately recessed and projecting, a design that must have given the buildings an appearance of great strength. The upper storeys are thought to have been built of masonry reinforced with timber, a type of construction that left the ends of the timbers projecting from the walls at the corners of windows and doors and at intervals along the wall surfaces. This constructional method (Fig. 4.4) is known from excavated archaeological evidence (e.g. Chittick 1974a: 190–1), from its representation on the largest examples of the stelae and from the tenth- or eleventh-century church of Debra Damo, studied by the German Axum expedition but also more recently by Matthews and Mordini (1959). With evidence from Debra Damo and elsewhere, Matthews was even able to attempt a reconstruction of the interior of a reception room on an upper floor of an Axumite 'palace' (Buxton 1970: 94–5). However, Anfray (1981: 370) has questioned whether the walls of such structures would have been strong enough to support more than two storeys. He considers that it is just possible, but rather unlikely, that some of these elite buildings had three storeys 'but to imagine more than that seems far-fetched'. Nevertheless, Anfray goes on to point out that in the sixth century AD Cosmas Indicopleustes wrote that in Ethiopia he saw a 'royal dwelling with four towers'. Whether the German reconstructions were correct in detail or not, it does seem likely that these monumental residential structures were attempting to achieve great height. After all, even two storeys, set on a solid masonry base, would have the appearance of a three-storey building. That they were in all probability quite imposing buildings has, in fact, been demonstrated again in more recent times with the excavation by Anfray himself of the so-called 'Dongur Mansion', on the western side of Axum.

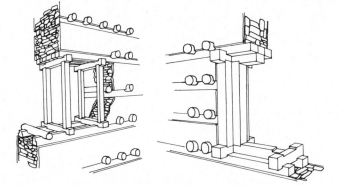

Fig. 4.4 Axumite constructional method: window to left, doorway to right. After Krencker (1913: Abb. 9, 15) as reproduced in Gerster (1970: Fig. 25).

Excavated in 1966–1968, this proved to be a 40-room complex occupying an area of approximately 3000 square metres and with its remains still standing in places to a height of 5 metres. The stone-built complex comprised a central structure and a series of interior courtyards that created separate blocks of rooms (Fig. 4.5). It is thought to date to about the seventh century AD. Rather smaller than

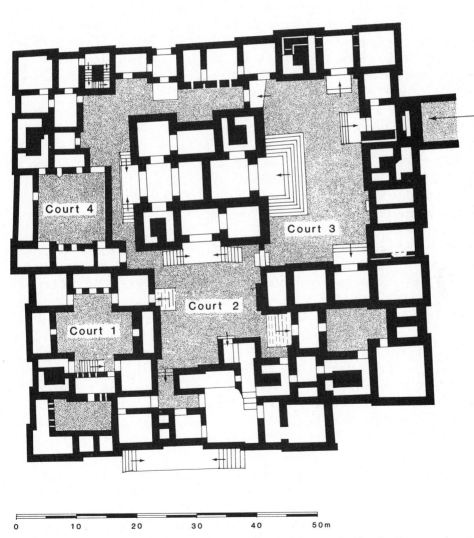

Fig. 4.5 Plan of 'Dongur Mansion' in Axum. After Anfray (1972b: Planche I).

Ta'akha Mariam, Anfray interpreted it as a villa of a member of the elite, not a royal palace (Anfray 1968: 360–3; Anfray 1972b: Plate I for plan; Michels, in Kobishchanov 1979: 7–8; Anfray 1981: 365–6).

Excavations by various people in other parts of Axum have indicated the existence of other stone buildings, some of which must have had more humble purposes than those discussed above. It seems likely, indeed, that Axum was a city of some importance during the first millennium AD. Excavations by Chittick, at the base of the hill behind the main stelae group at Axum (Chittick 1974a: 191) have also provided some indication of the impact of such a city on its immediate environment. The following erosional cycle has been suggested: (1) felling of trees on the hillside in early Axumite times; (2) cultivation of the hillside and the construction of houses on its slopes; (3) erosion of the hillside over a comparatively short period, ceasing before late Axumite times; (4) accumulation of recent colluvium. The hillside in question is now largely rocky, with little soil, leading one to wonder whether the eventual decline and disappearance of the city of Axum may have been linked to an environmental decline, triggered by a high density of population.

Amongst other Axumite sites, Matara is one of the most important and certainly one of the most extensively investigated. It lies about half-way between the Axumite port of Adulis and the Axumite capital of Axum and is likely, therefore, to have been a place of economic and political significance. Indeed, the site appears to have been a key urban centre, occupying about 20 hectares, and the deep deposits (up to 5 metres) contain evidence of two main phases of occupation: first a South Arabian period of about 500–300 BC and then (after a long abandonment) an Axumite period of about AD 700. Tombs, churches and residential buildings have been excavated by Anfray and amongst the latter both elite houses and ordinary dwellings have been discovered. Mound B yielded a large, multi-roomed mansion, comparable to those excavated at Axum and three other similar 'villas' were also uncovered. In addition, however, there were houses of only two or three rooms and others that were intermediate in size between these and the villas, suggesting a social hierarchy. Certainly some of the residents of Matara must have had considerable wealth, because there was recovered from this site a remarkable hoard of goldwork of Roman and Byzantine origin (Anfray 1963; Anfray and Annequin 1965; Anfray 1967; Michels, in Kobishchanov 1979: 14–16; Anfray 1981: 367–8).

There are also important urban sites of Axumite culture at Adulis, on the coast, and at Kohaito, north of Matara. Artefacts of both Axumite and Mediterranean origin have been found at Adulis, indicating its role in long-distance trade, and Kohaito is sometimes thought to be the Koloè which is mentioned in the *Periplus of the Erythraean Sea* (p. 73). Kohaito is perhaps best known for a dam, built of carefully fitted blocks of stone, that is 67 metres long and about 3 metres high (Anfray 1981: 368). This dam was designed to form an artificial reservoir of water, and Pankhurst (1961: 24) has called it 'one of the greatest engineering feats of the Aksumites'. A further Axumite site worth mention is Ouchatei Golo, about 7 kilometres from Axum itself. At this place was a quarry for the granite used for the dressed stones of Axumite building and for some of the stelae. A typical Axumite multi-roomed structure was excavated at this site by Contenson and undressed stelae were found in its vicinity (Michels, in Kobishchanov 1979: 10).

There are, however, far more Axumite sites known than have been excavated or concerning which there are individual published studies. Anfray (1973: 21) has published a site distribution map, which shows how the nuclear area of the Axumite state must have been located in the north-eastern corner of the Ethiopian Highlands, between Axum and Adulis. Anfray has also proposed a distinction between an eastern and a western Axumite province, the archaeological record suggesting that the eastern province was more prosperous but that the western was the centre of political power. To such traditional archaeological site survey, Michels has added a modern touch by carrying out a stratified random sampling procedure of all archaeological evidence in a 40 per cent sample of a 500-square-kilometre area, in the Axum-Yeha region. The result of this work is the discovery and documentation of about 250 sites, ranging from single compounds to large towns, and including temples, stelae fields, tombs and workshops. Such a survey reveals a sample of the Axumite settlement pattern and suggests that much evidence still remains to be located in other areas (Michels, in Kobishchanov 1979: 22–4).

Before leaving this discussion of Axumite archaeological evidence, one final point should be stressed. This is that inscriptions, coins and imported items have been found in most of the sites that have been investigated to any extent. Their repeated occurrence emphasizes, if such emphasis is needed, the level of sophistication achieved by Axumite culture. They also provide important historical data, of which scholars are able to make use.

Late in the tenth century AD the Axumite state was finally destroyed by an Ethiopian Agau chieftainess called Gudit. Subsequently, the political centre of gravity moved south to the Lalibela area, where it was to remain for some centuries (Buxton 1970: 44). The Ethiopian state survived down to modern times but for the earlier part of the present millennium it was feudal rather than urban in character, with its rulers leading a semi-nomadic life in an unending succession of camps, which Pankhurst (1979) has called 'moving capitals'. Such a camp might consist of as many as 100 000 people and continual movement seems to have been necessitated by the rapid exhaustion in any one area of the supplies of food and firewood. As a result, archaeological evidence for the first half of the present millennium is dominated by ecclesiastical structures, for not only did Christianity survive and flourish but it also constituted almost the only static element of importance in Ethiopian society. Some remarkable 'built-up' churches from this period have been studied, including Debra Damo, which has already been mentioned. Rock-hewn churches are more numerous, however, having survived rather more readily. These were made from about the tenth to about the fifteenth or early sixteenth century but the most remarkable of them seem to date from around the thirteenth century (Buxton 1970: 97–115). Best known of the rock-hewn churches are those of Lalibela but there are also many in Tigré Province and others scattered widely across the Ethiopian Highlands. They provide remarkable evidence of technical skill and of an ability to marshal the material resources implied by these often vast undertakings. The church of St George, at Lalibela, for instance, is a complex and sophisticated 'building' entirely carved, inside and out, from one gigantic block of stone (10.6 metres high) that had first to be isolated in a huge quarry-pit. Published accounts of Ethiopian rock-hewn churches include Buxton (1947), Gerster (1970), and Buxton (1971).

In the second half of the present millennium, 'static capitals', as Pankhurst (1979) has called them, tended to replace the frequently-moved camps, although even these more stable settlements were shifted periodically or used only seasonally. Beginning in the late sixteenth and early seventeenth century there grew up a practice of constructing stone castles, which formed the nucleus of capitals. It was one of these castles that was studied at Gouzara by Annequin (1965) but the most successful of these castle-based capitals was that at Gondar, north of Lake Tana, where no less than twenty successive emperors made their capital prior to the nineteenth century. In the meantime, churches continued to be built and right down to modern times Axum, much reduced in size, has continued to be important as a religious centre. It is popularly believed by Ethiopians that the true Ark of the Covenant is kept there and such emperors as were able to do so went there for their coronation (Pankhurst 1979: 4–6). It could be argued that this typifies the continuity that has so often been claimed to be characteristic of Ethiopian culture.

Subsistence economy

What light does archaeological evidence in Ethiopia throw on the origins of cities and of the state in that part of Africa? For instance, what is known of the subsistence economy on which these developments must ultimately have depended? The quick answer is that very little is known, as might be expected of a type of archaeology that has been mainly interested in architecture, sculpture, inscriptions, coins, objects of fine craftsmanship and artefacts generally. Animal bones and botanical remains do not appear to have had the same attention. Some indication of the character of much of the archaeological research in Ethiopia may be gained from the fact that Phillipson (1977a: 98) pointed out that 'no analysis of food remains from an Axumite site has ever been undertaken'. Similarly Michels (in Kobishchanov 1979: 29) complained that not a single radiocarbon date was available from any Axumite site!

Some scholars would argue that the lack of archaeological data for

subsistence hardly matters. Kobishchanov, for instance, has carefully reconstructed the Axumite subsistence base from information taken from inscriptions
and other historical sources. According to him, both terracing and irrigation
were practised and ox-drawn ploughs were in use. Wheat and other cereals were
grown, viticulture existed and large herds of cattle, sheep and goats were kept, as
well as asses and mules. He also claims that elephants had been domesticated but
were reserved for use by the royal court (Kobishchanov 1981: 383). All this is
very interesting but it is a pity that archaeologists have not tried to test some of it.

It seems likely that agriculture developed at an early date in Ethiopia. Portères
(1970: 54–5) regarded it as one of the 'primary cradles of agriculture of Africa'.
Simoons (1965) suggested that cereal-plough agriculture pre-dated the advent of
South Arabian migrants in the first millennium BC, to whom its introduction has
often been attributed as a modification of earlier cultivation practices. In
addition Ehret (1979) used linguistic evidence to argue for a substantial antiquity
of agriculture in Ethiopia. There are one or two pieces of archaeological
evidence that support this view. At Gobedra rock shelter near Axum, Phillipson
(1977b) recovered seeds of cultivated finger millet (*Eleusine coracana*). These
came from a 'later Stone Age' level in which pottery first appeared and which
yielded a radiocarbon date of about 5000 BC. A somewhat higher level, that gave
a radiocarbon date of about 1000 BC, produced one probable domestic ox tooth.
Phillipson thought that the tentative date for the millet seeds was in about the
fourth or third millenium BC and claimed that these seeds were 'the earliest
extant trace of any of the indigenous African cereal crops' (Phillipson 1977b: 82).
In addition, the excavation by Joanne Dombrowski of Lalibela cave, east of
Lake Tana (Phillipson 1977a: 69), produced evidence of cultivated barley,
chickpeas and some unspecified legumes, together with bones tentatively
identified as cattle and small stock bones. This evidence was associated with
stone artefacts and came from a first millennium BC context. Together with the
Gobedra evidence, it would suggest that by pre-Axumite and Axumite times a
strong subsistence base would have developed.

That such did exist is demonstrated by the number and size of settlements but
there are a few other pointers. Thus, for example, bronze sickles were found at
Yeha and Haoulti; the latter site also yielded pottery models of cattle, sometimes
wearing yokes; and grindstones were found at various sites (Contenson 1981:
356–7; Michels, in Kobishchanov 1979: 14). The evidence is tantalizingly
inadequate but archaeology does suggest that the subsistence economy of the
late first millennium BC in Ethiopia had already attained a level of some
complexity.

Technology

In contrast to the situation with subsistence economy, Ethiopian archaeological
evidence is highly informative on the technology of the periods under discussion.

As with the middle Nile, there exists some difficulty in discriminating between things made in Ethiopia by local craftsmen and those imported from elsewhere or made in Ethiopia by expatriate craftsmen (p. 54). An attempt must be made to separate the indigenous from the foreign, although some uncertainty will remain as to how reliably this can be done. In general terms, however, it does appear that the technological achievements, of the Axumite period in particular, must rank amongst the most sophisticated to be found in precolonial Africa.

First, some Axumite sites have provided evidence of remarkable engineering skills. To quarry and transport and erect such a monolith as the largest of the stelae at Axum, over 33 metres long and about 750 tonnes in weight, must have involved theoretical knowledge, practical skill and good organization. Furthermore, although this was the most outstanding achievement of this sort it was not alone. There is the giant 200-tonne granite slab of the Nefas Mawcha and there are substantial numbers of other stelae that although smaller still imply the existence of considerable engineering ability. It also appears that this ability could be directed to practical as well as ceremonial purposes. The dam at Kohaito and the Mai Shum rainwater cistern at Axum (Butzer 1981: 479) suggest that engineering expertise was applied to the task of water storage. Related to this, there was probably in addition extensive practice of both terracing and irrigation, as claimed from historical sources. So far as the archaeological evidence is concerned, however, it was in quarrying and carving and manipulating masses of stone that the Axumites evinced their main engineering ability. These skills had a long history, from the cutting of pre-Axumite subterranean tombs to the quarrying of the medieval rock-hewn churches and it seems reasonable to claim for them an indigenous origin. It should be no surprise that the inhabitants of an area as rocky as the Ethiopian Highlands should become expert in handling stone.

They also handled it with great skill architecturally and building construction was an area of technology where pre-Axumites, Axumites and medieval Ethiopians all excelled. Using mud-mortared stonework tied together with timber reinforcements, the Axumites were able to construct monumental multi-storeyed residences for the elite. It is possible that the architecture of these major buildings was influenced by Roman style, conveyed perhaps via Syria, with which early Christian Ethiopia had connections (Michels, in Kobishchanov 1979: 27), but whatever the source of the style the workmanship was distinctively Axumite. Building skills also extended to tombs, temples, early churches and structures of lesser importance. In addition to employing stone and timber, Axumite builders learned to both manufacture and use fired bricks (e.g. Chittick 1974a: 172, 186; Michels, in Kobishchanov 1979: 14), and the construction of brick arches and of brick barrel-vaulting were both understood. So far as ordinary domestic buildings are concerned, the rather limited number of excavated examples are supplemented by pre-Axumite and Axumite pottery models respectively from Haoulti (Contenson 1963a: Plates 38–9) and from Axum (Chittick 1974a: Figure 21a).

A number of other technical skills were associated with building construction. These included the dressing of fine stonework, the production of stone sculpture and the cutting of inscriptions. Because the latter included, at one time or another, both South Arabian and Greek characters, it seems likely that a foreign hand or at least a foreign-trained hand was sometimes in use here. Nevertheless, the gradual ascendancy of Ge'ez would suggest that even inscription cutting eventually passed into local hands. Another craft or art form associated with buildings was the creation of the fine wall-paintings that were such a feature of the interiors of many Ethiopian churches. Here again, the debt to foreign influences was great but the style that developed was distinctly Ethiopian (Buxton 1970: 136). The origins of Ethiopian wall-painting are not really known but perhaps it may be assumed that the churches of Christian Axum were already decorated in this way.

Metallurgical technology seems to have developed early in Ethiopia and to have remained at a high level of proficiency. In the first millennium BC there were still stone-using people at Gobedra (Phillipson 1977b) and Lalibela cave (Phillipson 1977a: 69) and the making of stone artefacts continued into Axumite times; but by the fifth century BC a literate urban culture using bronze and iron was established at Yeha. This apparently sudden technological transition has been explained in terms of a gradual infiltration of people from Southern Arabia, where iron had been in use from about 1000 BC, but it is possible that the use of copper had already reached Northern Ethiopia from the Nile Valley before this time (Phillipson 1977a: 91–2). Whatever the mechanism involved, however, it is clear that by pre-Axumite times a wide range of iron and bronze artefacts was in use. Mineral resources were such (p. 72) that iron must have been mined and smelted in Ethiopia, as perhaps some other metals were; but gold, known to have been exported from Ethiopia, was in all probability merely panned from watercourses.

Artefacts recovered from Axumite sites also indicate a variety of other manufacturing skills. The difficulty is to untangle the imported items from the locally-produced. Much pottery was made locally but a small amount came from the Mediterranean world, probably as containers for wine or olive oil. Leather working appears to have been practised (Chittick 1974a: Figure 24c) and it is surmised that textile production was important, although textiles of foreign origin were also in use. Bone is known to have been worked (Contenson 1963b: 12) and civet was probably already produced in Axumite times (Endt 1978). From historical and ethnohistorical sources, it seems that salt was probably produced from the Danakil Desert but there is no archaeological evidence for this. Coins were struck in Ethiopia in Axumite times, although some coins were also imported. Finally, there were numerous luxury goods: jewellery, glass and fine metalwork, for instance, that were clearly of foreign origin and therefore have no relevance for Ethiopian technology.

A final point needs emphasis. This is that the technological base of Ethiopia, in all the periods under discussion, remained agricultural. It could be argued that the most important aspect of Ethiopia's technology was the ox-drawn plough and the terracing and irrigation systems that went with it. Added to these was the use of the mule for transport. Collectively, these factors must have been contributory to the development of social complexity.

Social system

Ethiopian archaeological evidence suggests that at least by Axumite times a considerable degree of social complexity had been attained. The society which left so much material evidence in the north-eastern corner of the Ethiopian Highlands, and in some adjacent areas, must surely have been a stratified one. At the top was an absolute monarch, frequently depicted on Axumite coins wearing a crown and in one case shown seated on a throne (Fig. 4.6). Some of the inscriptions on the coins suggest that these rulers were, nevertheless, concerned about popular opinion: 'May the country be satisfied!' (Kobishchanov 1981: 394) and 'Joy be to the peoples' (Buxton 1970: 39), lack something of the usual tone of true autocracy. However, monarchical government, whatever its exact character, is indicated also by other elements of the archaeological evidence. Thus, some at least of the monumental, multi-roomed, multi-storeyed, residential buildings which have been investigated must have been royal palaces. At all events, it seems difficult to explain Ta'akha Mariam at Axum as anything else. In addition, there are monumental tombs that must have been for royal burials and those of other leading members of society. Other sorts of

Fig. 4.6 Bronze coin of Armah (seventh century AD).

monumental structures also occur that hint at the existence of a monarchical state: temples in earlier periods, churches in later ones and, of course, the largest of the stelae at Axum. One thing is common to many of these structures: they are large. Kobishchanov leaves us in no doubt of the historian's view of such evidence:

> The mania for the gigantic reflected the tastes of the Axumite monarchy and the monuments were the concrete realization of its ideological purpose, which was to instil awe-inspiring admiration for the greatness and strength of the potentate to whom the monuments were dedicated. (Kobishchanov 1981: 394)

Although the archaeologist might view the evidence with rather more circumspection, Kobishchanov cannot be far wrong. Perhaps it should merely be emphasized that not all the fine mansions or the large tombs may have been intended for royalty, they seem too numerous for that. Certainly stelae of small or medium size are too common for such a conclusion. In addition, the distribution of luxury goods, obtainable only from trade with the outside world, is too widespread. The conclusion seems inescapable that there was not only a monarchy but also an elite group of leading members of society, of the sort that usually form part of such an institution.

Equally, the archaeological evidence suggests the existence of a numerous mass of peasants and/or slaves. The existence of the latter might be assumed from the long survival of slavery in Ethiopia, condoned as it was even by Ethiopian Christianity (Pankhurst 1961: 372–3). It also seems likely that slaves were one of the exports of the Axumite state. In any case, whatever the exact status of the sweating humanity that must have toiled and suffered on such tasks as moving and raising the larger stelae, large labour forces must have been involved. Constructional work on the scale frequently achieved in Axumite times implies a numerous and an obedient labour force. If the modern world was built on machines, the ancient world was built on human backs. Indeed the necessarily-agricultural basis of Axumite society, and that of earlier and later times, would require the existence of a large peasant class. As is often the case, such a class is not so well represented in the archaeological record as that of the elite but the smallest houses of those excavated at Matara would seem to confirm its existence (p. 82).

Indeed, the intermediate-sized houses excavated at Matara would indicate that some form of middle class was also present, at least in Axumite times. It might be expected that such a class would include government officials, scribes, priests of temple or church, merchants and perhaps some of the more skilled craftsmen. Amongst such a class there would probably be some foreigners, permitted to live in Ethiopia because of their special skills or attributes.

Thus, in addition to social stratification, the archaeological evidence suggests the existence of functional specialization. In Axumite times, as well as rulers, government officials and farmers, there were also expert builders, including masons, brickmakers, carpenters and joiners. There must also have been miners, quarrymen, iron-smelters, blacksmiths, other metalworkers and workers of leather. Finally, one would expect that there were merchants, artists, scribes and temple or church officials. In this way an attempt can be made to reconstruct the society of the Axumite period, although that reconstruction will no doubt be incomplete. The picture that emerges is one of a degree of social complexity quite compatible with urbanization and state formation.

Population pressures

In general the Ethiopian Highlands were attractive to human settlement, providing climatic conditions and soils conducive to cereal-plough agriculture and stock-raising. True, much of the highlands were of limited or no use because they were too rocky, too exposed or too high but this was probably offset by the considerable benefits accruing from the great altitudinal range. This gave a diversity and a flexibility to the subsistence base that was clearly advantageous. Such other environmental constraints as there were consisted of occasional epidemics of disease and of periods of famine usually brought on by rainfall variability or crop destruction, the latter particularly caused by locusts (p. 73). It has already been suggested that the episodic character of these constraints would have meant that they had little overall inhibiting effect on the growth of social complexity in the highlands. Indeed, it is possible that one of these very constraints actually stimulated these developments by creating situations of localized and perhaps temporary population pressure.

The pre-Axumite and Axumite culture grew up in a part of the Ethiopian Highlands well placed for contact with the outside world. Indeed, it can be argued that the contribution of South Arabian migrants from that world had a lot to do with the emergence of social complexity in that part of Northern Ethiopia. It was, however, a part of the Ethiopian Highlands that in recent times has had less rainfall and a shorter wet season than areas to the south. As a result it was probably particularly prone to drought-induced famine and it is interesting to note that in medieval and modern times Ethiopia's centre of gravity has usually been considerably further south. It is possible to hypothesize a situation in which such an area, normally able to support a substantial agricultural population, suffered from recurrent episodes of population pressure caused by drought. In those circumstances, considerable power would be placed in the hands of those who controlled agricultural land with a potential for irrigation. Furthermore, the long-term effects of tree-clearance, cultivation and periodic drought, particularly on hillsides, could well have resulted in the destruction of some agricultural lands by erosion, another factor that could place pressure on subsistence agriculturalists. It is quite possible that the emergence of an elite was facilitated by such conditions.

Further light has been thrown on such matters by Karl Butzer, who in the early 1970s conducted a palaeo-ecological study in the Axum area (Michels, in Kobishchanov 1979: 21–2). On the basis of geo-archaeological evidence, Butzer has suggested that Axumite culture flourished at a time of better spring rains than at present and declined when: 'Intense land pressure and more erratic rainfall favored soil destruction and ecological degradation during the seventh and eighth centuries' (Butzer 1981: 471). The possibility of such a moister period might also be supported by other evidence. It is thought that during the first century AD the population of Anfray's western Axumite province (p. 83) gradually moved away from the plateau drainage system onto the broad plains (Michels, in Kobishchanov 1979: 27). Whether or not there were at one time more favourable climatic conditions, ecological degradation does seem eventually to have become a problem in some areas. There is, for instance, the evidence excavated by Chittick at Axum, that suggests that serious erosion of a hillside occurred following tree clearance and cultivation (p. 82). Indeed, it seems possible that resources were unequally distributed in north-eastern Ethiopia and that some land was under greater settlement pressure than other land. Partial confirmation of this may be provided by a settlement-pattern survey undertaken by Joseph Michels in the Axum area also in the early 1970s (p. 83). This stratified random sampling survey showed a distinct tendency for sites to cluster in certain areas and to avoid others (Michels, in Kobishchanov 1979: 24). Thus it seems likely that differential access to resources, in both space and time, could have brought about significant episodes of population pressure that played an important part in Ethiopian history.

Ideology

Archaeological evidence from Ethiopia indicates that religion played an important role in the emergence of the Axumite state and in the continued existence of its medieval successors. The evidence also suggests that religion contributed to the process of urbanization of pre-Axumite and Axumite times and to the eventual reappearance of urban living in the second half of the present millennium. For the pre-Axumites and early Axumites, religion consisted of a complex polytheism probably of South Arabian origin, in which the moon-god, Almouqah, and Mahrem, god of war and of monarchy, were amongst the more important deities. From the fourth century AD onwards, for both the later Axumites and medieval and modern Ethiopians, the principal religion has been Monophysite, Coptic Christianity of a distinctive Ethiopian type. Ullendorff (1960: 97) has called Ethiopian Christianity 'the most profound expression of the national existence of the Ethiopians' and it is quite possible that the beliefs that pre-dated it had a similar significance.

The most obvious indication of the role of religion, during the periods under discussion, consists of the numerous and impressive remains of temples and churches. The temple of Yeha was so well built that after approximately 2500 years its ruins still stand to a height of about nine metres; the surviving churches of medieval Ethiopia appear to constitute the only extant structures of their period. The direction of resources into such buildings must in all cases have been in the hands of the ruler and the elite, who no doubt expected in return an ideological legitimization of their position.

That such a legitimization was claimed by the monarchical Axumite state is clearly indicated on the coins that were minted. The earlier ones showed the crescent and disc, presumably representing the moon and the sun; the later ones included the cross, among the earliest coins of any country to do so according to Buxton (1970: 40). The stone-cut inscriptions of Ezana also demonstrate the support that the monarchy sought from religion, calling first on prechristian deities and later on the Christian god.

In addition there are the stelae, particularly the larger stelae at Axum. Anfray (1981: 371) thought that they had a funerary significance, Kobishchanov (1981: 397) thought that they were connected with an ancestor cult. Whatever the exact case, they would appear to have had some sort of religious role as well as being symbols of state authority. Groups of holes at the tops of these stelae have been thought to indicate the fixing of religious symbols to the stone: these symbols were probably made of metal, but none of them survive. As a result there has been some debate as to whether the symbols consisted of the crescent and disc or the Christian cross (e.g. Beek 1967: 118, 121) but whichever it was probably makes little difference to the role that these monuments played in reinforcing the power of the state.

Perhaps less obvious is the contribution that religion made to urbanization. The temple at Yeha and the tombs and stelae at Axum suggest that these urban developments were religious centres as well as commercial and administrative centres. The problem is that we do not know what their primary role may have been. Certainly it was as a religious and a ceremonial centre that Axum survived into modern times, so that Bent (1893) could call it 'the sacred city of the Ethiopians'. Also, in medieval Ethiopia it was religion that maintained almost the only static settlements: Lalibela may have been principally a religious centre but its archaeological remains imply that there must have been quite a number of people in its vicinity. When urban centres appeared again in the second half of the present millennium, the Church still played an important role: Gondar, for example, is said to have had no less than 44 churches (Pankhurst 1979: 5). Clearly, something more than religious fervour was involved, there was the politics of propitiating a powerful clergy and there was prestige.

External trade

Historical and archaeological evidence indicates that Axum had trading contacts with the Roman provinces of the eastern Mediterranean, with South

Arabia, Somalia, Meroë and India. Kobishchanov (1979: 175) has used both historical and archaeological sources to put together an impressive list of goods imported into the Axumite kingdom. They consisted of iron and non-ferrous metals, and articles made of them; articles of precious metals; glass and ceramic articles; fabrics and clothing; wine and sugar-cane; vegetable oils; aromatic substances and spices. From purely historical sources, Kobishchanov (1979: 172) has also reconstructed the exports of Axum. They comprised ivory, gold, obsidian, emeralds, aromatic substances, rhinoceros horn, hippopotamus teeth and hide, tortoise-shell, slaves, monkeys and other live animals. These details suggest that Axumite external trade was extensive and that, like the Nubian trade of the middle Nile, it was basically one involving the exchange of precious raw materials and African exotica for manufactured and luxury articles. It seems unlikely that pre-Axumite trade was anything like so widespread and it is apparent that medieval Ethiopia suffered from a comparative trading isolation, although even then contact was somehow maintained with places as far away as Armenia. It is tempting, therefore, to conclude that the Axumite state was a product of the international trade of its day. If Nubia was the corridor to Africa (Chapter 3), then it might be claimed that for a brief period Axum, through its port of Adulis, was a front door to the continent. Kirwan, indeed, is of the opinion that the rise of Adulis must have damaged the Nile Valley trade and contributed to the decline of Meroë after the first century AD (Kirwan 1972: 168). The question is, what light does the archaeological evidence throw on this subject?

As regards the commodities that were imported and exported, archaeology is at the same time informative and disappointing. As is the case with Nubia, exports are not well represented in the archaeological record, although an elephant tusk was found at Adulis (Anfray 1981: 377). The problem is that the commodities exported would either not have survived, or would not have survived in their original state and, furthermore, they would need to be identified as of Axumite origin in the archaeological record of the country to which they were traded. Archaeological evidence for imports is very much better, although durables tend to survive whereas consumables do not. In addition, soil and climatic conditions in the Ethiopian Highlands are not as conducive to the preservation of organic materials as they are in the middle Nile Valley. As a result, most of the evidence for imports is in the form of artefacts of metal, ceramic, and glass. For example, Axum has produced Byzantine bronze weights, and both bronze scales and weights of Byzantine origin have been found at Adulis. From Matara has come a Byzantine bronze lamp, two Byzantine gold crosses, a necklace of Roman silver coins of the second to third century AD and a fantastic bronze lamp of South Arabian origin depicting a dog in the act of catching an ibex (Kobishchanov 1979: 173–4). Even more remarkable is the hoard of 104 Indian coins of third century date which were found at Debra Damo (Munro-Hay 1982: 111). Examples of ceramic and glass imports are rather more numerous. Axum, for instance, has yielded amphorae of Mediterranean origin, pottery imitative of Roman fine ware and glass ointment flasks of Roman and Egyptian manufacture (Kobishchanov 1979: 173). Such imports as wine and oil, however, which must have been inside some of these pottery and glass containers, have left no trace. Even textiles, which were probably imported in significant quantities, are only represented by occasional discoveries such as that of silk fabrics at Debra Damo, which originated from Coptic, Mesopotamian and Islamic Egyptian sources of sixth to twelfth century AD date (Kobishchanov 1979: 174). Nevertheless, although archaeological evidence cannot provide a complete picture of the range of imported commodities, it does give some indication of the geographical reach of Axumite external trade. Clearly, that trade was of considerable importance.

Some confirmation that this was indeed the case is offered by several other pieces of evidence. Thus, Axum was the first state in tropical Africa to mint its own coinage, which was produced, at one time or another, in gold, silver and copper. It may be noticed that the Axumite monetary system was similar to the Byzantine system, in weight, standard and form (Kobishchanov 1981: 386), and it would seem very likely that coins were only introduced because of Axum's participation in an international trade which was accustomed to such a means of exchange. The earliest Axumite coins belong to the third century AD, the latest to the eighth century (Anfray 1981: 375) and it is surely significant that they ceased to be issued at a time when Axum's external trading interests were in decline. Nevertheless, it is a little strange that of the several thousand coins that are known, 90 per cent have been found in Northern Ethiopia itself, with the remaining ones being found primarily in South Arabia and only a few in Egypt (Kobishchanov 1979: 184). It would appear that the coinage of Axum did not have a circulation as wide as Axumite trading interests.

A further indication of the importance of external trade to Axum is the geographical location of this state. Situated as it was in the extreme northeastern part of the Ethiopian Highlands, it was in a decidedly advantageous situation for taking part in the Red Sea trade. It was, in fact, sitting at the side of one of the major sea routes of the ancient world. Just as the coinage died when Axum was excluded from that route, so too did the Axumite state fade away. Indeed, during the second millennium AD the political and cultural centre of Ethiopia was located far to the south. By then the need was not for access to the Red Sea but for maximum isolation from the enmity of Ethiopia's neighbours.

The geographical location of Axum in relation to the network of trade routes in this part of Africa, provides still more evidence of the role of external trade in the development of this state and of its cities. According to the *Periplus of the Erythraean Sea*, the journey from Adulis to Koloè (perhaps Kohaito) took three days and the journey from Adulis to Axum took eight, as it apparently still did at the beginning of the present century (Kobishchanov 1979: 185). By the standards of ancient trade routes, this was a brief journey and this route from Adulis to

Axum was, in fact, merely the beginning of a route that led from the Red Sea to the Nile Valley, ending near Meroë. Another route ran north-west from Axum to the Aswan region, across the Nubian Desert, a journey which took 30 days according to Cosmas Indicopleustes. Yet another route ran south from Axum to Lake Tana and Sasu, the latter reputedly the major source of Axumite gold. According to Cosmas Indicopleustes this journey took 50 days. Branches from this route led respectively to Shoa and into the region of the African Horn (Kobishchanov 1979: 185–6). Thus Axum was at the centre of a giant web of trade routes that tapped the resources of the African interior and injected them into the Red Sea trade. It can hardly be doubted that external trade was an important contributory factor in the rise of the Axumite state and in the growth of its cities.

Conclusion

It would appear that Ethiopian isolation was a relative thing; relative, that is to say, to the circumstances of the surrounding world. The Axumite state of the first millennium AD was able to benefit from its participation in the Red Sea trade, the Ethiopian state of much of the second millennium AD was able to isolate itself from hostile neighbours. Situated, as it were, on the roof of the world, the Ethiopians could join or reject that world as they wished. Thus can be explained the paradox of a people who have spent much of their history forgotten by the rest of humanity, but who have been, nevertheless, the creators of one of the earliest states and some of the earliest cities in Africa.

In general, therefore, it can be argued that Ethiopia's geographical location and its mountainous environment played a basic role in these developments. In particular, its accessibility to South Arabian settlers during the first millennium BC and the diversity of agricultural systems made possible by its great altitudinal range, provided a foundation for what was to follow. This is not to say that the state of Axum and its cities resulted from an injection of South Arabian migrants, but it is clear that Ethiopian technology, of the last few centuries BC and the first few centuries AD, benefited from alien contributions the source of many of which was Asiatic. Certainly the earliest state and urban developments took place in that part of the Ethiopian plateau most accessible from the Red Sea coast.

Compared with the surrounding lowlands, the Ethiopian Highlands were healthier, had better soils and a greater range of possible agricultural adaptations providing, therefore, a fertile seedbed for the growth of social complexity. It is also possible that episodes of stress, brought on by periodic drought-induced famine, created temporary population pressures that could be exploited by those with access to irrigated land. Such land may well have constituted a limited resource, the control of which could have provided a power-base for an emerging elite. On many aspects of these matters, archaeological evidence provides little information; nevertheless it does demonstrate that by Axumite times there had developed a stratified society consisting of monarch, surrounding elite, middle class, and peasant/slave class. It also indicates the presence of a fair degree of functional specialization. Furthermore, it is clear from the material evidence that the social order was confirmed and legitimized by religious dogma. Even the change from prechristian to Christian beliefs may be seen as a reinforcement of the prevailing social system.

To all this must be added the impact of external trade; not in itself a cause of social complexity but, nevertheless, a contributory factor of some importance. It is clear that the apogee of the Axumite state and cities was coterminous with Axum's involvement in the Red Sea trade but it is equally apparent that the state of Ethiopia, if not its cities, was able to survive many centuries of comparative isolation from international trade during the second millennium AD. The Red Sea trade, conducted by Axum through its port of Adulis, must not be seen in isolation, however, but as part of a widespread network of trade that Axum had developed throughout much of north-east Africa. Thus Axum profited from the role of entrepôt, acquiring wealth and prestige from commodities that were obtained from others. If Ethiopia appears isolated, this is clearly an isolation that has had its own particular benefits.

Chapter 5
An optimal zone: the West African savanna

'Amid all the world's misery, few people are worse off or face a bleaker future than the Sahelians.' This quotation comes from a leaflet circulated by an organization called 'S.O.S. Sahel International', centred on Dakar, in Senegal. This organization aims to raise funds to relieve the immediate effects of drought and to support small-scale technological innovations that can mitigate damage caused by future droughts. It defines 'Sahelians' as residents of the states of Mauritania, Senegal, The Gambia, Mali, Upper Volta (now Bourkina Fasso), Niger, Chad, Sudan, and Ethiopia. It is worth reflecting on the fact that three of the areas of precolonial urbanization and state formation which are considered in this book are situated within this group of countries. Clearly, their occupants did not always face the bleak future that, rightly or wrongly, is now forecast for them. Particularly this seems to have been the case in West Africa, where the savanna lands bordering the southern edge of the Sahara Desert were the setting for very important social and political developments during the first and second millennium AD. Some historical sources indicate conditions that were far from being bleak. For example, in the early sixteenth century Leo Africanus had the following to say about the kingdom of Jenne, situated in the Inland Niger Delta on the edge of the Sahel zone: 'This place exceedingly aboundeth with barlie, rice, cattell, fishes, and cotton: and their cotton they sell unto the merchants of Barbarie, for cloth of Europe, for brazen vessels, for armour and other such commodities. Their coine is of gold without any stampe or inscription at all' (Africanus 1896: Vol. 3, 822). This description was given by an outsider, for Leo Africanus came from North Africa. It is instructive, therefore, to see what a local scholar, al-Sa'di, writing in about 1655, had to say on the same subject:

> This city is large, flourishing and prosperous; it is rich, blessed and favoured by the Almighty ... Jenne is one of the great markets of the Muslim world. There one meets the salt merchants from the mines of Teghaza and merchants carrying gold from the mines of Bitou ... Because of this blessed city, caravans flock to Timbuktu from all points of the horizon ... The area around Jenne is fertile and well populated; with numerous markets held there on all the days of the week. It is certain that it contains 7077 villages very near to one another (al-Sa'di 1964: 22–4, translated by author).

Although Susan and Roderick McIntosh have pointed out that al-Sa'di may have been very biased in favour of Jenne, because he had lived and worked there for ten years (McIntosh and McIntosh 1980: Vol. 1, 49), E.W. Bovill (1968: 135) was of the opinion that this was a 'convincing tribute' because al-Sa'di was 'intensely jealous of the reputation of his own city of Timbuktu, of which Jenne was a rival in both trade and culture'. Notwithstanding the problems of interpreting such pieces of evidence, however, it does seem, from historical sources, from oral tradition, and from archaeological data, as if the West African savanna was in the past a zone that offered opportunities as well as constraints to the people who lived there. It is probably not too great an exaggeration to say that this was an optimal zone, so far as the attainment of increasing complexity by human cultures was concerned.

Geographical location and environmental factors

Throughout the history of the human race in Africa, the most important single ecosystem in the continent has probably been the savanna. Rich in faunal and floral resources, suitable for both cereal agriculture and livestock rearing, it offered conditions of relatively easy movement in which natural resources and manufactured products could be readily exchanged. The most extensive area of savanna in Africa consists of a broad zone which stretches almost across the continent from the Atlantic Ocean to the Gulf of Aden. This chapter is concerned with the western part of that zone, that is to say with the savanna lands to the west of Lake Chad.

It is important to understand the location of the West African savanna. Consisting of grassland, with varying densities of trees and shrubs, it is situated between the tropical rainforest to the south and the Sahara Desert to the north. In the past the Sahara formed what Bovill (1968: 1) called 'one of the world's greatest barriers to human movement', although, as Bovill was able to show so brilliantly, that barrier was repeatedly bridged by trade. Beyond that barrier lay the lands of the Mediterranean, heart of the Roman and of the medieval world and with contacts deep into Eurasia. To the south of the tropical rainforest, however, lay only the Atlantic Ocean, bordering a coast that until the middle of the second millennium AD was to remain isolated from the rest of the world. This is in such marked contrast to the East African coast, discussed in Chapter 7, where external contact is known to have been present for some two thousand years, that it is worth examining the reasons for this isolation. Much of the coast of West Africa is uninviting when approached from the sea: natural harbours are relatively few and most of the coast is fringed by mangrove swamps, or by exposed surf-pounded beaches, or backed by inhospitable desert. The real problem with this coast, however, is that south of Morocco, along the Saharan coast, the prevailing winds are always from the north. Given the sailing technology of the ships of the ancient and medieval worlds, it was possible to sail south but impossible to return (Mauny 1978: 292–3). As a result, Cape Bojador at about latitude 26° North remained effectively the furthest south to which outside ships were able to penetrate until towards the middle of the fifteenth century AD. It was only at that time that circumstances changed, according to Shaw (1975a: 54) because of the adoption of the lateen sail and of the stern-post rudder by seafarers of the western Mediterranean and Atlantic seaboard, which enabled ships to sail into the wind as well as with the wind. Bovill has also emphasized the importance of the discovery that it was possible to return from the West African coast, not by fighting contrary winds along the coast but by striking west into the Atlantic for several hundred miles to pick up winds blowing from the south and west. This discovery, which occurred about 1440, was made possible, Bovill suggests, by the Portuguese adoption of the caravel, a vessel that was much more manoeuvrable than earlier ships (Bovill 1968: 115). The caravel, it should be noted, was fitted with both lateen sails and a stern-post rudder.

If the ocean could remain a barrier for so long, it is perhaps surprising that so formidable a barrier as the Sahara Desert should have been successfully bridged by trade from such an early date. The fact that it was has often been explained as the result of another cultural innovation: the introduction to Africa of the domesticated camel, as a mode of transport over long distances through arid regions (Bulliet 1975). It will be argued below that the 'ship of the desert', as the camel has so often been called, did not inaugurate trans-Saharan trade but, in the hands of people who knew how best to utilize its peculiar physiology, it undoubtedly led to a very substantial development of that trade. The camel seems to have been brought into use in the Sahara during the first few centuries AD, coming originally from Arabia, although it had probably been known in Egypt for many centuries previously. It was not until after the seventh century AD, however, that the coming of the Arabs to North Africa brought about the development of trans-Saharan commerce based on the use of camel transport (Mauny 1978: 286–92).

It would be a mistake, however, to think of the West African savanna as merely a uniform zone, isolated to varying degrees through time by the desert, the forest and the ocean. It was a great deal more than this; it was a world of its own and a highly complex world, richly endowed with resources. Indeed, the West African savanna consists of a parallel series of different environmental zones, running roughly from west to east and forming a part of a greater series of such zones extending from south to north across West Africa. These zones have usually been characterized in terms of vegetation differences and one of the best known attempts to do this is the map produced by Keay (1959). Thus a hypothetical traveller, journeying due north from the Nigerian coast, could traverse in less than 1500 kilometres a whole range of environments, from coastal mangrove swamp to true desert (Fig. 5.1). On the way he or she would pass through tropical rainforest, forest-savanna mosaic, relatively moist woodlands and savanna, relatively dry woodlands and savanna, wooded steppe, and sub desert steppe. The close proximity of these different environments must have had an important influence on the development of human culture in West Africa. Because of the range of ecozones and ecotones that they presented, there was both the necessity and the occasion for the exchange of raw materials and products across environmental boundaries. Each environment possessed some resources but lacked others. Thus salt was available in the desert and along the coast but was relatively difficult to obtain in the savanna, where for cereal agriculturalists it was a physiological necessity. Thus the forest was deficient in meat but the savanna supported very large numbers of domestic animals. There are many other examples that could be given to illustrate this situation but the important point is that the complexity of the West African environment, as a whole, provided conditions conducive to the development of a complex network of regional trade. Within that network the West African savanna, relatively easy to traverse, played an essential part. It is quite likely that such trading activity was almost as old as West African food production and the beginnings of a trading network could well have been already in existence by about three thousand years ago.

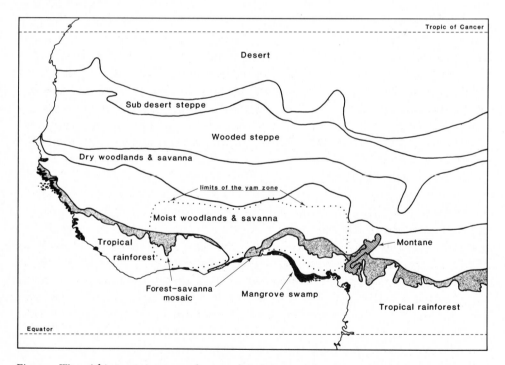

Fig. 5.1 West African environmental zones showing area of major yam cultivation. After
   Keay (1959) and Coursey (1980: Fig. 1).

It is worth pausing to consider the main resources that would probably have been available in the West African savanna two or three thousand years ago. Foremost of these would have been agricultural products: cereals such as sorghum, millet, *fonio*, and African rice; several indigenous yams; vegetable oils such as those obtained from the shea butter tree and the oil-palm; two African groundnuts; cowpeas; black beniseed; and other things (Harris 1976: 329–32). Also meat, dairy products and hides and skins from the numerous cattle, sheep and goats. Furthermore, food supplies could have been supplemented by hunting wild animals and by fishing, and such 'wild' resources could in addition have provided ivory. Important inorganic materials would have been available in the West African savanna, as well; particularly iron ore, alluvial gold, rocks suitable for making grindstones, good building earths and potting clays. Lastly, a relatively high population density would have provided a resource in itself that could have been exploited: the slave trade has a history in West Africa which goes much further back than the advent of Europeans on the Guinea Coast.

Nevertheless, the West African savanna was a zone of constraints as well as opportunities. Foremost of these constraints was water availability. The rainfall is markedly seasonal, the amount less and the wet season shorter the further north one goes. Also the temperature tends to increase as one goes north, leading to a greater loss of surface water to evaporation, so that much of the northern parts of the savanna consist for much of the year of a virtually waterless landscape. Although drinking water for both domestic animals and human beings is usually available by digging wells of varying depths, it is obvious that in such conditions the margins of perennial rivers and lakes must assume an especial attraction for agriculturalists. It is in such areas that 'floodwater farming' in its various forms has been of great importance. Such farming techniques – of which 'recessional cultivation' (the cultivation of naturally irrigated areas as floodwaters recede) is probably the most common – were one of the principal ways of intensifying African agricultural systems. It is of some significance that such techniques seem to have underlain the growth of social complexity in the Egyptian Nile Valley (Butzer 1976: 19) and that in West Africa they existed (and indeed still exist) both in the Inland Niger Delta in Mali (Harlan and Pasquereau 1969) and around the southern edge of Lake Chad (Connah 1985), as well as probably in other places. Nevertheless, there is a second major environmental constraint in the West African savanna that sometimes discourages human settlement from concentrating around the very bodies of water that attract it. Of the major diseases found in the savanna that can seriously damage the human or animal health sleeping-sickness and animal trypanosomiasis, malaria, schistosomiasis, filariasis, river blindness, and a whole range of intestinal parasites are associated in one way or another with water. Clearly the West African savanna was no earthly paradise but it did offer considerable opportunities to human groups that could adapt to its constraints.

Sources of information

Present day knowledge of the precolonial cities and states of the West African savanna is mainly based on historical sources. Some of these originated as oral traditions, either in the past or in recent times but the greater part of them consist of documentation, usually in Arabic and mainly written by outsiders who at best had only visited the area. The principal of these authors were al-Masudi, ibn Haukal, al-Bakri, al-Idrisi, Yaqut, al-Umari, ibn Battuta, ibn Khaldun, Leo Africanus, al-Maqrizi, ibn Said, al-Sa'di, and ibn Fartua. Collectively they throw light on the period roughly from the tenth century AD to the seventeenth century. Similar sources also provide brief references to the West African savanna back to the eighth century AD. Drawing on all these and other sources (including the writings of mainly nineteenth-century European travellers), modern historians have been able to reconstruct, in varying degrees of detail, the history of the most important states of this area over the last twelve hundred years or so. The old states of Ghana and Mali have been examined, for example, by Nehemiah Levtzion (1973) and those of Songhai, Borno, and Hausaland, for example, by John Hunwick (1971). In fact, there exists a very extensive literature on the history of the regions which were known as the Western and Central Sudan and it is not the intention here to attempt to add to it. It is the character of the sources on which that literature is based, however, that has determined the standard explanation of the development of cities and states in the West African savanna. That explanation has, perhaps, been most clearly stated by Levtzion. For example:

> *Sahil* is the Arabic word for 'shore', which is well understood if the desert is compared to a sea of sand, and the camel to a ship. Hence, the towns which developed in the Sahel ... may be regarded as ports. These towns became both commercial entrepôts and political centres. Those who held authority in these strategic centres endeavoured to extend it in order to achieve effective control over the trade. Thus trade stimulated a higher level of political organization, while the emergence of extensive states accorded more security to trade. Political developments in the Western Sudan, throughout its history, are related to the changing patterns of intercontinental and trans-Saharan trade routes. (Levtzion 1973: 10)

In other words, cities and states in this zone developed as a result of external stimulus, in the form of long-distance trade. In addition, this view usually emphasizes the role of Islam in these developments. Such an explanation might be expected, of course, if sources are limited to post eighth-century AD documents written by people of Islamic culture, most of whom belonged to lands beyond the Sahara. As a view of the later developments in the West African savanna, it is no doubt sound enough but the question is: does it adequately explain the origins of these developments? Fortunately, there is another source of information that can be drawn on, a source that has neither the chronological limitations of the historical sources nor their possible prejudices; this source consists of the archaeological evidence.

A quarter of a century ago, G.P. Murdock commented that the archaeologist had 'thus far lifted perhaps an ounce of earth on the Niger for every ton carefully sifted on the Nile' (Murdock 1959: 73). Many archaeologists might question his use of the words 'carefully sifted', but otherwise his remark is probably as true now as it was when he made it. In spite of some remarkable recent investigations, our knowledge of the archaeology of the West African savanna is still limited by insufficient fieldwork and excavation. Furthermore, much of what has been done was done many years ago and even by the standards of its time was technically inadequate. In addition, the publication of such work was often poor and some work was never published at all. There was also a tendency to adopt research strategies the main object of which was to throw more light on historically-known sites. This earlier work has been synthesized by Raymond Mauny in his book *Tableau géographique de l'Ouest Africain*... (Mauny 1961). In particular, the historical bias of such work has meant that we know so little about the later prehistory of the area that McIntosh and McIntosh (1979: 227) still call the three millennia immediately preceding the earliest historical documentation, the 'silent millennia', a description that has been in use for some years.

It is worth outlining the types of archaeological evidence that we actually have from the West African savanna, which throw light on the origins of cities and states in this area. First, and most obviously, are the sites of cities or towns which can, with varying degrees of certainty, be identified in the historical sources (Fig. 5.2). The best excavated and the best published of these is Jenne in the Inland Niger Delta of Mali (McIntosh and McIntosh 1980; McIntosh and McIntosh 1981a). The evidence from that site has provided the strongest challenge, to date, to the external stimulus model discussed above. With radiocarbon dates for its occupation back to the third century BC, 'Jenne-jeno is too big, too early, and too far south' (McIntosh and McIntosh 1980: Vol. 2, 448). The original excavations at Jenne were on a rather limited scale but further work in 1981 has confirmed and expanded their findings (McIntosh and McIntosh 1982; McIntosh and McIntosh 1983a).

Other important excavations have been conducted at Tegdaoust, far to the north in the Mauritanian desert. Here excavations over a number of years have revealed seven phases of occupation, the earliest of which were pre-urban, and occupation is thought to extend from the seventh or eighth to the seventeenth century AD (McIntosh and McIntosh 1980: Vol. 1, 18; Calvocoressi and David 1979: 14–15, 24–5; Devisse 1983, 556). The excavators of the site have tentatively identified it with the historically-known town of Awdaghust, which was a desert port-of-trade on one of the trans-Saharan trade routes. The excavated evidence certainly indicates that Tegdaoust was a flourishing town, heavily involved with trade beyond the desert. The investigations at this site have been the subject of a

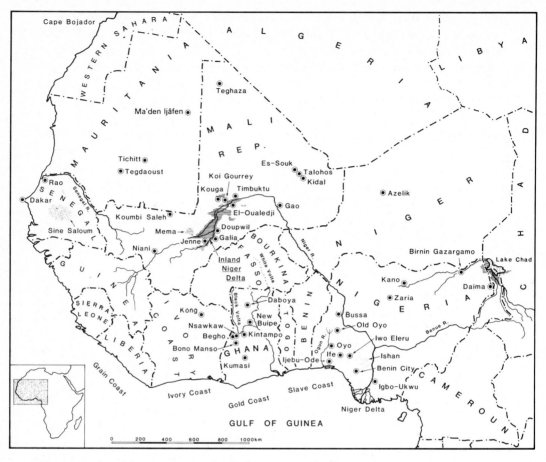

Fig. 5.2 Archaeological sites in West Africa.

number of publications which discuss the excavated evidence in some detail (D. Robert 1970; Robert, Robert and Devisse 1970; Robert and Robert 1972; Vanacker 1979; Devisse 1983). In comparison, the site of Niani, in Guinea, is of uncertain significance. Its excavator claims it to have been the capital of the old state of Mali but fairly extensive excavations have not revealed the wealth of Arab imports that might have been expected if this had been the case (Filipowiak 1966; Filipowiak 1969) and other writers (for example, Hunwick 1973) have suggested that the real capital was situated much further to the north-east. The radiocarbon dates for Niani cluster from the sixth to the tenth centuries AD and also suggest a later re-occupation in about the sixteenth and seventeenth centuries AD (Calvocoressi and David 1979: 15–16, 23; Sutton 1982: 306, 311). The gap in between could be seen as further reducing the likelihood that this was the capital of the state of Mali in the fourteenth century. In contrast, the site of Koumbi Saleh, in Mauritania, is thought by most scholars to have been the capital city of the old state of Ghana. Excavations have been conducted there on a number of occasions in the past, the best-known published work being that of Thomassey and Mauny (1951; 1956). This site, with its multi-storey stone buildings and extensive cemeteries is clearly of the greatest importance (Fig. 5.3). Although Thomassey and Mauny failed to explore its lower occupation levels, it seems that new excavations by Serge Robert in 1975–6 (which are as yet not published but see Robert and Robert (1972) for preliminary work) must have

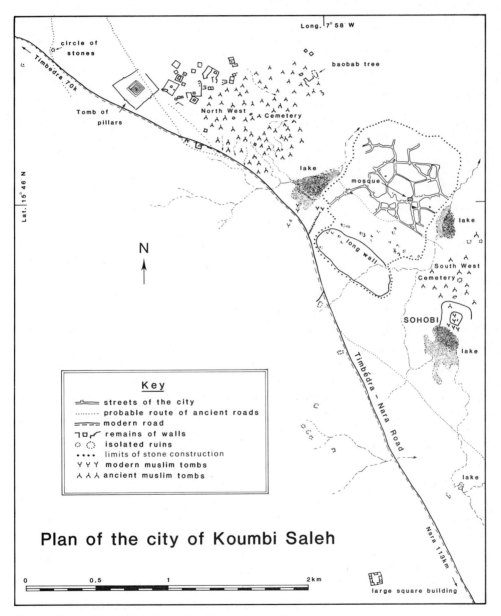

Fig. 5.3 Plan of Koumbi Saleh. After Mauny (1961: Fig. 95).

remedied that omission, because there is now a new series of radiocarbon dates for this site, extending from the sixth to the eighteenth century AD (Sutton 1982: 304–5, 311).

The problem with Koumbi Saleh, however, is that in the middle of the eleventh century al-Bakri described it as consisting of two towns: an Islamic town and, 'six miles away', the royal town' (Levtzion 1973: 22–3). It seems likely that it is the Islamic town that has been excavated; the other town does not seem to have been located. This is unfortunate because any evidence for indigenous origins for this urban development would be more likely to be discovered in the native town than in the strangers' town.

There are many other archaeological sites of cities or towns that can be identified, or tentatively identified, in the historical record but excavation at these places has been limited in scale, or absent. There is also the problem of relatively recent work which has not yet reached the publication stage. In one or other of these categories must fall: Birnin Gazargamo (Nigeria), one time capital of Borno but dating only from the fifteenth century AD (Bivar and Shinnie 1962; Connah 1981); Gao (Mali), where work seems to have been concentrated on the cemetery at Sané (Flight 1975); Kong (Ivory Coast), a trading town apparently dating only from the sixteenth century AD (Sutton 1982: 306–7, 311); and a whole collection of places still unexcavated such as Timbuktu and Teghaza in Mali and Kano and Zaria in Nigeria.

In addition to historically-known sites, there are also many other large settlement sites and burial sites which are relevant to our theme. For example, work by Bedaux and others (1978) on the two settlement mounds of Doupwil and Galia (Fig. 5.4) in the Inland Niger Delta of Mali, has investigated settlements that were first occupied in the eleventh century AD. Both of these sites were probably about 8 hectares in area, before erosion, which may be compared to the approximately 12 hectares of Tegdaoust (D. Robert 1970: 473), a figure which represents the area of stone foundations only and does not include a much larger surrounding area of mud and other less permanent architecture (R.J. McIntosh 1985). Other settlement mounds and related sites, with radiocarbon dates of the eighth to the twelfth century AD, have been investigated in the Mema area of Mali by Håland (1980; Sutton 1982: 305, 311) and some of the Borno settlement mounds on the *firki* plains of north-east Nigeria (of which Daima is the best known) constitute the remains of quite large settlements, whose origins date back three millennia (Connah 1981). In these examples, the settlements represented by the mounds were probably too small to be considered as urban themselves but they are relevant to an investigation of West African urban origins if using a regional approach to the study of urbanism, as discussed by McIntosh and McIntosh (1984: 77–9). It seems probable that they formed parts of regional site systems whose settlement hierarchy could be investigated as a means of achieving better understanding of the process of urbanization in the particular areas. To date, however, the McIntoshs remain amongst the few archaeological researchers who have used such an approach.

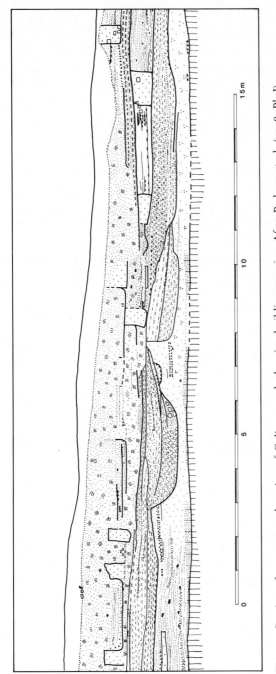

Fig. 5.4 Portion of an excavated section of Galia mound, showing building remains. After Bedaux et al. (1978: Pl. I).

It is clearly impossible to mention here all the settlement sites that might have relevance for our inquiry but there are also burial sites whose significance cannot be ignored. Best known of these are tumuli, or burial mounds, which are found particularly in Mali but also occur as far west as the coast of Senegal and as far east as the extreme north of Nigeria. McIntosh and McIntosh (1980: Vol. 1, 31–6) distinguish three types of burial mound in Mali: stone tumuli, in the Sahara, mostly dating from the first millennium BC to the end of the first millennium AD; earthen tumuli, in the dry savanna to the west and east of the Inland Niger Delta, of uncertain date but perhaps mostly older than the fourteenth century AD; and tumuli covering rock-cut tombs, in the wooded savanna, which probably belong to the first millennium AD. Both the size of the tumuli and the grave-goods buried with the dead indicate some differences in social status. Indeed, some of the larger earthen tumuli appear to have been quite remarkable structures in a number of ways. Thus some of them have their outer layers baked rock-hard by numerous small fires that were lit on the mound surface. An example of such a tumulus is the 15–18 metre-high mound of Koi Gourrey in Mali (Desplagnes 1903), where two individuals had been buried with varied grave-goods and with 25–30 other people, presumably entombed at the same time. Still more impressive, perhaps, was the tumulus of El-Oualedji (Fig. 5.5), also in Mali, which was 12 metres high and contained a wooden funerary chamber, in which two individuals had been buried with accompanying objects, and from which a vertical shaft extended to the top of the mound (Desplagnes 1951). These, and perhaps a small number of other tumuli, clearly indicate burial rites of the sort recorded in the middle of the eleventh century, by al-Bakri, for the kings of the state of Ghana:

> When the king dies, they build a huge dome of wood over the burial place. Then they bring him on a bed lightly covered, and put him inside the dome. At his side they place his ornaments, his arms and the vessels from which he used to eat and drink, filled with food and beverages. They bring in those men who

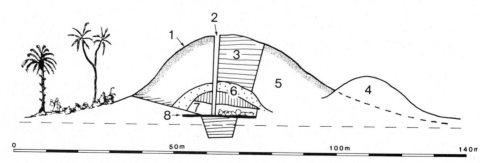

Fig. 5.5 Section through El-Oualedji tumulus.
1: Fired clay surface. *2:* Shaft. *3:* Excavated area. *4:* Spoil heap. *5:* Clay mound. *6:* Domed roof of wood and straw. *7:* Burial chamber. *8:* Layer of sand. Vertical scale double that of horizontal scale. After Desplagnes (1951: Fig. 3).

used to serve his food and drink. Then they close the door of the dome and cover it with mats and other materials. People gather and pile earth over it until it becomes like a large mound. Then they dig a ditch around it so that it can be reached only from one place. They sacrifice to their dead and make offerings of intoxicating drinks. (al-Bakri, as quoted by Levtzion 1973: 25–6)

The dating of these large earthen tumuli is not very satisfactory but, interestingly, one of them (at Kouga in Mali) has produced a single radiocarbon date of AD 1000 ± 150 (McIntosh and McIntosh 1980: Vol. 1, 31), and tumuli associated with the Tondidarou standing stones in Mali have been dated by radiocarbon to the first half of the seventh century AD (Saliège et al. 1980). Some of the grave-goods from these mounds suggest an unusual level of wealth but the most impressive evidence of that sort comes from a number of tumuli in the Rao region of north-west Senegal. Collectively these mounds yielded a remarkable collection of grave-goods, including jewellery of silver and gold (one item of gold is a decorated disc of exceptional workmanship, of 184 mm diameter and 191 grams weight (Fig. 5.6)), an iron sword, beads, and objects of copper (of which two were Moroccan lidded-bowls). When first published, these finds were of unknown date but were subsequently dated to the thirteenth and fourteenth centuries, although it was admitted that they might be later in date (Joire 1943; Joire 1955).

It would appear that all the tumuli discussed above represent non-Islamic burial practices. However, such practices seem to have been quite varied, so that not only was there inhumation in one sort of tumulus or another but some small earthen tumuli west of the Inland Niger Delta contained cremations in pottery urns (Szumowski 1957). In addition, the usual burial rite in the Inland Niger Delta itself seems to have consisted of inhumation in large pottery urns (McIntosh and McIntosh 1980: Vol. 1, 36–7). Nor does this exhaust the variety of non-Islamic burial practices recorded archaeologically from the last three millennia in the West African savanna. It is important to realise, however, that although many of these burials are probably pre-Islamic in date, some of them could also be later than the introduction of Islam to the area, which was certainly in progress by the eleventh century AD. This is because the replacement of traditional practices by Islamic rites is likely to have been a gradual process, rather than an abrupt change.

Other relevant archaeological evidence consists of the megalithic sites of Senegambia and Mali. These arrangements of standing stones, in Senegambia apparently with associated burials (Thilmans and Descamps 1974; Thilmans and Descamps 1975), have proved difficult to date but radiocarbon dates indicate that they belong principally to the second half of the first millennium AD, although some might be much later (Sutton 1982: 304). According to Posnansky (1973: 152) pottery from the megalithic sites is similar to pottery from the tumuli of the Rao and Sine Saloum regions of Senegal, the dating of which had (by the time that Posnansky wrote) been revised, as a result of new excavations, to around AD 1000. More recent work by Gallay et al. (1982) has confirmed this similarity of pottery and further excavations of tumuli in north-west Senegal by Descamps and others have revealed collective inhumations often accompanied by grave-goods of iron, copper, brass and gold, at dates indicated by radiocarbon to range between the eighth and twelfth centuries AD.

Fig. 5.6 Gold disc from Rao, diameter 184mm. From Joire (1943: 49).

In addition, excavations of tumuli along the middle Senegal River by Ravisé and Thilmans have shown that copper, brass and silver were reaching that area as early as the sixth century AD (McIntosh and McIntosh 1983b, 247).

Subsistence economy

The problem is, what light does the archaeological evidence outlined above throw on the origins of cities and states in the West African savanna? To begin with what *ought* to be the easiest question to answer, what does it tell us about the subsistence economy on which such developments must have been based?

It is probable that livestock husbandry and cereal cultivation were firmly established in West Africa by the first millennium BC (Shaw 1977a). However, direct evidence for this is limited. There is evidence for *Pennisetum americanum* and *Brachiaria deflexa* (Guinea millet) at Karkarichinkat (Mali) in the second millennium BC and there is Munson's discovery at Tichitt, in Mauritania, that *Pennisetum* sp. (bullrush millet) was being grown by the beginning of the first millennium BC. There is also direct evidence for the cultivation of *Oryza glaberrima* (Afrian rice) *Pennisetum* and sorghum at Jenne from the third century BC onwards and of the cultivation of *Sorghum bicolor* at Daima and Niani from late in the first millennium AD (Munson 1976; McIntosh and McIntosh 1980: Vol. 1, 6, 172; Connah 1981: 188–9; McIntosh and McIntosh 1983b, 238). Jenne, in addition, has direct evidence of livestock-rearing involving cattle and perhaps sheep or goats, and of augmentation of food supplies by hunting and fishing. The occupation of the Jenne site extends from about the third century BC to about the fourteenth century AD. It appears that Jenne was already about 12 hectares in extent by early in the first millennium AD and reached a maximum area of about 33 hectares by the middle of that millennium (Fig. 5.7). In addition, the McIntoshs have demonstrated, from the distribution of archaeological sites on the floodplain near Jenne, that towards the end of the first millennium AD the population density of the Inland Niger Delta was probably greater than it is at present. After discussing climatic and geomorphological data, they suggest that between about the middle of the first millennium AD and the middle of the second millennium AD the climate of the Inland Niger Delta was wetter than before or since, so that this would explain the greater population density (McIntosh and McIntosh 1980: Vol. 2, 428; McIntosh and McIntosh 1982; R.J. McIntosh 1983). It is probably a reasonable assumption that the dense population of the Jenne area about a thousand years ago was based mainly on the recessional cultivation (the cultivation of naturally irrigated areas as floodwaters recede) of rice, and elsewhere I have argued that recessional cultivation can constitute a form of agricultural intensification (Connah 1985). It could perhaps be suggested, therefore, that urban growth in the Inland Niger Delta was supported by one of the relatively rare examples of African intensive agriculture. Indeed, the McIntoshs suggest that it was the agricultural surplus of the Inland Niger Delta that provided much of the food for urban centres situated in less fortunate areas such as Timbuktu and Gao and even places further afield. In such movement of foodstuffs, canoe transport on the Niger River seems to have played a major role (McIntosh and McIntosh 1980: Vol. 2, 448–50).

Other parts of the West African savanna were probably not quite so fortunate as the area around Jenne, nor is there enough evidence to say much about them at the present time, but it is probable that most of the urban and state developments of this zone had a sound agricultural base with the potential to produce a surplus. The probability that such a surplus was frequently in the form of grain, of one sort or another, that could be readily stored or transported, should not be overlooked. This meant that some urban centres strategically situated on trade routes at the edge of the desert could be supported by the surplus produce of more fortunate regions. It also meant that various specialists could be supported within the different urban centres. Finally it is becoming apparent, as suggested above, that climatic and environmental deterioration may now have rendered the West African savanna less agriculturally viable than it was a thousand years ago. The McIntoshs' evidence for this in the Inland Niger Delta does not stand alone. An overall drop in the level of Lake Chad over the last millennium would indicate that such a deterioration may have been general in the West African savanna (Sutton 1982: 310). A similar impression is given by the abandonment of

Fig. 5.7 Artist's reconstruction of life in the city of Jenne about 1000 years ago. Photograph from a painting by Charles Santore. Reproduced by permission of National Geographic Society and of R.J. and S.K. McIntosh.

Tegdaoust, after changes in well design which are thought to indicate an increasing water supply problem (D. Robert 1970).

Technology

It is now apparent that iron technology emerged in West Africa no later than the middle of the first millennium BC (Sutton 1982: 297). On the basis of the evidence excavated at Jenne, it would seem that the occupants of the settlement mounds in the Inland Niger Delta were iron-using from the time of their arrival in the area late in the first millennium BC. In addition, the builders of the tumuli and of the megaliths discussed above all seem to have been iron-users. Although the condition of excavated iron is often poor, it is clear that the metal was being used for a variety of purposes by the first millennium AD, ranging from weapons and tools to bracelets and other jewellery. There is also ample evidence that these were indigenous products, in the form of slag and other indications that smelting and black-smithing were widespread. Judging by the evidence from Jenne, copper was also worked by the middle of the first millennium AD (McIntosh and McIntosh 1980: Vol. 1, 193) and the unfortunately undated tumulus of Koi Gourrey produced copper and bronze items, some of which appear to have been made by the lost-wax casting technique (Desplagnes 1903: 165). More satisfactory as evidence, Bedaux and others (1978) excavated a mould for lost-wax casting from a context dated to the end of the eleventh century and the beginning of the twelfth century, at their settlement mound of Doupwil in the Inland Niger Delta. As the excavators claim, this discovery demonstrates that items of copper and copper alloys were manufactured locally. Less certain in this respect are the occasional items of silver and even gold jewellery that have been recovered from some of the tumulus burials. Gold, which is mentioned so often in the historical sources, is rare in the archaeological record. This is, perhaps, understandable in view of its value in the past as in the present. Nevertheless, a remarkable hoard of gold and silver excavated at Tegdaoust included five gold ingots as well as gold jewellery (D. Robert 1970) and excavations at Jenne–Jeno in 1981 produced a gold earring from a context dated to AD 800 (McIntosh and McIntosh 1982: 30).

In addition to metalworking of one sort or another, there was probably a fairly wide variety of other technological skills. There must have been miners, particularly of gold (and in this case panners also), but (with the exception of Kiéthéga, 1983) archaeology has little to tell us of their techniques. This is in spite of the general location of the gold deposits being quite well known (for example Curtin 1973) and in spite of the existence of ethnohistorical observations of traditional gold-mining methods in West Africa (Addo-Fening 1976). There may also have been specialist builders because, whether or not this was the case, mud architecture dates from early in the first millennium AD at Jenne (McIntosh and McIntosh 1980: Vol. 1, 188–9) and (although it was hardly an urban settlement) from a similar date at Daima in north-east Nigeria (Connah 1981: 147). Pottery-making had reached an impressive technical level by the beginning of the first millennium AD. Although hand-made, like most traditional African pottery, it was generally thin-walled, symmetrically shaped in many forms and well fired. It was also painstakingly decorated, often with impressions and sometimes, in parts of the northern savanna, with painted patterns. The production of textiles, on the other hand, as indicated by the archaeological occurrence of spindle-whorls, may not have developed until the end of the first millennium AD, by which time the spinning and weaving of cotton was probably becoming established. Prior to that time, such clothing as was worn was probably of leather, and with the longstanding traditions of livestock husbandry in the area, it is reasonable to guess that the working of hides and skins had a long history. Overall, it seems that by the first millennium AD there was probably a varied technological base for the societies of the West African savanna.

Social system

It is always difficult to determine social organization from archaeological evidence and in the area under discussion it is made the more so by the very little fully controlled excavation that has been done until recently. In particular, there has been insufficient area excavation to inform us much about urban layout or house plans. Nevertheless, the tumuli and the megaliths should have something to tell us on the subject of social organization. Posnansky (1973: 151), for instance, sees the megaliths of Senegambia (and presumably the tumuli that he associates with them) as evidence of chiefs who perhaps derived their power from controlling local iron and gold deposits. He is of the opinion that 'the social organization of the megalith builders predates the Arab contact'. He then goes on to discuss the rich contents of some of the tumuli of the Niger Valley and has the following to say of all the megaliths and tumuli:

> This affluence was almost certainly due to the control of the gold resources and to the agricultural potential of the upper Niger area and particularly the Niger delta.
>
> We probably have to think of a continuing process of the accumulation of social wealth and power in this Sudanic area, leading to the growth of the indigenous Ghana Kingdom before the eighth century. (Posnansky 1973: 152)

When compared with the ideas of Haas, discussed in Chapter 2, such an interpretation would suggest that state formation was already in progress before the growth of trans-Saharan trade with Arabic North Africa. It appears, indeed, quite likely that Posnansky's view is correct and that during the earlier first millennium AD ranked chiefdoms were gradually giving way to stratified societies. At the same time, it seems, the development of urban centres was already in progress, as the 12 hectare extent of Jenne early in that millennium would suggest. The culmination of such development can be seen in the site plans of Tegdaoust or Koumbi Saleh, the latter with its stone-built houses and tombs, and in the great walled city of Kano, which in 1929 had about 50000 inhabitants enclosed by a defensive wall over 23 kilometres in circumference (Logan 1929). It may be some years, however, before we have plans of West African urban centres during the early, formative stages of their growth, when they were relatively free from external influences.

Population pressures

As already discussed in the section on geographical location and environmental factors, the conditions in the West African savanna are such that the margins of perennial rivers and lakes have a particular attraction for agriculturalists. From the McIntoshs' work, it would seem that this was certainly the case in the Inland Niger Delta, where the unusual hydrological conditions allowed the intensification of agriculture by means of the recessional cultivation of rice. Coupled with the availability of other agricultural produce and the movement of commodities both along the Niger River and across it from one environmental zone to another, this could well have encouraged a concentration of population within this area. Certainly the work done by the McIntoshs seems to have revealed an amazing density of settlement by the middle of the first millennium AD. In addition, the area of the Inland Niger Delta is confined and, as the McIntoshs have shown, its complex variety of landforms is highly susceptible to environmental fluctuations. Such an area, richly endowed with resources and yet subject to stress, could well have provided an inception point for social developments in the West African savanna. It is unlikely, however, that it was the only place where such developments took place. Population pressures must have varied a great deal in the different environments of the savanna and it is probable that there were a variety of circumstances that brought about the social changes leading to urbanization and state formation.

Ideology

Historical sources indicate that Islam had an important influence on the course of West African urbanization. The Islamic world of the early second millennium AD was a world of independent states in which substantial numbers of people lived in towns and cities. It was also a proselytizing world, seeking, with fluctuating degrees of enthusiasm, to convert the infidel not only to its religious beliefs but also to its way of life. Archaeology has revealed the remains of early mosques in a number of places: at Koumbi Saleh, Tegdaoust, Es-Souk, Kidal, Talohos, and Teghaza (Mauny 1961: 472–6; D. Robert 1970) and indeed some mosques still in use, such as that at Jenne, are reputed (in origin at least) to be of great age. However, archaeology has also confirmed the historical evidence that indicates that the inhabitants of the earliest cities and states of the West African savanna were definitely not Muslims. The tumuli, in particular, indicate non-Islamic practices, as also do the urn burials of the Inland Niger Delta and the making of clay figurines in that same area. Some of this evidence might merely represent a survival of traditional practices after Islam had already been introduced to the West African savanna, and we know from historical sources that this did happen to a considerable extent. Nevertheless, the McIntoshs' evidence of urban development at Jenne by early in the first millennium, would appear to confirm the impression that the origins of urbanization and state formation in the West African savanna *were* pre-Islamic. The people involved with these developments must have been animists of one sort or another and the variety of non-Islamic burial practices in the archaeological record of the West African savanna would suggest that there was considerable diversity of belief between different human groups.

External trade

Drawing on historical sources, Bovill came to the conclusion that trade was 'a dominant factor in the history of the north-western quarter of the continent' (Bovill 1968: 236). Indeed, Levtzion, whose opinion has been quoted above (p. 102), clearly saw long-distance trade as a vital stimulus to developments in the West African savanna. What do the archaeological sources have to reveal on the matter? Certainly, evidence of the trans-Saharan trade that Bovill and Levtzion were mainly thinking of has been found often enough. Thus, for example, Koumbi Saleh produced stone plaques with Arabic inscriptions and Islamic decorations painted on them, not to mention stone houses said to show Maghrebian influence (Thomassey and Mauny 1951; Thomassey and Mauny 1956). Thus also, Tegdaoust yielded imported pottery, oil lamps, glass vessels, glass weights and ingots of both copper and gold (D. Robert 1970). Perhaps the most impressive of the archaeological evidence for the trans-Saharan trade, however, is amongst the group of twelfth and thirteenth-century gravestones found at Sané, near Gao on the Niger in Mali. Some of these are marble gravestones with inscriptions in Kufic, an early angular form of the Arabic alphabet that was often used in decorative work. These inscribed stones have been closely dated to AD 1100–1110 and are thought to have been made to order in Spain and carried by camel across the Sahara (Flight 1975: 82). In fact, there is even archaeological evidence of the difficulties that could assail such trans-Saharan camel transport, in the form of the abandoned loads of a caravan buried in a sand-dune in the lonely Majâbat Al-Koubrâ, halfway across the desert. Dated to the twelfth century AD, these loads consisted of large numbers of brass rods and of cowrie shells of the species *Monetaria moneta* (Monod 1969).

There is, indeed, a considerable amount of archaeological evidence for the trans-Saharan trade. In mentioning some of the more remarkable examples, as has just been done, it should not be forgotten for instance that countless sites in the West African savanna contain beads of glass or semi-precious stones; many of the earlier of these must have originated from that trade. Also, the location of some of the West African cities and towns should not be overlooked. Pushed well forward of the most viable agricultural lands of the savanna or even into the desert proper, places like Timbuktu, or Tegdaoust, or Teghaza were clearly located at strategic points on the trade-routes, rather than in hinterlands that could support them. Also, it is interesting to note that many of the savanna urban centres appear to have grown up at environmental interfaces, between transportation systems. Thus at Timbuktu goods were transferred from camel to canoe and at Kano from camel to donkey. A comparable situation will be seen in Chapter 6: trading centres growing up at the junction of the forest and savanna, where the tsetse fly made it necessary to transfer goods from donkey back to human head.

It may be noticed, however, that archaeological evidence does not give anything like a true picture of the Saharan trade as seen by historians (Fig. 5.8). Where in the archaeological evidence is any indication of the literally millions of tons of salt that must have travelled south from the desert itself to the savanna? Similarly, where is the evidence of the cloth that, we are told, was carried south from North Africa, or of the thousands of slaves who were taken north, or of the ostrich feathers and fine leather? For that matter, who would realise, from the archaeological evidence, just how important the gold trade was? Such questions lead to others. If West African agriculture is at least three thousand years old, as the evidence appears to indicate, then why should we believe that the salt trade developed only towards the end of the first millennium AD with the advent of the Arabs and of the camel? According to Nenquin (1961) it has been calculated that a fully-grown person on a mixed diet needs 12–15 grams of salt per day. In the West African savanna, salt could be transported from the coast where it has long been extracted from seawater, or transported from the Sahara where it is quarried from rock-salt deposits, or obtained by filtering plant ashes, which is possible only in certain areas and not very efficient as a source of supply (Bloch 1963). In practice, there are extensive areas where the local supply is deficient but where diet and climate make salt an absolute necessity. Implicit in this situation are two probabilities: (1) that trade networks within West Africa are likely to be almost as old as food production, as already suggested on p. 100 and (2) that trading contacts with the desert are likely to be nearer to three thousand than to one thousand years old. In addition, no one has ever suggested that gold mining in West Africa commenced because of economic or technological stimulus from across the desert. On the contrary historical source after historical source tells us that West Africans were so secretive about the location of the mines that outsiders had very little idea where the gold came from. Furthermore, there is now evidence of gold at Jenne by AD 800. There thus seem to be several reasons

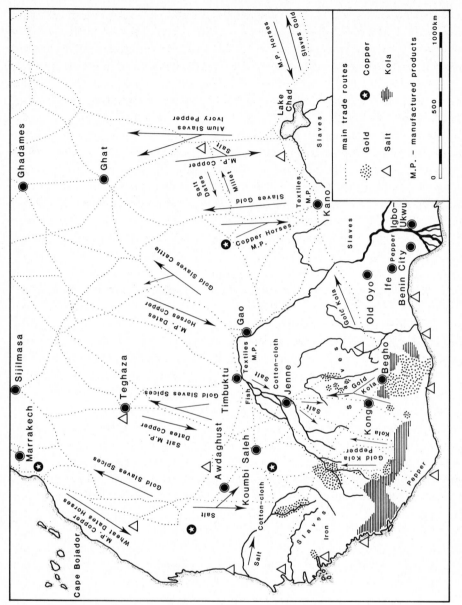

Fig. 5.8 Precolonial trade routes and commodities in West Africa. After Mauny (1961: Fig. 55).

for supporting the McIntoshs' idea that a regional network of trade routes grew up in West Africa before the advent of the Arab trans-Saharan trade. The McIntoshs (1980: Vol. 2, 444–6) point out that because Jenne was iron-using from the time of its earliest occupation, and because there was no iron ore in the vicinity, then supplies of raw materials or of finished iron would have had to be brought from over 50 kilometres away. Also, situated at the interface of the dry savanna and the Sahel, on a fertile alluvial plain, and at the highest point on the River Niger for reliable seasonal river transport, Jenne was well-placed to play an important role in a developing trade network. That such a network could also have had earlier connections with the desert, and perhaps even beyond it, is suggested by the enigmatic paintings and engravings of horse-drawn chariots and ox-drawn carts on rocks in the Sahara, that have so often been discussed (Mauny 1978; Law 1980a). These are distributed along two main axes across the desert, both of which stretch from North Africa to the Niger, axes which have been called the 'chariot tracks'. It has been assumed that these rock-drawings date from the first millennium BC, more likely from its second half. Most scholars now doubt that these are representations of vehicles used in commerce, however, and Camps (1982) has rejected the idea of 'routes', pointing out that the distribution of this rock art merely reflects the distribution of rock outcrops in the Sahara. Nevertheless, whatever else this art may mean, it is important in indicating that horse and ox traction and wheeled vehicles were known in the desert before the advent of the camel during the first few centuries AD (p. 99). Even Bovill could admit, with characteristic wisdom, that: 'There is certainly no reason to suppose that caravan traffic in the Sahara only became possible with the arrival of the camel' (Bovill 1968: 17). Indeed the McIntoshs (1980: Vol. 2, 445) have commented on the presence of copper at Jenne from the middle of the first millennium AD; the three closest known sources are all in the Sahara. It is relevant to note that there are now radiocarbon dates indicating that copper ores were being smelted at Azelik, in Niger, by the middle of the first millennium BC and perhaps earlier (Calvocoressi and David 1979: 9–10, 25). Overall, the McIntoshs could well be correct when they argue that 'the rapid establishment and expansion of Arab trade in the Western Sudan was possible because it keyed into an already-extant system of indigenous sub-Saharan trade networks' (McIntosh and McIntosh 1980: Vol. 2, 450).

Conclusion

The emergence of urbanism and political centralization in the West African savanna has long been attributed to contact with the Mediterranean world, resulting from long-distance trade. Suspiciously, the origins of that trade have usually been dated to the period of the earliest historical sources that touch on the subject. Archaeology has until recently played a confirmatory, some might even say a subservient, role in the stock historical interpretation. It has been a case of so much historical information being available that archaeologists have failed to ask the sort of questions that they might have asked otherwise. As a result, the quality of the archaeological data available to shed light on the origins of cities and states in the West African savanna is poor. Fortunately, there have in recent years been some exceptions to this general rule. The work at Jenne is a notable example. Reviewing such new evidence, along with the older evidence obtained over the last eighty years or so, leads to questioning the long-accepted external-stimulus explanation. It would appear that the West African savanna at the beginning of the first millennium AD already had a sound agricultural base, with the potential for intensification of production in some more fortunate areas, and already had a varied iron-based technology. It seems quite probable that during the first millennium AD, and prior to Arab contact, stratified societies were already emerging in the West African savanna, on the basis of resource control. In addition, it is possible that localized population pressures were stimulating social developments leading to urbanism. Such developments seem to have taken place before the advent of Islam but, nevertheless, with the ideological support of a variety of probably animistic religions. Finally, although adequately dated evidence is very limited, it seems most likely that an extensive trading network existed within West Africa before the Arab trade across the Sahara was developed. The savanna towns were indeed 'ports' at the edge of the 'sea of sand', as Levtzion (1973: 10) has said (p. 102), but they were ports with a vast trading hinterland that was already developed. After all, what ship would ever visit a port unless there was a chance of a cargo to collect?

Chapter 6

Brilliance beneath the trees: the West African forest and its fringes

It was in the second half of the fifteenth century AD that European sailors first set eyes on the southerly coast of West Africa. What they saw was hardly encouraging. From a distance, a vague grey line pencilled in between an immensity of sea and sky. From close-in, either a dangerous, surf-pounded, sandy beach or an uninviting network of mangrove swamp, creek and river mouth. Whatever the character of the shoreline, however, behind it there was nearly always an impenetrable tangle of trees and other vegetation. Experience soon taught such visitors that this was a coast to be reckoned with: ships' crews died of fever, shipworms (*Teredo* spp.) ate the bottoms out of their ships. As the centuries went by, it was this coast that became known as 'The White Man's Grave': a name that to many proved to be no exaggeration. Yet it was neither altruism nor curiosity that tempted most Europeans to such a region, it was profit. The very names that they gave to different parts of this coast indicate their motives: 'The Grain [pepper] Coast', 'The Ivory Coast', 'The Gold Coast', 'The Slave Coast' (Bosman 1967: frontispiece map). For Europeans had quickly discovered that behind the coast itself lay a forested hinterland rich in resources, where the inhabitants were able and willing to trade on a considerable scale. Not only that, but those inhabitants lived in highly organized communities, some of which took on a size and density which left the visitors in no doubt about what they were dealing with. Within some parts of the West African forest there were, indeed, hierarchical states and there were towns and cities. Because of their tangibility, it was these large settlements that particularly attracted European attention (Fig. 6.1). Thus, writing in AD 1507–8, the Portuguese Duarte Pacheco Pereira described Ijebu-Ode (in what is now Nigeria) as 'a very large city called Geebuu' (Bascom 1959: 38). Thus also, in about 1600, the Dutchman 'D.R.' (thought to have been Dierick Ruiters) described the main street of Benin City (also now in Nigeria) as 'a great broad street, not paved, which seemeth to be seven or eight times broader than the Warmoes street in Amsterdam' (Hodgkin 1975: 156). In a similar vein, the Englishman Towerson, writing in 1557, could claim, perhaps with some exaggeration, that a town in what is now Ghana, was 'by the estimation of our men, as big in circuit as London' (Blake 1942: Vol. 2, 406).

These quotations have been deliberately selected from *early* in the history of European West African contact. This has been done because state development and urbanization in the West African forest have sometimes been written about as if they were developments resulting from that contact rather than pre-dating it. For instance, this is the impression given by Goody when he discusses what he calls the 'gun states of the forest' (Goody 1971: 55, and see p. 13). Although there is no doubt that European seaborne trade did play an important part in the later development of the forest states and their towns and cities, historical sources suggest that some of them at least were in existence before that trade started. In so far as they can be trusted, some oral traditions give a similar impression and, in recent decades, archaeological evidence has become available that points in the same direction. It seems likely that there was increasing social complexity in some parts of the West African forest from late in the first millennium AD onwards. The question is 'why?'; why should such developments take place in the West African rainforest, an environment that to many outsiders has seemed to constrain rather than to encourage human endeavour?

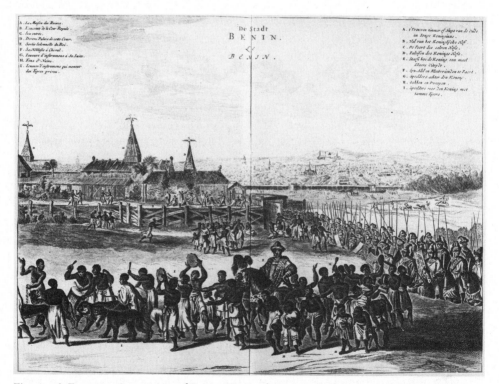

Fig. 6.1 A European impression of Benin City in the seventeenth century. From Dapper (1686: 308–9).

Geographical location and environmental factors

Compared with the West African savanna, discussed in Chapter 5, the tropical rainforest of West Africa occupies a relatively small area. An extension of the equatorial rainforest, it stretches from Cameroon to Sierra Leone but is broken between the western frontier of Nigeria and eastern Ghana by a gap where forest-savanna mosaic and also relatively moist woodlands and savanna reach the ocean. The belt of rainforest is never wider than four hundred kilometres and in many places it is far narrower than this. To the south it is bounded by coastal mangrove swamp or by the Atlantic Ocean itself. To the north it merges into forest-savanna mosaic, often called 'derived savanna' because there is a strong suspicion that it results from human agricultural exploitation, over many centuries, of what was originally tropical rainforest. The northern fringes of the forest form, in fact, an ecotone that has been particularly important in the history of the human race in West Africa.

The West African forest consists of dense tropical rainforest. A few large trees grow to a height of about 42 metres and many others to a height of about 27 metres, but they protrude above the main leaf canopy that is formed at about 10 metres by most of the trees. Smaller trees and bushes densely occupy the zone below. It is possible that in its natural state the forest often lacked this dense tangle of lower growth and the forest floor may have been relatively easy to traverse (Richards 1952: Figure 6, pp. 29–31). Nowadays, however, much of the forest has been taken over by a dense tangle of secondary growth, often of no great height but virtually impenetrable unless one chops a path through with a machete. To some extent, this secondary growth results from the extensive timber exploitation of the last seventy years or so. Nevertheless, it seems probable that much of it has existed for a far longer time than this and results from the long practice of rotational bush-fallow agriculture. In the area around Benin City, for instance, it has been shown that most of the apparently 'well-grown forest of considerable age' has probably 'been farmed at one time or another during the past few hundred years' (Allison 1962: 243, 244). Thus, in 1897, Boisragon and Locke, fleeing for their lives after the so-called 'Benin Massacre', found it very difficult to travel through the forest. Boisragon described the Benin 'bush' as follows:

> ... if one tries to imagine a thick wood in which big and little trees all intermingle their branches, with a tremendous dense undergrowth of shrubbery of all sorts, with brambles and various other evildoing thorns, all woven together into a maze so thick that neither man nor beast can press through it, one comes somewhere near the idea. (Boisragon 1897: 94)

It is quite possible that Boisragon exaggerated the difficulties, but an earlier account in a different part of the forest gives some idea of the problems of travel, even when fear was not forcing the traveller to attempt to go cross-country. This is how Bowdich described part of the Asante forest, in what is now Ghana, when he journeyed through it in 1817 on his way from the coast of the Gulf of Guinea to Kumasi:

> The doom and iron-wood trees were frequent; the path was a labyrinth of the most capricious windings, the roots of the cotton trees obstructing it continually, and our progress was generally by stepping and jumping up and down, rather than walking; the stems or caudices of these trees projected from the trunks like flying buttresses, their height frequently 20 feet. Immense trunks of fallen trees presented constant barriers to our progress, and increased our fatigues from the labour of scaling them: we were also frequently obliged to wait the cutting away of the underwood before we could proceed, even on foot [they had been travelling at times by hammock]. The large trees were covered with parasites and convolvuli, and the climbing plants, like small cables, ascending the trunks to some height, abruptly shot downwards, crossed to the opposite trees, and threaded each other in such a perplexity of twists and turnings, that it soon became impossible to trace them in the general entanglement. (Bowdich 1966: 20–1)

It is descriptions such as these that make it so difficult to understand how the West African rainforest could have been the setting for the cultural developments that undoubtedly took place there. In reality, the forest is much more complex and much more varied than descriptions by culture-shocked Europeans, writing to impress other Europeans, would make it appear (Fig. 6.2). In the area around Benin City, for example, it seems that vegetation on the upper interfluves may originally have been less dense than that of the lower valley slopes and it has been shown that farming has tended to concentrate on those more easily cleared areas (Darling 1982: Vol. 1, 33–48). Darling suggests that the forest environment around Benin varies in part because of the ever-changing mosaic of plant succession following agricultural clearance and fallowing but also in part because of differences in soil characteristics. In addition, if we look at local perceptions of the environment, we find not the European notion of continuous forest broken only by clearings for settlements but a three-part division of the 'forest' itself into farmlands, fallow, and 'wild' forest. What Darling has found around Benin could in all probability be applied also to other parts of the West African rainforest.

In one important respect the forest has a considerable advantage over the savanna lands to its north: it has more water. Rainfall is higher, the wet season is longer, humidity is greater and evapotranspiration is lower. As a result, the forest is well supplied with rivers and streams, many of which run all the year round. Also as a result, the rate and ease of vegetal growth is phenomenal, even fences take root and grow into thriving hedges or rows of trees. Although fertility is a somewhat subjective concept, it is apparent that many forest soils are moderately fertile, if this is measured in terms of productivity. This is providing

Fig. 6.2 Rainforest in the Ivory Coast in the late nineteenth century. From Binger (1892: Vol. 2, 269).

that farming practices are adopted which minimize erosion and which alternate brief cropping periods with long periods of fallow, during which the 'bush' is allowed to invade the fields.

It is important to note the main resources that would probably have been available in the West African forest some two or three thousand years ago. The most important of these would have been plant foods, including several species of yam, the oil-palm, kola, coffee, *roselle*, okra, fluted gourd and *akee*. At the western end of the forest belt there may also have been African rice and Melegueta pepper, the so-called 'Grains of Paradise' (Harris 1976: 329–33). So important have introduced plants of South-East Asian and tropical American origin now become in the forest (such as certain yams, plantain, banana, sugar-cane, citrus fruits, cassava, sweet potato, maize, papaw and chili pepper) that it is easy to forget that the West African forest was already well-endowed with plant foods before these others arrived. Particularly important amongst the indigenous plants would have been the various West African yams and the oil-palm, the former providing carbohydrates and the latter supplementing these with both fat and vitamin A (Harris 1976: 351). It should be noticed, however, that both yams and oil-palms seem originally to have belonged in the forest-savanna ecotone and must have been introduced to the forest proper by Man planting them on cleared land. Thus Coursey's West African 'yam zone' includes extensive areas of the southern savanna as well as the more northerly parts of the forest (Coursey 1980: Figure 1). In contrast to the plant food situation, the forest was not so well provided with animal foods as was the savanna. The presence of tsetse flies precluded the keeping of domesticated livestock in the forest, with the exception of small numbers of trypanosomiasis-resistent dwarf goats and cattle. Furthermore, the forest had fewer wild animals that could be hunted than did the savanna, although a wide selection of those that were present have probably been eaten at various times in the past, including elephants, baboons, monkeys, bats, large rats, the giant land snail (*Achatina* spp.) and anything else that could be caught. In addition, fish from the sea, from coastal lagoons and from rivers have almost certainly been an important source of animal protein for a long time. As well as food, the forest possessed numerous other resources, however. Perhaps most important was the availability of a great many different types of wood, suitable for everything from house-building, to canoe-making, to carving, to firewood. Various sorts of wood could also be burnt to produce such things as charcoal, potash, salt and ashes for 'native soap' and 'native butter' (Darling 1982: Vol. 1, 41). In addition, the forest could supply numerous medicinal substances, beeswax, gum, bark, rope and many other things. There was also ivory which could be obtained in some quantity, and inorganic raw materials included gold, iron ore, rocks suitable for making grindstones, good building earths and potting clays. Lastly, a population density that in many places was probably higher than could be found in the savanna, provided a resource that could be exploited as a source of slaves.

As already indicated in the case of trypanosomiasis, the West African forest zone suffered from constraints as well as benefiting from substantial resources. The most important of these constraints must have been the heavy burden of human diseases. Malaria, in particular, has been so serious a problem for so long a time that some populations in the forest have developed a greater than normal incidence of the sickle-cell gene, a blood anomaly that provides a measure of protection against this disease (Livingstone 1967). Other serious diseases would have included yellow fever, dengue fever, filariasis, yaws and a wide selection of parasitic infections, particularly of the human intestinal tract. This list by no means covers the full range of suffering that was risked by occupants of the West African forest. One suspects that disease levels in the forest may have been higher than those of the savanna, particularly of the drier savanna. Another constraint within the forest was the availability of water during the dry season. For in spite of a more plentiful water supply than in the savanna, a long dry season together with the generally permeable forest soils and high temperatures on cleared surfaces, meant that women and children frequently had to carry water long distances from rivers and streams. Various strategies were used to alleviate this problem, including digging wells, underground cisterns and even artificial ponds. The extent to which dry-season water supply could be a problem, however, particularly for large groups of people on the move, is illustrated by the experience of the British expedition against Benin City in 1897, for which water was a major worry (Home 1982). That same expedition also serves as a reminder of just how difficult communication within the forest could be, with movement restricted to narrow paths and head-loading the only means of shifting burdens. Communication problems have, indeed, been another of the forest's traditional constraints, particularly during the wet season when forest paths are frequently reduced to a sea of mud. Nevertheless, it is possible to exaggerate such difficulties, for the people who lived in the forest adapted well to them. Thus canoe transport on rivers and coastal lagoons was extremely important (Smith 1970) and the very impenetrability of the forest could be turned to good use as a defence by leaving a ring of uncleared land around settlements, as was recorded in the nineteenth century for both the 'war-towns' of Sierra Leone (Siddle 1968) and the towns of the Yoruba (Ajayi and Smith 1971: 23).

It is all too easy for outsiders to underestimate the potential for cultural growth in the West African forest and forest fringes. To people not accustomed to living in such environments and adapted to them, the constraints would seem sufficient discouragement from developing the undoubted resources. However, cities and states did grow up in some parts of those zones and these developments probably took place without external interference, because both distance and environment insulated the forest and its fringes from the communities of the northern savanna. Nevertheless, the forest was probably closely linked with the savanna in a wide-ranging, regional, trading network. It was only the appearance of European traders on the coast of West Africa that reversed this economic orientation and turned what had been a remote hinterland into a major contact-zone of long-distance trade.

Sources of information

Most of what is known about precolonial urbanization and state formation in the West African forest and its fringes comes from historical sources. These are of two main sorts that give us information on different aspects of the subject: the outsider's view and the insider's view. The outsider's view is represented by the numerous contemporary written accounts of European visitors from the late fifteenth to the late nineteenth century. These visitors included people of different national backgrounds: particularly Portuguese, English, Dutch, French, Danish and German; and with a variety of professional orientations: including sailors, traders, explorers and missionaries. To their number must be added others, who merely stayed at home and compiled books and maps on the basis of information collected from those who had actually visited the Guinea Coast. Some of the principal accounts by outsiders are those by Adams, Barbot, de Barros, Bosman, Bowditch, Burton, Dapper, de Marees, Landolphe and Pacheco Pereira; and this list does considerable injustice to the many it does not mention. Such sources throw a good deal of light on some of the forest societies of West Africa during the 400 years prior to colonial takeover. A.F.C. Ryder, for instance, has been able to use them as the main basis for a detailed study of European relationships with the state of Benin (Ryder 1969). They are limited, however, not only by their sometimes imperfect understanding of what they observed but also by their short time range. Whereas external sources for the West African savanna reach back for a little over a thousand years, those for the forest zone extend over only half that time. Fortunately, however, they are complemented by the insider's view, represented by the oral traditions of the West African societies themselves. Many of these have been collected by European scholars in recent times but some have actually been recorded by representatives of the people to whom they refer. Perhaps the most notable of these are Samuel Johnson's *History of the Yorubas*, originally published in 1921 (S. Johnson 1921) and Jacob Egharevba's *Short history of Benin*, first published in 1934 (Egharevba 1968). Such sources do throw a little light on the centuries before the first appearance of the Europeans on the Guinea Coast, they take us back perhaps to the beginning of the present millennium. Unfortunately, however, their information on the earlier periods is limited and of doubtful reliability. Their chronologies are particularly uncertain, as Bradbury was able to demonstrate in the case of Benin City (Bradbury 1959). Overall, therefore, the written and oral historical sources have comparatively little to tell us about the *origins* of cities and states in the forest, except that such developments either took place during, or had already taken place by, the first half of the present millennium. From such sources, it has sometimes been implied that these developments were generally later than those of the savanna because it took rather longer for long-distance trade routes and postulated migrations to reach so far into the hinterland (for example Oliver and Fage 1962). In other words, as in the savanna, external stimulus has been advanced as an explanation. Clearly, it becomes important to examine such relevant archaeological evidence as we have, in order to see whether this alternative source of information can throw any light on these matters.

Archaeological research, into the last two or three millennia, commenced in the West African forest rather later than in the savanna. As a result, it was spared some of the uninformative destruction that took place further north and it has, in general, been more adequately published. Nevertheless, there has been a similar tendency to pursue research programmes aimed at providing more information on historically-known sites. In the case of the forest, however, two particular circumstances have exaggerated this tendency to a marked degree. The first is that archaeological field prospection and survey is so difficult in the forest that sites are not easily found and there has been a disinclination amongst archaeologists even to make the attempt. It is so much easier to excavate sites which are known from documentary sources or from oral traditions to have been important. Patrick Darling's work on the linear earthworks of Benin and Ishan (Darling 1974; Darling 1976; Darling 1982) is one of the rare cases where deliberate, systematic search has revealed previously unknown sites. Second, the remarkable artistic traditions associated with some of the historically-known sites of southern Nigeria has tended to concentrate archaeological field research at those sites and to influence the sort of research that is carried out (see for example Willett 1967 on the subject of Ife). The overall result is that archaeological field research, in particular archaeological excavation, has been limited to relatively few sites, although a substantial amount of work has been done at some of those sites. So far as the subject of the present enquiry is concerned, such work has been restricted to Ghana and Nigeria and in some ways it is surprising how little it has yet told us.

It is instructive to examine the main examples of archaeological evidence presently available that are relevant to the origins of urbanization and state formation in the forest and its fringes. Perhaps the most interesting of these examples results from archaeological investigations into the origins of the Akan states, in what is now Ghana. It is with some justification that James Anquandah (1982: 85–112) has written of what he calls: 'The Akan – "a golden civilization" in the forest', for these states seem to have controlled a part of the gold trade from the forest north to the Inland Niger Delta (Dumett 1979). The Akan states already existed by the late fifteenth century AD, when they were mentioned by the earliest European visitors to the West African coast, and a considerable amount is known about the last major Akan state, that of Asante, in the eighteenth and nineteenth centuries (McLeod: 1981). The earliest of these states were situated on the fringes of the forest and excavations at the site of Begho, in this region, have revealed the remains of a large market town made up of four different 'quarters', which are 1–2 kilometres from one another. According to local traditions these belonged, respectively, to the Akan-speaking Brong, to the Kramo, who were Muslim merchants presumed to have come from Mali to the north-west, to the Tumfour or artisans, and to the Nyaho, who were a mixed group. Each of these quarters consists of a group of mounds, about 1.5 metres high and 30 metres across, which are often L-shaped and which are the remains of mud-walled houses. At first, oral tradition and radiocarbon dates indicated that the town was occupied between about AD 1400 and 1725 and attained a peak of prosperity towards the beginning of the seventeenth century (Posnansky 1976: 51), but radiocarbon dates from subsequent excavations have indicated that settlement probably began as early as the eleventh or twelfth century (Crossland 1976; Posnansky and McIntosh 1976: 166, 189). At Bono Manso, another town site in the same region, occupation appears to have commenced about the thirteenth century (Anquandah 1982: 96). There seems at the moment to be no evidence of urban developments in the Akan area earlier than the beginning of the second millennium AD, although the second phase of the occupation site excavated at New Buipe represents an iron-using community and appears to date from late in the first millennium AD. Consisting of three mounds with a total diameter of less than 200 metres, it is perhaps too small to be relevant to the present enquiry, although it does seem to have been part of a larger site complex (York 1973). It may be significant, however, that the area of the early Akan states on the forest fringes (the centre of Akan power shifted south into the forest proper only after European contact) is the same general area that has provided the bulk of the evidence for the early food-producing Kintampo Culture of the late second millennium BC. It is also an area rich in iron ore and it has provided a second century AD radiocarbon date for iron-smelting at Hani, near Begho (Posnansky and McIntosh 1976). The major problem has been the lack of data to link these developments to the growth of urban communities in the second millennium AD. The recent excavations by Shinnie and Kense at Daboya, further north in the savanna, now offers some hope of an improvement in this situation. Daboya (a source of salt, at least in more recent centuries) has produced a series of radiocarbon dates ranging from the eighth century BC to the seventeenth century AD, with the earliest evidence for iron in about the first century BC (Sutton 1982: 297–8, 307, 312). However, the exact significance of Daboya and of some other recent excavations in Ghana will not be clear until they are adequately published.

The second example of archaeological evidence relevant to urbanization and the growth of the state in the West African forest and forest fringes, relates to the Yoruba people of south-western Nigeria. Yoruba urbanization, in particular, is a subject that has attracted the attention of many scholars. As Bascom could write:

The Yoruba of Western Nigeria have large, dense, permanent settlements, based upon farming rather than upon industrialization, the pattern of which is traditional rather than an outgrowth of acculturation. They are undoubtedly the most urban of all African peoples, the percentage living in large communities being comparable to that in European nations. (Bascom 1955: 446)

Indeed, as Bascom pointed out, in 1931 nine out of the ten largest cities in Nigeria were Yoruba, the only exception being Kano. Studies of this interesting phenomenon, however, have concentrated on the present time and on historical sources, most of which are of nineteenth-century date (for example Mabogunje 1962; Ojo 1966a; Ojo 1966b; Krapf-Askari 1969). There has been less concern about remoter origins, except from a theoretical point of view. This is probably because many people are persuaded, like Eades (1980: 43), that 'the impressive scale of urban development' observed by modern scholars 'in most cases does not predate 1800'. Indeed, the early nineteenth century Fulani attacks on Northern Yorubaland, and the Yoruba civil wars that followed, do seem to have played a substantial part in the development of the urban pattern that now exists. Nevertheless, some large urban centres clearly did exist amongst the Yoruba at an earlier date and archaeological investigations are beginning to give some idea of how they developed. Excavations and survey during the 1970s by Soper at the important site of Old Oyo, in the southern savanna, should provide useful data when they are eventually published (but see Darling 1984: Vol. 2, 360 for a transect plan of compound banks). Old Oyo was, however, only the most important of numerous towns abandoned in the southern savanna as a result of the Fulani attacks and Babayemi has located the sites of a substantial number of these in the Upper Ogun area (Babayemi 1974). It is interesting that even now the greater number of Yoruba towns and cities tends to be concentrated in the transitional zone between grassland and forest (Mabogunje 1962: Figure 4). From the point of view of our enquiry, the most important of those in the northern part of the forest itself is Ife, where according to Yoruba traditions the world was created. Ife has remained of spiritual and ceremonial importance to the Yoruba and the remarkable terracottas, 'bronzes' and stone sculptures discovered there during the present century have focussed archaeological activity on this site (Willett 1967). The art itself has been interpreted as evidence of emerging social stratification, for some of it appears to represent personages of importance and, in addition, art on such a scale must surely imply patronage, particularly as the items of copper-base alloys are made from materials that must have been imported to the area (Fig. 6.3). Excavations at various sites in the present city of Ife (which covers the area of the ancient city) by Willett, Eyo and Garlake have produced a radiocarbon chronology suggesting that occupation commenced during the late first millennium AD (Shaw 1980: Figure 1). Archaeological deposits at Ife have proved technically difficult to excavate and

Fig. 6.3 'Bronze' casting of an Oni of Ife. Height 46.7cm. Reproduced by permission of Frank Willett.

rarely has mud-walling been isolated in the generally shallow deposits. Nevertheless, some indication of the layout of domestic buildings has been provided by the successful excavation of extensive pavements of recycled potsherds and small stones (Willett 1967: Figures 16 and 17, Plate 66; Garlake 1974: Figures 3 and 4; Garlake 1977: Figures 4 and 8). The main period during which such pavements were made has been dated by radiocarbon to approximately the twelfth to the fifteenth century and both radiocarbon and thermoluminescent dates have been used to suggest that the most important period of the Ife art was in the late fourteenth to early fifteenth century (Shaw 1980: 376). Little, however, can be said of the growth of the city itself, although a series of concentric city walls (Fig. 6.4) suggest a complex series of phases in

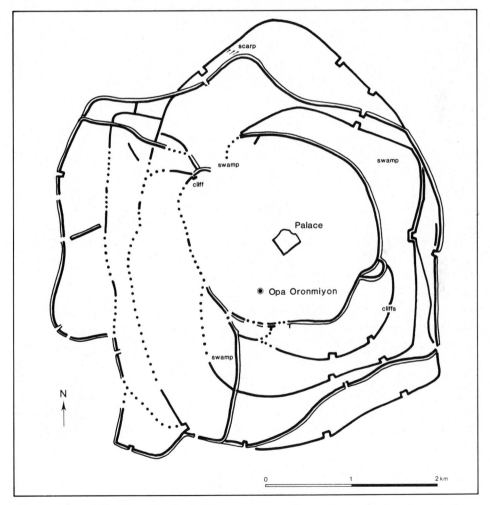

Fig. 6.4 Map of Ife city walls. Single lines represent earlier walls, double lines later walls. The Opa Oronmiyon is a monumental stone pillar of early date. After Ozanne (1969).

which the city grew up around the palace of the ruler (Ozanne 1969). Unfortunately these walls have not been adequately dated and it is known that at least some of them belong to only the last few centuries. It does seem, nevertheless, that the ancient city must have covered a considerable area. Garlake (1977: 92) has suggested that it was probably at least as large as the nineteenth century walled town, because two of the excavated sites lie outside the western wall of that town while another lies beside and just beyond the eastern wall. He has also claimed that: 'There are strong indications that buildings were sufficiently compact and close together for the settlement to be ranked as urban'.

A third example of relevant archaeological evidence is Benin City in Nigeria. Benin seems to have mesmerized European visitors for centuries and, indeed, it is archaeologically fascinating not only because it is situated deep in the rainforest itself but also because its origins are still unclear. Excavations during the 1950s by Goodwin (1957; 1963) and by myself during the 1960s (Connah 1972; Connah 1975) revealed substantial post-European-contact deposits on the site of the old palace. My own work was also able to demonstrate occupation of the city by about the thirteenth century AD. The principal evidence for this consisted of radiocarbon dates for a mass burial of at least 41 young women, who lay at a depth of over 12.5 metres in a narrow well-like cistern (Fig. 6.5). Wearing clothing, bracelets, finger-rings and beads, they appeared to have been dropped down the deep shaft in which they were found and must surely represent ritual sacrifice of a sort indicative of strongly centralized authority. Good documentary evidence exists for the continued practice of throwing the bodies of sacrificial victims into such pits, as late as 1897 (Roth 1903). Deep beneath the modern, developing city of Benin there must surely be other similar pits, still preserving their evidence of fear and of power, and it is possible that some of them could be earlier in date than the one that was excavated. The excavations of the 1960s also made it apparent that potsherd pavements had been made in Benin City during or prior to the fourteenth century AD, and this was a practice that appears to have ended before European contact. The existence of such pavements suggests formal architecture like that of which Garlake has revealed indications at Ife. More important, however, is the evidence of the so-called 'Benin City walls', the innermost of which has been demonstrated by radiocarbon dating, historical documentation and oral tradition to have been constructed before European contact, quite possibly around the middle of the fifteenth century. Consisting of a massive earthen bank and ditch, with a total vertical height, from the excavated bottom of the ditch to the top of the surviving bank, of as much as 17.4 metres and a circumference of 11.6 kilometres, this earthwork alone represents an enormous investment of human effort that must clearly have been directed by a powerful centralized authority. Calculations have suggested that its construction would have absorbed 5000 men continuously occupied for ten hours a day, if it had been completed in one dry season. Such rapidity of construction is perhaps unlikely but, even if spread over five dry

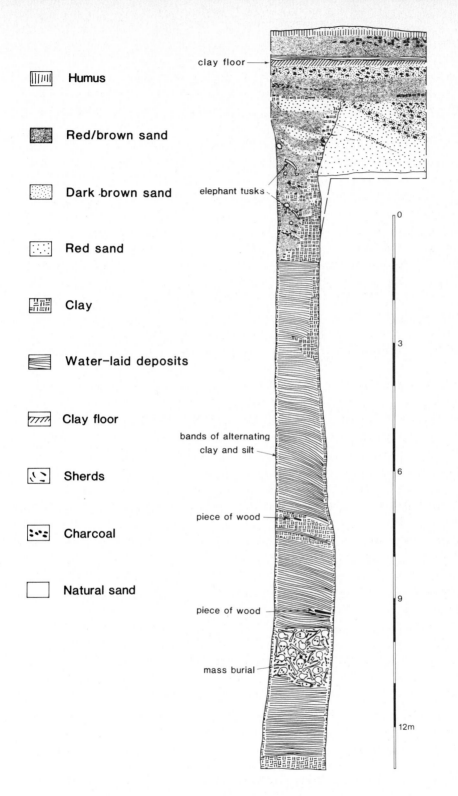

Legend:

▥	Humus
▦	Red/brown sand
▦	Dark brown sand
▦	Red sand
▦	Clay
▦	Water–laid deposits
▨	Clay floor
▨	Sherds
▨	Charcoal
▢	Natural sand

clay floor

elephant tusks

bands of alternating
clay and silt

piece of wood

piece of wood

mass burial

0

3

6

9

12m

Fig. 6.5 Section of shaft containing mass sacrifice, Benin City. After Connah (1975: Fig. 18).

seasons, a labour force of 1000 men (and/or women?) would have been necessary. The direction of such a labour force on a massive project of this sort must, indeed, have implications of the very greatest significance for our enquiry into state formation. That is not the whole story, however, because surveys during the 1960s in the tangled vegetation around Benin City revealed a vast network of further interlocking enclosures, consisting of over 145 kilometres of earthworks. These appeared to hint at the process of synoecism ('the union of several towns or villages into or under one capital city' (*Oxford English Dictionary* 1933)) by which a group of villages had developed into a city, at a date prior to the construction of the innermost and most massive of the 'walls'. Nevertheless, subsequent work by Darling (Darling 1974; Darling 1976; Darling 1982) and by other researchers (Maliphant et al. 1976; Roese 1981) has shown that even this outer network that was mapped by me (Connah 1975) was only 'a small peripheral part of a much more extensive pattern of rural earthwork enclosures' (Darling 1982: Vol. 1, 387). This overall pattern has been found to cover an area of about 6500 square kilometres, and has been estimated to have a total length in excess of 16 000 kilometres (Fig. 6.6). It is thought to imply at least 150,000,000 man-hours of work over a period of several centuries (Darling 1982: Vol. 1, 392). It is little wonder that the Benin earthworks, or *iya* as they are known locally, have got themselves into the *Guinness book of records* (McWhirter 1980: 125)! As Darling (1982) has shown, they probably have more to tell us about the process of state formation than about the origins of urban growth that produced Benin City itself. Nevertheless, it is a great pity that a satisfactory series of radiocarbon dates for the land surfaces beneath these earthworks has still not been obtained. Six radiocarbon determinations are available, it is true, but two of them give 'modern' dates, one a nineteenth century date and three give dates in the thirteenth to fifteenth centuries (Sutton 1982: 309, 312). Clearly, much more excavation time and money will have to be invested if this enormous complex of earthworks is to be sorted out chronologically. Indeed, the same might be said also of the artistic use of copper-base alloys in Benin. My own excavations of the 1960s showed that these materials were used artistically as early as the thirteenth century AD but those excavations recovered no evidence of *casting* these metals prior to European contact. In spite of the numerous artistic studies that have been made of the famous Benin castings (for example Forman et al. 1960; Dark 1973) we still have very little evidence about their detailed chronology. In view of the implications of these castings, implying as they do both an hierarchical power structure and considerable artistic patronage, it is a great misfortune that so few have ever been recovered from properly controlled and adequately published stratigraphic excavations. However, a small number of Benin castings has been dated on the basis of the thermoluminescence of the fragments of fired clay core remaining within them and it is interesting that they were all found to date from about the fifteenth century AD or later (Willett and Fleming 1976).

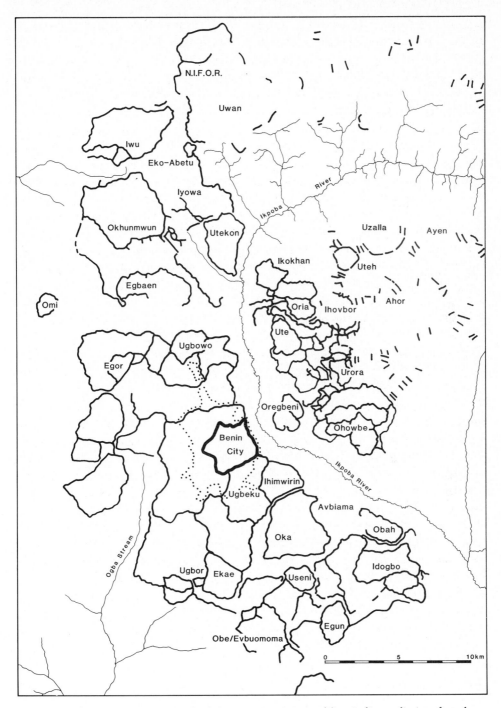

Fig. 6.6 Earthwork enclosures in the Benin City area. Dotted line indicates limits of modern city. After Darling (1982).

It is impossible to leave the subject of archaeological evidence for state formation and urbanization, within the West African rainforest, without some consideration of a collection of evidence that at first sight appears irrelevant. This evidence comes from Igbo-Ukwu, east of the River Niger in Nigeria, from an area now occupied by the Ibo people, who have long interested anthropologists precisely because apparently they neither developed cities nor states until recent times, in spite of a high population density. What, then, is one to make of Igbo-Ukwu, where the burial of a clearly important individual (Fig. 6.7), a repository of sophisticated regalia, and a ritual disposal pit produced, amongst other things, 685 copper and bronze objects (many of them highly ornamented) and some 165 000 stone and glass beads? Thurstan Shaw, the excavator of this remarkable site, has suggested that this evidence indicates the former existence of a local 'priest king', who was the holder of the highest politico-ritual title in the democratized title-taking system of the Ibo of this area (Shaw 1970; Shaw 1977b). There is some ethnohistorical evidence that supports this interpretation, although it is not clear whether this should be applied to archaeological data a thousand years old. This date, at the end of the first millennium AD, is based on a group of radiocarbon dates that have been the subject of some argument (Lawal 1973; Posnansky 1973; Shaw 1975b) but more recently there seems to be a greater readiness to accept them at their face value (Posnansky 1980; McIntosh and McIntosh 1981b). As the Igbo-Ukwu evidence appears to imply trading connections between the West African rainforest and the Mediterranean world, its early date raises more questions than can be answered at the moment. Clearly there was an early participation in long-distance trade by people living in the Igbo-Ukwu area, and clearly there was some sort of local authority capable of concentrating a considerable quantity of the products of this trade on one individual. Elsewhere, such archaeological evidence would probably be thought suggestive of the sort of social stratification indicative of an emergent state or at least of a ranked chiefdom. In the case of Igbo-Ukwu the ethnohistorical evidence would require considerable qualification of such an interpretation. Until we know far more about the late first millennium AD in this part of Nigeria, there are two tentative conclusions that suggest themselves. First, that we should be very careful when deducing socio-political organization from such archaeological evidence as 'rich burials'. Second, that the social and political organization observed in any area during the last two centuries does not necessarily indicate the situation a thousand years ago: societies are dynamic not static and change exists in forms other than unilinear evolution.

Subsistence economy

What can these rather fragmentary examples of supposedly relevant archaeological evidence tell us about the origins of cities and states in the West African rainforest? To begin with, what about the subsistence economy on which these

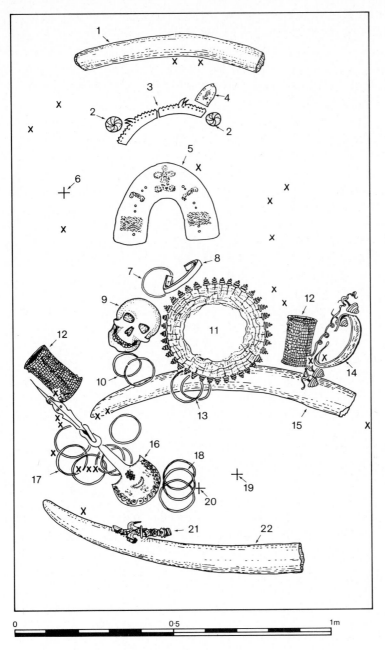

Fig. 6.7 Plan of the burial at Igbo-Ukwu.

1, 15, 22: Elephant tusks. *2:* Decorated copper roundels. *3:* Crown. *4:* Decorated copper plate. *5:* Pectoral plate. *6, 19:* Position of point of bracket. *7, 10, 13, 17, 18:* Copper anklets. *8:* Copper strap. *9:* Skull. *11:* Spiral copper bosses set in wood: remains of stool. *12:* Beaded armlets. *14:* Copper handle for calabash. *16:* Copper fan-holder. *20:* Position of point of rod supporting bronze leopard's skull. *21:* Bronze horseman hilt. X: Iron nails and staples. After Shaw (1970: Fig. 14).

entities must have been based? It must be admitted at once that we have very little direct evidence. Forest soils are usually destructive of bone and the recovery of botanical evidence by means of flotation does not seem to have been adequately attempted as yet. However, the excellent preservation of bones, wood and cloth in the Benin cistern containing the sacrificed women, suggests that exceptional conditions do exist if the archaeologist can but find them. Until that happens, the evidence from the late second millennium BC Kintampo sites, at the junction of forest and savanna in Ghana, will remain of value even for this later period. From these sites there is evidence of small domesticated cattle and domesticated dwarf goats, and of the use of cowpeas and oil-palm, although it is unknown whether these were domesticated or not (Carter and Flight 1972; Flight 1976). Faunal and artefactual evidence indicate, nevertheless, that hunting and fishing remained a significant part of the basic subsistence. From sites of the late first millennium AD, or of the early second millennium AD, there is virtually no published evidence for subsistence economy. The early Akan sites seem to have nothing of relevance and there is definitely nothing from Benin City. Ife has produced slight evidence of sheep or goat associated with potsherd pavements (Garlake 1977: 91) and terracottas of a bull and of a ram's head were found at Lafogido (in Ife) in a twelfth century context (Eyo 1974). The ritual disposal pit at Igbo-Ukwu yielded a moderate number of bones but all of wild though edible fauna, a circumstance perhaps explained by the presumed ritual character of the pit (Shaw 1970: Vol. 1, 247–8).

With so little direct archaeological evidence, it is necessary to fall back on indirect archaeological evidence and on evidence from non-archaeological sources. As already discussed (p. 126), there were substantial plant-food resources in the rainforest and it should be noted that all the sites that have been mentioned are situated within the West African 'yam zone'. Furthermore, those sites tend to be in the more northern parts of the forest or in the southern savanna, where yams and oil-palm originally grew more readily. These, and the complex of other plants already reviewed, would have provided a sound subsistence base. The main deficiency would probably have been animal protein, as in recent times, but small numbers of dwarf goats and cattle, large quantities of fish and extensive hunting in the forest could have rendered this less of a problem than it is with an exploding modern population. Overall, this food-production system was almost certainly indigenous in its development and of substantial antiquity. Thus it may be significant that pottery, ground stone axes and possible sickle components appear at the Nigerian rock shelter of Iwo Eleru some time after 4000 BC (Shaw 1978: 47) and that during the last few millennia BC many of the stone-using peoples of the forest made pick-like and hoe-like implements, that some archaeologists have interpreted as digging tools for the collection and eventual cultivation of yams. Certainly those trypanosomiasis-resistant goats and cattle must have taken a considerable length of time to acquire the resistence that enables them to survive in the forest.

It would appear that by the end of the first millennium AD, and perhaps one or two thousand years earlier, a sound agricultural system had grown up on the interfluves of the more northerly parts of the forest. This system was based on the rotational bush-fallow cultivation of extensive areas of forest land, that was cleared by slashing and burning and then abandoned to regeneration when soil exhaustion reduced productivity. One of the main crops was probably yams and it should be noted that yams are a food source that can be stored and can be transported. In such circumstances, it seems likely that by the early second millennium AD the subsistence economy of the rainforest was able to produce a surplus and to provide adequate support for the growing social complexity of which the archaeological record provides evidence.

Technology

As stated above (p. 130), iron-smelting was already being practised at Hani in Ghana, just north of the forest, by about the second century AD. It seems reasonable to assume, therefore, that the technology of at least some of the occupants of the forest included iron-working from early in the first millennium AD. Certainly the iron-working skills of West African forest peoples grew in time to a high level of sophistication; there is ample evidence of this by the end of the first millennium AD at Igbo-Ukwu (Shaw 1970: Vol. 1, 97–103). Also, ethnohistorical data such as that of Bellamy (1904), who recorded the operation of a most impressive induced-draught furnace near Oyo in Yorubaland, indicate a long-established tradition. The adoption of iron, by people living in and on the fringes of the West African forest, must have made the agricultural exploitation of those zones very much more practicable than previously. Iron tools were almost certainly not a precondition of forest cultivation, as was once thought, but it was probably their existence that made cultivation possible on a scale that could support communities of increasing size.

In addition to the working of iron, copper and copper-base alloys were also being handled with great skill by the close of the first millennium AD. The evidence from Igbo-Ukwu shows that both lost-wax casting and smithing and chasing techniques had been mastered. Indeed, by the second quarter of the second millennium AD, metalsmiths in Ife were producing copper-base alloy castings of a technical excellence and an artistic refinement that is very impressive. A little later, craftsmen in Benin City were excelling in a similar fashion and the Akan were producing their intriguing little weights for weighing gold. Only those who have watched a modern West African 'brassworker' attempt to emulate his forebears can appreciate how difficult this craft of casting is and how very skilled were the artisans and artists of the past.

Perhaps the most impressive aspect of the forest-dwellers' technology, however, was its diversity. Thus the artists of ancient Ife excelled in the making of terracotta representations as well as ones of copper-base alloy. Also at Ife, the complex pavements of potsherds and stones hint at considerable architectural sophistication, a sophistication that can perhaps still be seen in the much later but nevertheless imposing traditional mud palaces of some Yoruba rulers (Ojo 1966b). Indeed, some of the coursed-mud architecture of the West African forest seems to have been quite remarkable. That of the Asante, for instance, with its polished red and white walls decorated with low reliefs, is still an impressive demonstration of what is possible in this building material, as also is that of Benin, with its polished, fluted red walls. Benin City has, in fact, provided us with a time-capsule of traditional technology, in the form of the massive and varied collection of objects looted from the city at the time of its capture by the British in 1897 (see for example Pitt Rivers 1900). It is apparent that the Bini were proficient not only in iron-working, 'brassworking' and building but also in carpentry, wood-carving, ivory-carving, mud and terracotta sculpture, pottery, leatherworking, weaving and beadwork (Dark 1973).

The full range of technological skills amongst some forest communities, during the last 500–1000 years or so, is too great to discuss in any more detail here. There were, however, two other areas of expertise that particularly deserve a mention. The first is that a number of sites at Ife have yielded evidence of glass-melting, in the form of fragments of crucibles coated with waste glass (see for example Garlake 1977: 89–90). The exact significance of this evidence is not clear, because it might only mean that imported glass was being melted to turn into beads or other small objects (Willett 1977: 22), or it could mean that glass was being made from its basic ingredients. Whatever the case, it is interesting that radiocarbon dates for a recently-excavated site, that is described as a glass-bead-making factory, point to a date between the late eleventh and the fourteenth centuries (Sutton 1982: 309, 312). The second area of expertise that deserves special mention is that of mining, specifically of gold mining, particularly in the area of the Akan states in southern Ghana. As stated in Chapter 5, little archaeological research has yet been conducted at West African gold mining sites but there are some interesting ethnohistorical accounts which indicate that mining in the Akan forest was carried to a depth of as much as 46 metres (Addo-Fening 1976). Clearly, miners who could engage in that sort of enterprise must have known a considerable amount about their craft.

Thus it would appear that by early in the second millennium AD, if not before, there was a varied and sophisticated level of technology in at least some of the West African forest communities. There is, in short, good reason to suspect that there would have been a growth in specialization amongst the societies concerned.

Social system

Ethnohistorical and oral sources have much more to tell us about social organization in the West African rainforest during the last half millennium, than does archaeological evidence. Nevertheless, the latter has an important part to play in amplifying the other sources, and it is our only source of information for the crucial earlier formative periods. From the examples of archaeological data that have been examined, it would appear that by late in the first millennium AD, or early in the second millennium, there was growing social stratification based on the control of trade resources and of agricultural surplus. This took place particularly in the northerly parts of the forest and in the forest-savanna ecotone. It led in some places to increasing centralization of authority, particularly in the form of the much-discussed institution of divine kingship. The copper-base alloy castings of Ife and Benin provide eloquent representations of that institution and, in the case of Benin, of the social and political hierarchy that supported it (Fig. 6.8). The thirteenth-century sacrificial victims at Benin and the scale of the earthworks with which that city and its surrounding

Fig. 6.8 'Bronze' plaque from Benin City, showing a seated Oba with kneeling attendants.

settlements were protected, give some idea of the power of the centralized authority of that place. In the terms defined by Haas (p. 10), it is possible to see evidence here of the scope, the amount and the extension of power, if not indeed of more of his variables for the measurement of power. Similarly, whatever the precise socio-political significance of the Igbo-Ukwu evidence, it clearly indicates a concentration of 'wealth' on one individual, an individual who must have held institutionalized power of some sort. However, even without the Igbo-Ukwu evidence, there do seem to be signs of emergent states in the forest by early in the second millennium AD.

There are also clear signs of urbanization by this time; at the very least Begho, Ife and Benin were already expanding communities and they are only the ones of which we know something. Although our archaeological evidence for the beginnings of urbanization in West Africa is so poor, as Andah (1976) has pointed out, the technological developments discussed above (p. 141) suggest a growth of specialist crafts and with this a growth in functional specialization within society which, as Mabogunje has argued (p. 12), is fundamental to the development of urbanization. Furthermore, it seems that by the early second millennium AD, Mabogunje's 'limiting conditions' (Chapter 2) for urbanization were also being met in some parts of the West African forest. There was almost certainly a surplus of food production, there were in some areas small groups of people able to exercise power and very likely there was a class of traders and merchants. In some places, however, these conditions were apparently not met and urbanization did not take place. Thus there is the example of the Ibo people of eastern Nigeria, who developed a different form of socio-political organization. The origins of Ibo society would merit careful archaeological examination, for surely it is not enough to explain their case, as Hull (1976: 25) has done, by claiming that 'while the Ibo were urbanites, they were not city dwellers in the classical sense'?

Population pressures

At first sight, the West African rainforest would seem to be an unlikely place for population pressures to build up. To the outsider, there seem to be almost limitless supplies of unused land and farmers have none of the problems of water stress that characterize the savanna. Indeed, it is possible that the iron-using farmers of the first millennium AD did enjoy for some centuries a virtual 'frontier' situation, in which there was always sufficient fresh land to meet increases in the population. This might even be the reason why urbanization and state development were conspicuously later phenomena in the forest than they were in the savanna.

It is clear from Darling's work around Benin, however, that forest soils and environments varied in their attractiveness to farmers. It seems probable that the best farmlands were situated on the upper interfluves, where the vegetation may have been easier to clear and the soils were better drained. Also there seems to have been a preference for ecotonal environments on the fringes of the forest. Given a rotational bush-fallow agricultural system of the sort that has been traditional in the forest, each piece of farmland would have to be fallowed for 10–15 years, after only three or four years of cultivation (Grove 1978: 77). During those brief periods of cultivation each piece of land would be relatively productive and capable of producing a surplus of food. Such a surplus could stimulate population expansion but a time would come when the best land became harder to find, unless the farmer was willing to reduce the fallowing period, a solution that would be detrimental to productivity and therefore to food supplies. All this is supposition, of course, but it may be significant that Allison (1962: 244) citing E.W. Jones (1956) was able to produce evidence that most of the forest around Benin City had been farmed at one time or another. Indeed, surely the vast pattern of earthworks mapped by Darling (1982) is indicative of an expanding farming population competing for land? Human communities do not indulge in such monumental labour unless there is a very good reason. Whether such competition existed also in other areas of the West African forest, remains to be seen. It is quite possible, however, that population pressure was one of the factors which led to an increasing elaboration of social hierarchies and to an increasing size of human communities, in the earlier part of the second millennium AD.

Ideology

Prior to European contact, the religions of the West African forest peoples seem to have consisted of a very complex collection of animistic beliefs. From ethnohistorical sources and from oral tradition, it appears that whole pantheons of deities as well as ancestor-worship, played a part in many of these beliefs and that the ruler or leader of a community often fulfilled the function of its chief priest. Thus in Benin City the Oba appears to have been the principal officiant in the most important religious ceremonies and some of these at least involved human sacrifices in which the victim or victims were asked to carry a message to the gods. Likewise the Oni of Ife was a spiritual leader of importance, and the Akan chiefs seem to have had spiritual as well as temporal powers. Thus it would seem that ideology may have played an important part in the emergence of West African forest states, particularly as a means of reinforcing centralized authority. In view of the importance of a food surplus in both the development of states and cities, it is interesting that in many parts of the forest and its fringes some of the most important ceremonies of the religious year were concerned with the yam harvest.

There is a little archaeological evidence that suggests that the role of religion, indicated by ethnohistory and oral tradition, may have been similar in the early centuries of the present millennium. In Ife, for instance, Garlake has excavated the remains of fourteenth-century altars built into the edge of potsherd pavements and comparable with those dedicated to past Obas that are still to be seen in the royal palace of Benin (Garlake 1977: 69). At Benin itself there is evidence of human sacrifice being practised in the thirteenth century. In addition, many of the Benin copper-base alloy castings of sixteenth to nineteenth-century date apparently represent former Obas and originally were important pieces of shrine furniture. The 'bronze' and terracotta heads from Ife of fourteenth to fifteenth-century date were perhaps intended for a similar use or, in some cases, intended to be used in second-burial ceremonies. Finally there is the thousand-year-old Igbo-Ukwu evidence for the existence of what its excavator has called a 'priest king' (Shaw 1977b). Whatever its precise significance may be, this site seems to indicate that the combining of spiritual and temporal authority is indeed an ancient practice in the West African forest.

External trade

In Chapter 5 (p. 100) it was argued that the range of environments in West Africa would have provided both the necessity and the occasion for the exchange of raw materials and products across the boundaries between those environments. Thus one might expect an early development of regional trading both within and between the various ecozones and ecotones of West Africa. The forest and forest fringes must have played an important part in such development. Forest products that were probably both exchanged in local markets and traded to greater distances could have included yams, vegetable oils, palm wine, miscellaneous vegetable food, dried fish, salt, Melegueta pepper, kola nuts, dyewoods, various gums, cloth, pots, canoes, charcoal, ivory, gold and slaves. Among these commodities were a number that were sought after by long-distance trade, particularly gold, ivory, slaves, pepper and kola nuts. By the end of the first millennium AD some of these were being carried across the Sahara and by the middle of the second millennium AD seaborne European traders were seeking them on the coast and, in addition, gradually developing what was to become an almost insatiable demand for vegetable oils. In return for their various exports, the forest and forest fringes received an assortment of goods, of which luxury goods that gave status to the recipients formed a substantial part. This is not to deny that regional trade in meat-on-the-hoof from the savanna was important in the forest probably from an early date, or that some of the salt from the trans-Saharan trade must have reached as far south as the forest. Nevertheless, it appears that amongst the most important of the commodities reaching the forest from the Saharan trade were copper-base alloys, either in ingot or manufactured form. These were much sought after by the peoples of the forest and from the time of their first arrival on the West African coast, European traders were quick to take advantage of this demand. Clearly, copper and its alloys were luxury materials of considerable socio-political and economic importance in the forest (Herbert 1973). In addition, cowrie shells were an important commodity traded into the forest, originally across the Sahara but eventually to the coast on European ships (M. Johnson 1970a; M. Johnson 1970b). Used both decoratively and as a form of currency, their possession was again an important indicator of status. The same could be said of many of the other imports to the West African forest. As indicated by European records of ships' cargoes, there was a demand for a variety of manufactured goods, particularly glass beads, coral beads, fine cloths, metalware of all sorts – especially iron knives, iron bars, alcohol, tobacco, gunpowder, guns and mirrors; and this is only to name a selection of the goods that were carried at one time or another (Ryder 1969). One of the most remarkable status symbols, however, was the horse. Used in the forest fringes, horses were also known as deep in the forest as Benin City; they were imported there from the savanna and, in later times, occasionally from European traders on the coast (Law 1980b). Given the trypanosomiasis problem in the forest, it is unlikely that horses could have lived very long in such an environment. It would seem that their use in Benin represented a remarkable example of conspicuous consumption.

The above discussion is based on a mixture of ethnohistory and oral tradition, and its major weakness is that so much of the information is drawn from post-European-contact times. Thus, to find evidence of external trade in the forest, from any time before about 500 years ago, we must turn to archaeology. The most obvious piece of such evidence, and perhaps the earliest, is Igbo-Ukwu. The very large quantities of items of copper-base alloy and of beads at that site imply early trading links, but what could the people of Igbo-Ukwu have been giving in exchange? Shaw (1970: Vol. 1, 284–5) suggested ivory, in the form of elephants' tusks, and added that probably slaves and perhaps kola nuts had also been exported from this part of the forest. He thought that in addition to copper-base alloy, salt and perhaps textiles were imported. His suggestions seem reasonable but the location of Igbo-Ukwu in the northern margin of the forest, near to the Niger River and not very far from the Niger Delta, makes one wonder whether salt, dried fish and perhaps some other Delta products (Alagoa 1970) may not also have been amongst the goods traded to the north.

Further to the west, the location of Begho and other sites thought to relate to the early Akan states is surely indicative of an early trade in gold and other forest commodities? To the south of Begho lay many of West Africa's gold mines and substantial resources of kola. To the north lay more gold mines, and the Akan states would seem to have developed astride a major trade-route from the coast, through the forest, up the Black Volta River, to the region of Jenne in the Inland Niger Delta (Wilks 1962). Some confirmation of the importance of this trade exists in the form of a number of copper-base alloy basins and bowls which have survived in eight or more localities in the Akan area. These appear to have had a north African origin, indeed three items from Nsawkaw have Arabic inscriptions and one of those three is thought to be possibly of fourteenth-century date.

More remarkable still, perhaps, is the fourteenth-century English bronze jug which was amongst the loot taken by the British from Kumasi in 1896 (Posnansky 1973: 155–6). However, there was probably a far wider range of imports into the Akan area than such items would suggest. Similarly, the commodities exported could well have consisted of things other than just gold and kola. Other likely trade goods would have been ivory, dried fish, slaves and salt. With respect to the latter, it was on this part of the coast of West Africa that an eighteenth-century European visitor recorded salt production (by seawater evaporation) on such a scale that a number of storehouses were seen, each containing about 50 tonnes of good clean salt (Nenquin 1961: 115–6).

At both Ife and Benin City the only really firm archaeological evidence for external trade prior to European contact consists of the presence of items of copper-base alloys. As an indication of external trade, it is interesting that by the fourteenth century AD such items were even getting down into the Niger Delta, implying that canoe-borne trade had already developed (Nzewunwa 1980: 247). In the case of Ife, it has been suggested that a trade-route ran north from Yorubaland to a crossing of the Niger below Bussa, where a remarkable group of copper-base alloy castings known as the 'Tsoede bronzes' were found (Shaw 1973). It seems likely that this could have been so, and the most probable commodities that could have been traded out of Yorubaland would have been kola nuts (long important in the savanna because kola is the only stimulant permitted by Islam), ivory, salt, dried fish and slaves. Similar trade-goods would probably have been exported from Benin City, although Melegueta pepper was probably more important than kola. Also trade in vegetable oils is likely to have long pre-dated European contact. The location of Benin City seems never to have been adequately explained in terms of trade-routes, however, although it was quite well placed to maintain contact with both the Niger Delta to its south and the Niger River to its east.

Although the direct archaeological evidence is very limited, there seems to be no doubt that external trade was important for the peoples of the West African forest and its margins long before European traders arrived on the coast. It seems probable that such trade had commenced at least by the first millennium AD and its origins may be much earlier. Although long-distance contacts with trans-Saharan trade must have had a stimulating effect on the movement and procurement of certain types of commodities, there seems no good reason why the inauguration of such contacts should be claimed as the beginning of forest zone trade. In Chapter 5 it was argued that a regional network of trade-routes existed in West Africa before the advent of the Arab trans-Saharan trade. It seems logical that such a network must have included the forest and its margins.

Conclusion

Why did cities and states develop in the West African rainforest and its fringes? Why should there have been such apparent cultural brilliance beneath the trees?

Inevitably, many explanations have drawn on external trade to explain such developments and indeed, the approximate contemporaneity of these socio-political changes with the appearance of Arab trade across the Sahara, has been seen as particularly significant. Such an external stimulus hypothesis remains untested, however, until we know far more about the archaeology of the first millennium AD within the forest. Until then, it seems more likely that the origins of these cities and states lay within the forest and its margins, rather than remote from them. The forest possessed abundant resources and the potential to produce a food surplus. By early in the first millennium AD there existed an iron-based technology sufficiently sophisticated to exploit the forest environment more successfully than ever before. The diversity of this technology in time gave rise to functional specialization and this, probably combined with population pressure, helped to stimulate the growth of larger more heterogeneous communities. It was possibly population pressure also that led to an increasing stratification of society, in which control of resources fell into fewer and fewer hands. In some places this culminated in centralization of authority on one individual, whose power was frequently reinforced by the assumption of spiritual as well as temporal attributes. This state of affairs seems to have existed by the early second millennium AD, if not before.

It would be a mistake, however, to ignore the part that trade, both local and external, did undoubtedly play in the development of urbanization and state formation in this zone. Although this role has been frequently over-emphasized (see for example Morton–Williams 1972), there is no doubt that it was an important contributory factor in the growth and situation of cities in the West African forest. Thus there was a tendency for such cities to be located in the northern part of the forest or even in the southern savanna, so that they were situated at the interface between donkey transport and human portage. There was also a tendency for them to be located on important trade-routes. In addition, the growth of states within this zone was undoubtedly stimulated by control of trading resources or of the trade-routes. As Law (1978) has shown, for instance, West African rulers in later times drew their incomes both directly and indirectly from trade. Furthermore, imported commodities provided both status symbols to enhance the position of local rulers and a source of movable wealth which could be used to reward supporters. It is little wonder that rulers of the West African forest so often insisted that it was their right to control the trade that was carried on in their territories. Trade, however, was only one factor in the appearance of cities and states in the West African forest and, like the other factors, its origins were probably within that zone rather than external to it.

Chapter 7

The edge or the centre: cities of the East African coast

'Kilwa is one of the most beautiful and well-constructed towns in the world.' It was in such words that the much-travelled ibn Battuta described, first-hand, 'the principal town on the [East African] coast' in 1331. Apparently, Kilwa (properly called Kilwa Kisiwani), situated at 9° South in what is now Tanzania, was no isolated phenomenon. Over 1500 kilometres along the same coast, at 2° North in what is now the Somali Republic, was Mogadishu, of which ibn Battuta could write that it was 'a very large town' (Freeman–Grenville 1975: 27–31). Ibn Battuta can be seen as representing the scholarly opinion of the fourteenth-century Islamic world. By the end of the following century, however, there were less-scholarly visitors from the Christian world of Western Europe and they also seem to have been impressed with the towns and cities that they saw on the East African coast. Thus in 1498, the unknown author of the *Journal of the first voyage of Vasco da Gama, 1497–1499*, could compare 'the town of Malindi' (now in Kenya) with Alcouchette, a town near Lisbon in his native Portugal (Freeman–Grenville 1975: 55–6). Indeed, it is in the account of Vasco da Gama's second voyage (1502) by Gaspar Correa (written long after the event about 1561 but Correa probably visited the East African coast in 1514) that there occurs one of the most detailed early descriptions of an East African coastal city. This again concerns Kilwa and is worth quoting extensively:

> The captain-major told the pilot to show him the port, and that he wished to go to Quiloa, which he did; and on sighting it, he entered the port with the whole fleet, which anchored round the city, which stands on an island which is surrounded and encircled by the sea water, but on the land side there is little water, which at high tide is knee-deep. The city is large and is of good buildings of stone and mortar with terraces, and the houses have much wood works. The city comes down to the shore, and is entirely surrounded by a wall and towers, within which there may be 12,000 inhabitants. The country all round is very luxuriant with many trees and gardens of all sorts of vegetables, citrons, lemons, and the best sweet oranges that were ever seen, sugar-canes, figs, pomegranates, and a great abundance of flocks, especially sheep, which

150

have fat in the tail, which is almost the size of the body, and very savoury. The streets of the city are very narrow, as the houses are very high, of three and four stories, and one can run along the tops of them upon the terraces, as the houses are very close together: and in the port there were many ships. (Freeman–Grenville 1975: 66)

Clearly, the East African settlements would be expected to make a favourable impression on sailors several months outward bound from Portugal, who had just endured a long journey through the eastern Atlantic on a dull if not inadequate diet. Nevertheless, historical sources like those that have just been quoted demonstrate that settlements of considerable size had already developed on the East African coast before the middle of the present millennium. Archaeological and oral traditional evidence supports this conclusion. The main problem is to explain how such a development took place, a development that was limited to a 10-kilometre-wide strip comprising 2400 kilometres of coastline, from the southern Somali Republic to northern Mozambique and including various offshore islands, to which should be added the Comoro Archipelago and the northern coasts of Madagascar.

The distinctive culture that eventually developed along this coastal strip was at least in part urban, mercantile, literate and Islamic. Modern scholars often refer to it as the 'Swahili Culture', because of the fact that many of the inhabitants of the strip are now speakers of one or another form of ki-Swahili, a north-eastern Bantu language rich in loan-words from Arabic and from a number of other languages; although it is doubtful if the term 'Swahili' should be used in contexts earlier than the last few centuries. Nonetheless, whatever one calls the developments along this coast prior to the arrival of the Portuguese, they were clearly impressive. One can sympathize, although not necessarily agree, with the view that: 'There is little doubt that this civilization, at its zenith in the fourteenth century, was the highest in the material sense that has existed until recent times in Black Africa' (Chittick 1971: 136). Given sentiments such as these, it is not surprising that external stimulus has been advanced as the most likely explanation for such developments. Thus we have been told that: 'We should picture this civilization as a remote outpost of Islam, looking for its spiritual inspiration to the homeland of its religion ...' (Chittick 1971: 137). In recent years, however, this 'colonial-origins interpretation' has been rejected by some (Allen 1980: 361; see also Allen 1974), and new archaeological evidence is suggesting that the development of the coastal culture owed far more to its African origins than to any external influences, contributory though these obviously were (Horton 1983). It is an interesting case of the edge or the centre: was the East African coast merely the edge of the Islamic world, or was it the centre of an indigenous African development of substantial significance? There are exciting indications that the latter was the case.

Geographical location and environmental factors

The area with which this chapter is concerned consists of a long, narrow coastal strip. Extending from about 2° North to about 16° South and perhaps to as much as 22° South, this comprises a very large part of the eastern coast of Africa (Fig. 7.1). The cultural developments with which we are concerned seem to have been

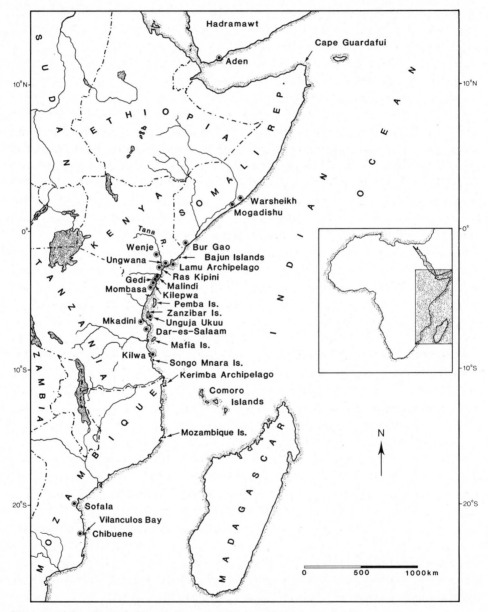

Fig. 7.1 Archaeological sites on the East African coast.

restricted to that coast and not to have penetrated inland. Therefore, these developments clearly had a maritime and mercantile orientation. This situation contrasts very much with that of West Africa, discussed in Chapters 5 and 6. In that case, cities and states developed in the northern savanna before they did so in the forest and when such developments did take place in the forest they were always inland and often in or near the forest-savanna ecotone. Until the advent of European sailors in the fifteenth century AD the coast itself remained relatively remote and was not the scene of any major cultural developments. The explanation of this contrast can be found in the different locations and maritime environments of these two coasts. On the West African coast, the Atlantic Ocean was a barrier rather than a highway, until changes in sailing technology in the fifteenth century allowed European ships to sail against the prevailing northerly winds, that had previously made it impossible to return from a visit to this coast. In addition, the more environmentally attractive parts of the West African coast are a very long way from Western Europe: a voyage from Lisbon to Ghana, for instance, would be roughly 5500 kilometres as indicated by modern marine distance tables (Caney and Reynolds 1976). The East African coast, on the other hand, has the very great advantage of ease of navigation from maritime southern and western Asia. The winds and currents of the Indian Ocean are seasonal and reverse their direction every six months. Thus, from December to March the prevailing wind on the East African coast is the north-easterly monsoon but from April till November it is the south-westerly monsoon. This enables voyages to be made from the southern Arabian coast, the Persian Gulf and the north-west coast of the Indian subcontinent. Furthermore, it is possible to return to such places from the East African coast within the same year. Also, the length of such a voyage need not be so great as those to the West African coast. Thus a voyage from southern Arabia to the Kenyan coast, for example, would be roughly 2800 kilometres (Caney and Reynolds 1976). Currents also contribute to the ease of navigation to and from East Africa. In particular, the main Indian Ocean currents flow east-west, reversing each half year, and thus make it easier to sail to and from western and southern India, Indonesia and South-East Asia. These differences between the west and east coasts of Africa have had a marked effect on their respective histories: on the west coast, seaborne contact with the outside world has existed for only 500 years but on the east coast such seaborne contact has certainly been a reality for over 1000 years (e.g. Ricks 1970) and, judging by the first-century *Periplus of the Erythraean Sea* (Freeman-Grenville 1975: 1–2), such contact also existed during the Roman period.

As might be expected, the environment varies to some extent within this long coastal strip. To its north, the coast of the Somali Republic from Cape Guardafui to round about Mogadishu is open, has few harbours and an arid hinterland. From Mogadishu to near the present border of the Somali Republic and Kenya, harbours are more numerous but the coast is still exposed, hazardous and somewhat barren. From the Somali Republic/Kenya border, however, there is a fair rainfall and the coast is frequently broken by drowned valleys that provide natural harbours. Along the northern part of this coast there is also a string of coral islands, close offshore, known as the Bajun Islands. Between them and the mainland is a sheltered channel and at their southern end are the important islands of the Lamu Archipelago: Pate, Manda, and Lamu (Fig. 7.2). Only a narrow, mangrove-fringed channel separates these islands from the mainland and from here southwards there is an almost continuous offshore coral reef, providing protected inshore waters along which there are many small creeks and harbours. Much of the mainland coast is fringed with mangrove swamps but there are also stretches of steep sandy beach, the foreshores of which shelve so gradually that at low tide the sea retreats for long distances. The more protected of these beaches provide ideal landing places: the lightly-built sewn boats that were traditionally used along this coast could be anchored on the high tide and unloaded at low tide while they were high and dry. On the islands along the coast, fresh water could usually be obtained by digging wells and consequently they provided obvious locations for human settlements. To the south, the large ocean islands of Pemba, Zanzibar and Mafia, which are

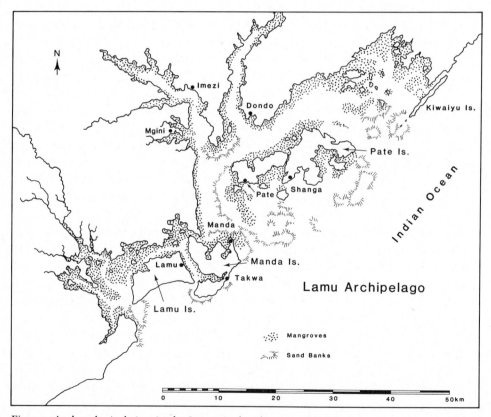

Fig. 7.2 Archaeological sites in the Lamu Archipelago.

less than a day's voyage from the mainland, are particularly important but south of them are the inshore islands of Kilwa and Songo Mnara and further south again the Kerimba Archipelago and Mozambique Island, which are the last islands of the coral reef. South of the Zambezi estuary the temperature of the sea is too low for coral growth and beyond Vilanculos Bay the coast is not relevant to the discussion here (Chittick 1971: 108–9; Garlake 1978a: 95–6).

In general, the environment of the coastal strip from the southern Somali Republic to northern Mozambique would have been attractive to human settlement. Much of the strip has an adequate rainfall of about 1000 millimetres per year and its maritime, tropical climate has encouraged agricultural exploitation in areas where there are suitable soils. The character of the coast and of its inshore waters and their resources would inevitably have stimulated the early development of coastal shipping and, because of the winds and currents of the Indian Ocean, the people of the East African coast were bound to come into contact eventually with other maritime peoples of that ocean.

In contrast to this narrow coastal strip, the environment of the interior has often been described as relatively unattractive. Behind the generally narrow, sandy, often fertile coastal plain, where fresh water could be found in many places, lies a gently rising belt of dry, scrubby, savanna bushland, 100–200 kilometres in width, difficult to penetrate, harbouring tsetse flies and offering little to interest people adapted to a maritime environment. Furthermore, there are few permanent rivers, and of these only the Zambezi, at the southern end of the coastal strip under discussion, is navigable for any distance (Chittick 1977: 185–6). Consequently, it has been assumed that, although there was contact between the coast around Sofala and the Zimbabwe Plateau, there was little between the Kenya/Tanzania coast and the interior until recent centuries. For instance, Posnansky has attempted to explain the apparent slightness of contact between the East African lacustrine peoples and the coast (Posnansky 1975: 217). The reality of this situation will be discussed later but it is appropriate to question here the basic idea of an attractive coast and an unattractive hinterland. A closer examination indicates a rather greater variety of environment, at least in some areas. Thus, in the stretch of coast and hinterland between Bur Gao (Somali Republic) and Ras Kipini (Kenya) Horton (1983) has identified a remarkable range of ecological areas. These include: *driest woodland*, the predominant inland vegetation which was traditionally exploited by pastoralist groups; *riverine woodland*, where the fertile land of perennial river flood-plains has been densely settled by agriculturalists; *lowland wet forest*, along the narrow coastal strip, and traditionally important both because of the large wild animals it contained and because of its agricultural production; *coastal swamps*, filled with rapidly-growing mangroves that were an important source of building timber; *island savanna*, where the soils are poor but fresh water is available at locations close to the sea; and *the reefs and littorals*, which fringe the coast and support rich fishing grounds.

The East African coast possessed a variety of resources that must have played an important part in the cultural developments of the last millennium or so. To begin with, there was probably substantial food production in some areas. By the middle of the present millennium, millet, rice, sorghum, cocoyam, coconuts, bananas, citrus fruits, pomegranates, figs, sugar-cane and vegetables were being grown. Fat-tailed sheep, goats, cattle and chickens were raised, fish and probably other marine foods were extensively exploited and bees were kept in specially constructed hives (Chittick 1971: 136; Chittick 1974b: Vol. 1, 236, 248–51; Chittick 1977). It should be noted, however, that the list of food plants given here includes a number that were introduced to East Africa from India and South-East Asia at some unknown date before the arrival of the Portuguese on this coast (Gwynne 1975). The most important indigenous African plant foods were probably limited to millet, sorghum and a number of vegetables. Nevertheless, it is apparent that in time food resources became extensive and varied, and that the environmental diversity of this coast must have necessitated the early development of local exchange systems handling these resources. Indeed, by the nineteenth century the East African coast was exporting an increasing quantity of grain, including sorghum, maize and sesame (Spear 1978: 81–2). The last two grains were introduced to Africa and the volume of this trade was probably much greater than in previous centuries but it is probable that grain export to the dry lands of southern Asia had a long history. Thus Chittick (1977: 217) has claimed that records in Aden show that rice was imported there from Kilwa prior to Portuguese contact, and he has suggested that much of the rice actually came from Madagascar.

It was on the basis of other East African resources, however, that the remarkable export trade of this coast was principally developed. Most important of these seems to have been ivory, already mentioned in the *Periplus of the Erythraean Sea* in the first century AD (Freeman-Grenville 1975: 2) and still important in the nineteenth century (Spear 1978: 81–2). The *Periplus* also mentions rhinoceros horn and tortoise-shell, which actually would have been obtained from sea-turtles, and pearly shell (on the latter see Chittick 1981: 186). At a later date there were, in addition, numerous other resources that became important trade commodities during the first half of the second millennium AD. From Sofala, in the south, came gold and copper, both of which must have been obtained from the interior. From the Horn of Africa, to the north, came frankincense and myrrh, aromatic gum resins much sought after in some parts of the world. From more central parts of the East African coast, mangrove poles, ebony and perhaps other timbers were exported, as was iron, ambergris and sandalwood. Slaves were probably exported from the more northerly parts of the coast (Chittick 1977) but there was no substantial slave trade till late in the eighteenth century. Nineteenth-century exports included other commodities which may or may not have been exported at an earlier date but which are an additional indication of the range of East African resources. Excluding some of obviously late introduction, these comprised copal (a tree resin used in the manufacture of varnish), hides, wax, hippopotamus teeth, coconuts, orchilla (a vegetable dye), beans, shell and livestock (Spear 1978: 82).

Some of these non-food resources would have been important for local use as well as for export. This would have been the case with iron, copper and perhaps ivory. Timber would also have been important, particularly for building construction and shipbuilding. In addition, there were other resources that were of local significance only or formed the basis of production for trade with the interior. Thus the coral reefs and the outcrops of coral on dry land, provided important building materials: both stone and lime for mortar and plaster. A considerable amount of cotton was grown on the coast and manufactured locally into cloth. Even silk was produced. Furthermore, the coast probably produced salt and also made use of some of the numerous marine molluscs, either as raw material for beads or, in the case of cowries, perhaps for both decoration and currency. The various species of coastal palms provided many things: including coconuts, wine, rope, matting, and caulking for ships. Finally, the coast had fresh water, so often a problem in the dry hinterland and so essential both for human settlements of substantial size and for ships' crews anxious to replenish their supplies (Chittick 1977).

With such a diversity of resources, it is difficult to understand why so many settlement sites of the first half of the second millennium AD were abandoned, in some cases prior to the arrival of the Portuguese. What were the constraints that could have operated on this seeming coastal paradise to produce such disasters? The most important was probably dependability of water supply. Horton (1983) has pointed out that in the Lamu Archipelago, for example, the best fresh water is found in wells closest to the sea, where it floats on the heavier, salt water. If the wells are overdrawn or the well shafts made too deep, the supply becomes salty and unusable. In fact, the wells at the abandoned settlements on these islands are today salty. As there is little or no surface water on this coast, the only alternative to such fragile well supply would have been rainwater cisterns: never a very reliable source. Another constraint on this coast would have been soil fertility, which in some places seems to have been poor and may well have been easily damaged by agricultural exploitation. A range of tropical diseases could have provided further problems and one would very much like to know whether or not the extensive maritime contacts of this coast complicated this situation still further, by introducing and reintroducing such diseases as smallpox, cholera and plague. There were also other constraints. Problems of overland communication, particularly with the interior of East Africa, have probably been exaggerated in the past but nevertheless it would have been so much easier to move by boat along the coast that communications would have tended to be concentrated around a coastal axis. The coast-clinging locations of the larger settlements, however, would have rendered them vulnerable to attack, both by those inland peoples over whom they had no control and from the very sea that brought them so much of their livelihood. That vulnerability was clearly demonstrated during the fifteenth and sixteenth centuries AD by the Galla and the Zimba from inland and by the Portuguese from the sea (Chittick 1977: 229–31).

Sources of information

Compared with West Africa, the East African coast is well supplied with sources for the study of its past. Historical documentation is particularly extensive, commencing with the first-century *Periplus of the Erythraean Sea*, which is now thought to have been an official report by an agent of the Imperial Roman government (Mathew 1975: 154) and may in fact be as late as the third century (Chittick 1981: 185). Another early historical source is Claudius Ptolemy's *Geographia*, originally written in about AD 150 but in its final form probably an edited compilation of about AD 400 (Freeman-Grenville 1975: 3). Both of these sources contain information about the East African coast but it is difficult to use them and there is no further information with which to compare their contents until the ninth and tenth centuries. From then on there is a series of documentary sources, mostly from Arabic authors but with some contributions from Chinese writers, until the arrival of the Portuguese on the East African coast at the end of the fifteenth century. Perhaps the most informative of these historical sources are al-Masudi in the tenth century, al-Idrisi in the twelfth century, and ibn Battuta in the fourteenth century. Only the last of these, however, includes an eyewitness description of some of the East African coastal cities and none of these sources provides the wealth of ethnohistorical evidence to be found in the sixteenth-century accounts of Portuguese writers, such as the anonymous authors of the *Journal of the first voyage of Vasco da Gama, 1497–1499*, and *The voyage of Pedro Alvares Cabral to Brazil and India*. Other similarly useful early Portuguese sources include Gaspar Correa's *Lendas da India*, João de Barros' *Da Asia* and an account written by Duarte Barbosa but there are also a number of other sources (Freeman-Grenville 1975). Collectively, these Portuguese sources give us a surprisingly detailed picture of some of the towns of the East African coast in the middle of the present millennium. In addition, there is information from a variety of European sources concerning the last few centuries before colonial rule, although the greater part of this dates only from the nineteenth century.

All the historical documentation discussed so far, however, consists of the writings of outsiders, visitors to East Africa who at times either did not understand or did not wish to understand what they had observed, or even writers who had never been there at all and were merely repeating information that was at best secondhand. It is fortunate, therefore, that it is possible to complement such sources with the oral traditions of the people who lived in some of the East African coastal settlements. Best known of these is the 'Kilwa Chronicle', available both as a sixteenth-century Portuguese version and as an

Arabic version that was copied in Zanzibar in 1862. Collectively, these two versions record the traditions about Kilwa that were current in the earlier sixteenth century and give some account of its origins (Chittick 1974b: Vol. 1, 13–14). There are also a number of other traditional accounts but they seem to have been written down only in the nineteenth or early twentieth century. Perhaps the best known of these is the 'History of Pate', written down about 1910 but covering the period back to 1204 (Freeman-Grenville 1975: preface, 241). Although some of these traditional histories include useful information concerning the life of the coast, much of them consists of a mixture of myth and genealogy which is difficult to use historically. For example, a substantial literature has grown up on the question of how one should interpret the Kilwa Chronicle story of a 'Shirazi' immigration to the East African coast from the Persian Gulf (e.g. Chittick 1965; Allen 1982). Nevertheless, oral sources do have something to tell us and Thomas Spear with his work on the traditions of the Mijikenda peoples and J. de V. Allen on those about Shungwaya have been able to demonstrate how some of the inland traditions indicate a far greater indigenous contribution to the coastal culture than the better-known oral histories would suggest (Spear 1978; Allen 1983). The fact remains, however, that historical sources, whether oral or documentary, are not able to explain adequately the origins and early development of the coastal cities. To throw more light on that problem, we must turn to the very substantial archaeological evidence that exists.

Archaeological research on the East African coast commenced shortly after the Second World War and it is fortunate that its principal exponents – James Kirkman, Neville Chittick, Peter Garlake, Hamo Sassoon, Thomas Wilson and Mark Horton – have all been able fieldworkers, most of them excavating extensively. Nevertheless, until recent years work has tended to focus on sites with stone ruins, rather than looking at these sites in their overall archaeological context. This has resulted from the assumption that the remarkable stone buildings on the coast derived ultimately from the cultural influence of Muslim immigrants from the Persian Gulf and parts of the Arabian coast, an assumption that the emphasis on stone buildings has in turn helped to perpetuate. It was admitted that such Arab immigrants had been rapidly integrated with the local people, but it was insisted of the resulting culture that:

> ... one can detect little in it that appears to have been derived from the indigenous peoples of the continent. On the hinterland of the coast this civilization had little impact, except for the stimulus to trade ... From the point of view of the homelands of Islam, from which they drew their spiritual inspiration, these cities represented a frontier of the civilized world. (Chittick 1977: 219)

This interpretation of the culture of the East African coast has already been referred to (p. 151). The important point here is to realise that it is this view that has shaped much of the archaeological research that has been conducted on this coast. While the coastal cities were thought of as semi-alien trading centres clinging to the edge of the African continent and relevant only as the periphery of an international trading system, there seemed little point in investigating their relationship with the 'indigenous' settlements of the coast or the interior, nor in bothering much about their local antecedents. As a result, much of the archaeological survey and excavation conducted on this coast has concentrated on the highly visible stone ruins of mosques, tombs and houses (e.g. Kirkman 1954; Kirkman 1959; Kirkman 1963; Kirkman 1964; Kirkman 1966; Garlake 1966; Chittick 1974b; Wilson 1978; Wilson 1980) and there has been relatively little investigation of those parts of settlements built in mud, wood and thatch or of those settlements only built of such materials. In addition, the presence of complex architectural features, of inscriptions, of coins and of imported glazed earthenwares, porcelains, glassware and beads has tended to concentrate much of the work on artefact studies and particularly on the detailed chronology that they have provided. By the 1970s, however, the emphasis was changing, as some archaeologists came to realise the basically indigenous character of the coastal culture and began to see the cities as part of an ongoing process of African social and economic change, rather than the result of alien colonization (e.g. Allen 1980; Horton 1980; Wilson 1982). These contrasting approaches in East African coastal archaeology must be kept in mind when reviewing the archaeological evidence relevant to the origins of urbanization and state formation.

Allen (1980) has listed 173 settlement sites with stone ruins, between Warsheikh (north of Mogadishu) and the Tanzania–Mozambique frontier. In addition, there are sites relevant to our discussion in Mozambique, the Comoro Archipelago and northern Madagascar (on Madagascar see Verin 1976) and there must also be many relevant sites that have no stone ruins and have, therefore, not yet achieved notice. Thus, in total, there must be a large number of sites spread over a great length of coast but most of the archaeological investigations that have been carried out have been on the Kenyan or Tanzanian coasts and, indeed, Kenyan sites have had rather more attention than those of Tanzania. One of the first sites to be excavated was the city of Gedi (Fig. 7.3), on the mainland of Kenya, where Kirkman was able to reveal a curiously skeletal city plan (Kirkman 1954: 185). Thus he was able to demonstrate the layout of its city walls, which clearly represented two structural phases: an earlier city of about 18 hectares and a later, smaller city of about 7 hectares (Kirkman 1975: 239). Within that city were plotted a so-called 'palace', several houses, some of which were concentrated in a group near the palace and a number of mosques and tombs. The excavations were extensive but although the Jamia (or main congregational mosque) and the palace were published in detail (Kirkman 1954; Kirkman 1963) the houses, city walls and other details of this important urban site are still not in print. In particular, it is unclear whether Kirkman's city plan shows all the stone ruins or not. If it does, then it must be the case that much of the apparently empty space on his plan was filled with buildings of mud, wood and thatch: that is to say with the houses of the bulk of the inhabitants. Certainly the strange angular outline of the city walls, which may be compared with that at Shanga (Horton 1980: Figure 3), would suggest that they enclosed tightly an irregular mass of houses (compare Fig. 7.3 and Fig. 7.5).

On the basis of the dating of imported ceramics, some of them excavated from beneath a tomb with an inscription containing a date equivalent to AD 1399 (Kirkman 1960), Kirkman suggested that Gedi was founded in the thirteenth century, abandoned in the early sixteenth century and briefly reoccupied in the late sixteenth century, at which time the inner town wall was constructed (Kirkman 1975: 237–9). Most of the buildings that were excavated were, in fact, of fifteenth-century date and the house-plans that were revealed (Garlake 1966: 194) are of particular interest in throwing light on pre-Portuguese social organization. The coral ragstone houses comprised a number of narrow oblong rooms, averaging about 2.4 metres wide, their width dictated by the maximum

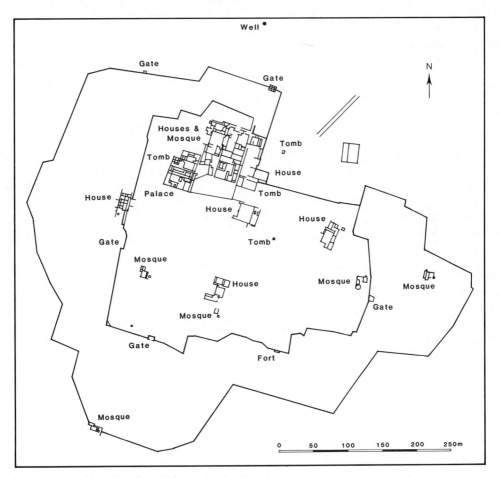

Fig. 7.3 Plan of Gedi. After Kirkman (1964: Fig. 7).

available rafter span (Fig. 7.4). Although there was some variety of plan at Gedi, the basic house-plan both here and in other coastal settlements consisted of two of these long narrow rooms, one behind the other, with the first one fronting on an enclosed courtyard and the rear one opening into two or three smaller rooms behind. None of these rooms had external windows but sometimes there was another courtyard situated behind the smaller rooms. It seems probable that each house was intended for a separate family, with the rooms providing a graded privacy: most public in the front courtyard, most private in the back rooms. As argued by Allen (1979) the stone houses in archaeological sites such as

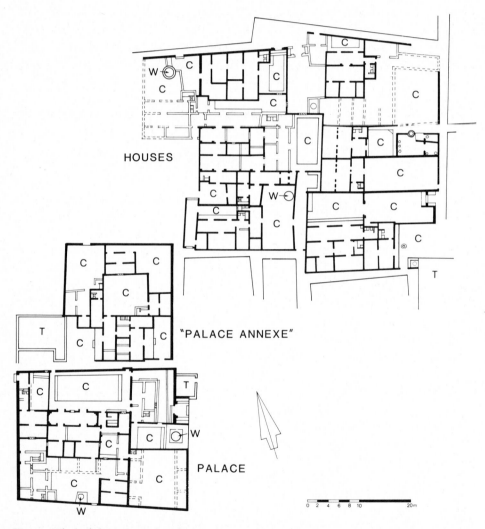

Fig. 7.4 Plan of the centre of Gedi.
C: Court. W: Well. T: Tomb. Original buildings shown solid, alterations in outline. After Garlake (1966: Fig. 76).

Gedi are in the same tradition as the mostly eighteenth-century, stone-built mansions of Lamu, some of which are still occupied. This would suggest that there was already in existence a class of cultured, wealthy, mercantile urbanites (similar to that later known as the *wa-ungwana*) who reinforced their position by reserving to themselves the exclusive right to build their houses in stone, thus making use of what Linda Donley has called 'house power' (Donley 1982). Looking at the Gedi house-plans, it seems as if a number of such families sometimes built their houses in interlocking groups, each group representing a distinct lineage or kin. Certainly such people seem to have lived at a level of material comfort higher than that of most of their contemporaries. Houses had plastered walls, inside toilets, washplaces with bidets, underfloor soakaways and rainwater drains. Indeed, at Gedi one apparent group of houses was identified by Kirkman as a palace. With its monumental arched entrance and its generous provision of courtyard space, this might well represent the houses of a particular lineage who, having become the hereditary ruling family, had adapted their dwellings to suit their new duties (Allen 1979: 24).

Kirkman also excavated at a number of other sites in both Kenya and Tanzania. Most significant of them was probably that of Ungwana, on the northern Kenyan coast near the estuary of the River Tana (Kirkman 1966). Here is the remains of a large walled city covering about 18 hectares and occupied from the thirteenth to the seventeenth century but the excavator concentrated on the mosques and the tombs, although the ruins of some stone houses were present. According to Kirkman's plan, however, extensive areas of this city consisted of empty space (Kirkman 1966: 71) and, as with Gedi, it seems likely that much of this space must have been filled with buildings of mud, wood and thatch. It seems probable that Kirkman's excavation strategy was not designed with this possibility in mind. Thus at Kilepwa, a small thirteenth to sixteenth century settlement near Gedi where he also excavated (Kirkman 1952), the remains consisted of a small mosque, two pillar tombs and a group of houses. According to its excavator, this was 'clearly a family unit, corresponding perhaps to the European manor'. Yet we are also told that 'sherds of *sgraffiato* [imported glazed earthenware of eleventh and twelfth-century date] were found all over the site, so it may have had a large population in the pre-building period' (Kirkman 1975: 239–40). The last phrase is surely significant: it would appear that, to this excavator, a building that was not made of stone was not a building.

Thus, the first major point that emerges when one begins to examine the settlement archaeology of the East African coast is that buildings of mud, wood and thatch must have constituted a large part of some of these settlements and, if this was the case, then the indigenous African contribution to the growth of these settlements must have been far more important than has sometimes been admitted. For example, the town of Songo Mnara, on the island of that name off the Tanzanian coast, must have consisted of more structures than just a collection of uniformly planned stone houses, a so-called palace and several

mosques, loosely distributed within a large walled area. These, after all, appear
to have been recorded without resorting to excavation (Garlake 1966: Figure
74). Similarly, at Kilwa, in the same area, where there have been extensive
excavations, it has been estimated that the city site covers about one square
kilometre but the stone ruins consist of only a scatter of structures. As its
excavator has admitted: 'Many, and perhaps most, of the buildings at Kilwa,
even at the height of its prosperity, were built of mud-and-wattle, evidently in a
similar style to that which can be seen on the coast today. The original settlement
was probably entirely of such buildings ...' (Chittick 1974b: Vol. 1, 24).
However, it appears that the ratio of buildings of stone to buildings of less
permanent materials did vary to a considerable extent from site to site. For
instance, the final phases of Shanga, abandoned in the fifteenth century and
comprising a walled town of some 5 hectares situated on the shore of Pate Island
(Kenya), probably consisted mainly of stone structures (Fig. 7.5). The city wall, 3
mosques, 300 tombs outside the town, other tombs within the town, and 139
houses were all built of stone, leaving some but not much space for buildings of
other materials (Horton 1980). A similar but slightly less convincing case might
be made for Takwa, a comparatively short-lived town occupied during the
sixteenth and seventeenth centuries. Situated near the shore of the Kenyan island
of Manda, this stone-built walled town of a little over 4 hectares in extent
contained a mosque, a well, and 137 other structures, most of which were
probably houses (Fig. 7.6). Allowing for open spaces for gardens and markets,
there were still some empty areas that could have contained mud, wood and
thatch buildings but they were limited (Wilson 1982: Figure 2). In contrast, the
stone remains at Dondo, on the coast of the Kenyan mainland close to Pate
Island, consist of only two mosques, two wells, two groups of tombs and a
building and well suspected to be Portuguese. The excavator of this site has
concluded that this unwalled town, which is about 2 hectares in extent, was
occupied between the fourteenth and sixteenth centuries by people of sufficient
wealth to build lavish tombs and two mosques who were, nevertheless, 'living in
non-stone structures' (Horton 1980). Indeed, a comparable site exists at Mgini,
on the same part of the Kenyan coast. In this case there are scatters of fifteenth
and sixteenth-century sherds over an area of some 10 hectares but there are no
traces at all of stone buildings (Horton 1983). I am also indebted to Mark Horton
for information about a third site on this same piece of coast, that is relevant to
this discussion. The site of Imezi consists of a large oblong enclosure with a
single gate. Within the enclosure is a mosque and a well and nothing else; but a
surface scatter of pottery, both local and imported, indicates occupation in the
fifteenth and sixteenth centuries. Horton points out that the plan of this site is
similar to that of enclosures found on the southern Kenyan and northern
Tanzanian coast, which are believed to have been built by the Segeju in the
nineteenth century. It was the Segeju, a mixed Bantu-Galla people, who in 1590
stopped the Zimba in their tracks as they were in the very act of attacking the city

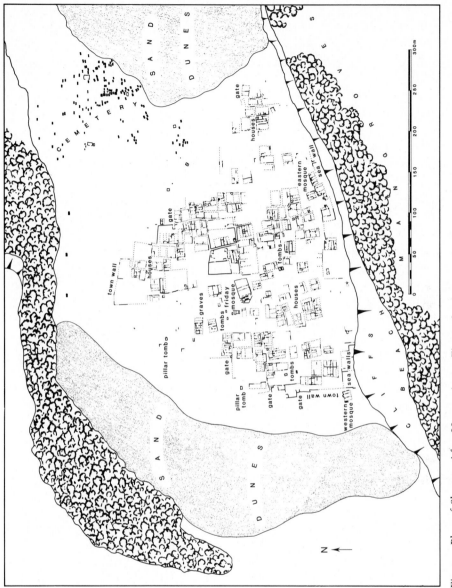

Fig. 7.5 Plan of Shanga. After Horton (1980: Figs. 2 & 3).

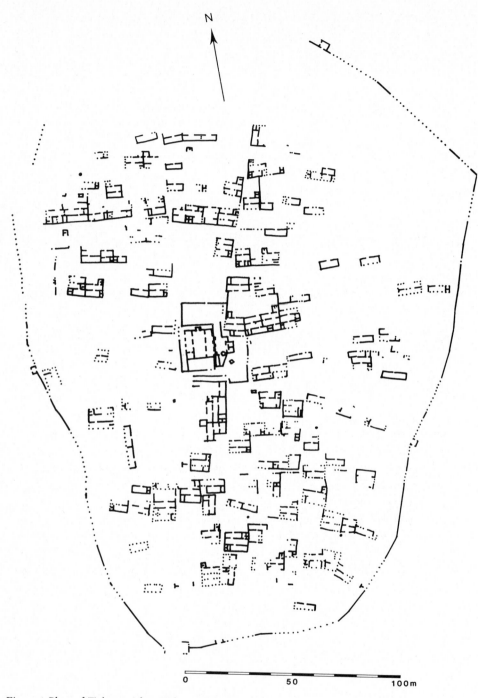

Fig. 7.6 Plan of Takwa. After Wilson (1982: Fig. 2).

of Malindi (Kirkman 1964: 93). It is difficult to escape the conclusion that mud, wood and thatch buildings, and the African peoples who built them, contributed greatly to the East African coastal settlements.

If mud, wood and thatch buildings meant indigenous contribution, does this imply that stone buildings meant alien contribution? At one time many writers would have answered with a categorical 'yes'; now the question would be considered far more difficult to answer. Garlake, seeking the origins of the architectural styles of the stone buildings, could find various parallels in different parts of south-west Asia but came to the overall conclusion that before the eighteenth century the architectural style of the coast was, 'to a large extent, indigenous to the coast' (Garlake 1966: 116). Clearly, alien influences might be seen in the fourteenth-century palace and commercial centre of Husuni Kubwa, just outside the city of Kilwa, with its audience court, open-sided pavilion, bathing pool, domed and vaulted roofs, and its Arabic inscriptions (Fig. 7.7). The same might be said of the nearby site of Husuni Ndogo, a large rectangular enclosure of unknown purpose that could have been a mosque, a market, or a barracoon. These sites, however, are exceptional and the stone buildings of the coast have a far wider range of quality. Thus, Takwa, which Allen has called 'the poorest stone settlement so far excavated', consisted mainly of small houses whose 'comfort was little if any greater than that enjoyed by mud and thatch dwellers (and well below that enjoyed by some mud and thatch dwellers today)' (Allen 1979: 27). Indeed, as has already been argued, stone buildings, whether houses, mosques, tombs or other structures, were only one aspect of these coastal settlements. Thomas Wilson has shown that coastal sites in the southern Somali Republic and Kenya can be subdivided into five classes, based on their size, ranging in area from over 15 hectares to less than 2.5 hectares. Significantly, the smaller sites tended to have fewer buildings built of stone and tended to lack stone-built houses (Wilson 1982). In this way, we begin to see the stone buildings as an integral part of an overall settlement pattern, rather than as the major features of coast-clinging, trading cities of alien merchants, that some might once have thought them. Moreover, when that settlement pattern is analysed for location and date, it appears that this supposedly coast-clinging culture has 30 per cent of the southern Somalian, Kenyan and Tanzanian sites located in places that have 'poor or no harbours' (including six that are actually inland) and it also appears that 'although . . . Swahili society became overwhelmingly sea-oriented, it looks as if it might have been much less so in earlier centuries' (Allen 1980: 362).

In the end, the question of the significance of stone-building is bound up with the question of the origin of these coastal settlements and here the archaeological evidence is beginning to be helpful. The earliest indications of settlements relevant to the present discussion belong to the closing centuries of the first millennium AD. In spite of the mention by the *Periplus of the Erythraean Sea* of an East African port called Rhapta, it has not been possible to identify this early-first-millennium site (Datoo 1970) and none of the supposed discoveries of early-

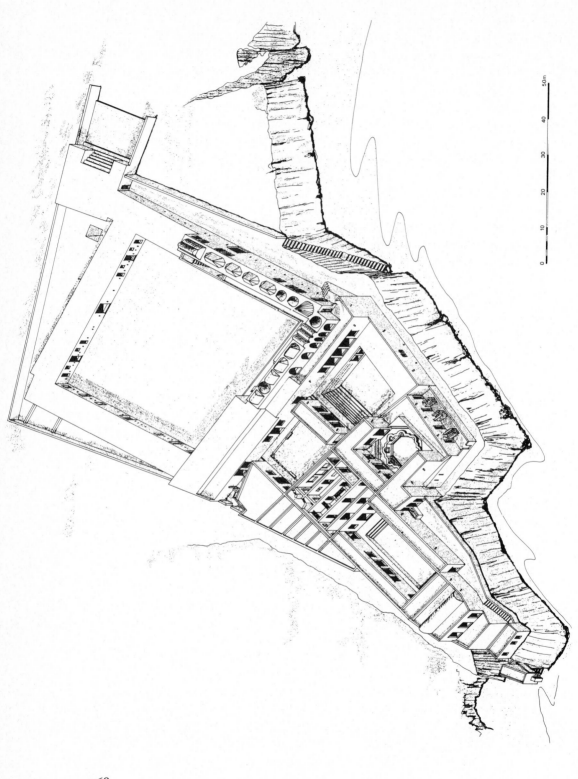

Fig. 7.7 Axonometric reconstruction of Husuni Kubwa. After Garlake (1966: Fig. 69).

first-millennium coins on this coast are thought to be reliable (Freeman–Grenville 1960; Chittick 1966). Some of the best-published early evidence that is reliable is that from Kilwa, where it is thought settlement commenced about AD 800. Neville Chittick's excavations at Kilwa are probably the most important and certainly the most extensive on the East African coast but they are particularly interesting for the light that they throw on the early occupation of this site. The dating of the various excavated 'periods' was partly on the basis of imported ceramics, indicating that the settlement had overseas trading contacts from its very beginning. In Period Ia (ninth century (?) to about 1000) buildings were first of all lacking and were then in mud and thatch with a little coral stone used with mud mortar. Similar buildings were found in Period Ib (about 1000 to late twelfth century) and it was only in Period II (late twelfth to late thirteenth century) that the first substantial building in lime-mortared stone was found, at the same time that the first coins appeared. It was, indeed, only in Periods IIIa and IIIb (late thirteenth century to about 1400, and about 1400 to about 1500, respectively) that the real floruit of stone-building occurred. Chittick interpreted the evidence as indicating that the earliest settlement was a pre-Islamic fishing village, with Islam beginning to arrive in Period Ib and becoming firmly established by Period II, by which time 'Kilwa had become a substantial and prosperous town' (Chittick 1974b: Vol. 1, 18–19, 28–9, 235–41). Although it might be remarked that it is difficult to visualize a fishing village that indulged in overseas trade and smelted iron, the early evidence at Kilwa suggests the gradual development of both building techniques and settlement complexity rather than any sudden arrival of these cultural characteristics from outside.

Another site with evidence of early settlement is that of Manda, on the island of the same name in the Lamu Archipelago. This has also been excavated by Neville Chittick and has provided enough information to demonstrate the existence of a flourishing town as early as the ninth century. Again there was evidence of overseas trade from the beginning of the settlement but in this case buildings of both mud, wood and thatch and of stone were constructed, the stonework of the latter sometimes being set in lime mortar, sometimes in red earth. There were also 'sea walls', some of which were of massive masonry that was set without any kind of mortar. In addition, unique for the East African coast, there were structures made of burnt brick set in mud mortar and it has been suggested that these bricks could have been imported from the Persian Gulf, perhaps as ships' ballast. From the overall evidence, Chittick has deduced that the town was founded by immigrants from the Persian Gulf and that at least some of the inhabitants were Muslim from the settlement's beginning (Chittick 1967; Chittick 1971; Chittick 1984). In contrast to Kilwa, the alien input in the earliest periods at Manda would seem to have been greater. However, that evidence should also be compared to that which has recently become available from Shanga, on Pate Island. There, Mark Horton has established a building sequence from mud, wood and thatch to stone, with imported ceramics present throughout. This sequence extends from the ninth century to the fifteenth; mud mortar and stone buildings first appear in the eleventh century and lime-mortared stone buildings not perhaps until the thirteenth century, becoming more important in the fourteenth century (Horton 1980). Again, this sequence seems to emphasize the indigenous evolution of coastal culture, as also does the increasing number of sites that now appear to have an early origin. Thus, Mombasa has been shown to have been occupied by about AD 1000 (Sasoon 1980); Pate by about AD 900 (Wilson 1982: 214–15); and, most remarkable of all, Chibuene, an occupation site far away on the southern Mozambique coast, was probably occupied by the late eighth or early ninth century and contained imported glazed earthenwares similar to those from the early periods at Kilwa and Manda (Sinclair 1982).

Therefore, it seems that early sites are so widely distributed along the coast and so likely, as research progresses, to prove more numerous that one would have to postulate a huge migration from southern Asia to attribute their simultaneous development to external stimulus. Such stimulus doubtless existed to some degree but its relative importance is perhaps indicated by the very small percentage of total pottery in excavated sites that is constituted by imported wares (as little as 0.2 per cent in Period Ia at Kilwa (Chittick 1974b: Vol. 2, 302)). The bulk of the recovered sherds are of indigenous wares and in the earliest periods there is considerable uniformity amongst pottery from widely separated areas. For instance, Chibuene has some indigenous pottery that is similar to the 'Early Kitchen Ware' at Kilwa and Manda (Sinclair 1982: 155, 162). Indeed, Horton (1983) reports that similar pottery has also been found in the basal levels of Unguja Ukuu (Zanzibar Island, Tanzania) Mombasa, Pate, Lamu and Shanga and he has compared it with the undated pottery from Wenje, 100 kilometres up the Tana River in Kenya (Phillipson 1979). If such similarities prove on closer examination to be confirmed, then the preponderantly Bantu origins of the East African coastal culture will surely have been established once and for all?

Subsistence economy

It remains to examine the archaeological evidence reviewed above, to ascertain what can be learnt from it about the origins of cities and states on the East African coast. The basis of these developments must have been the subsistence economy, so what does the archaeology have to tell us about this? In the past, archaeologists have not been very interested in the subject, probably because the ethnohistorical sources from the end of the fifteenth century onwards are so informative and, indeed, it is these which have already been used to discuss the food resources available at the middle of the present millennium (p. 156). However, we cannot be sure that the descriptions in such sources can necessarily be applied to the end of the first millennium AD, unless we also make use of such archaeological evidence as is available. For example, the cultivation of sorghum in the eleventh and twelfth centuries is presumably attested by the recovery of carbonized sorghum from a layer attributed to Period Ib at Kilwa (Chittick 1974b: Vol. 1, 52–3). Also the early deposits at Kilwa produced plentiful evidence for the eating of fish and shellfish, while the filling of a well dated to the late thirteenth to fourteenth centuries produced the mandible of a very immature camel, an animal not now found on this coast and not recorded there historically (Chittick 1974b: Vol. 1, 28, 43, 98). The evidence from Chibuene is of rather more value, although it is as yet only published in a preliminary form. It indicates the presence of sheep and cattle and the exploitation of fish and shellfish at this site, dating from the end of the first millennium AD (Sinclair 1982: 152, 162). Another site that promises to yield very important evidence when it is fully published is Shanga. At this site seafood seems to have been particularly important and included fish of reef, inshore and deep-sea type, dugong, turtles and shellfish. In addition there were domesticated cattle, sheep or goat, camel and fowls. Cats and dogs were also kept and the hunting of wild animals contributed a very small part to the diet. Mark Horton, to whom I am indebted for this information, concludes that a mixed economy was being practised, although there seems to be no evidence available for the extent to which plant foods were used (Horton 1983).

The last site worth mentioning in the present discussion is Manda. Excavations there have provided evidence of goat or sheep, of cattle and of the domesticated cat. In addition, dugong, turtles and fish were exploited. Camel was present and a very little land game was hunted. Again, this site seems to lack evidence for plant food (Chittick 1984).

This is little enough evidence but it does suggest that by the end of the first millennium AD, when the earliest-known of the coastal cities and towns were first settled, there already existed a varied mixed economy in which the resources of both sea and land played a part. Livestock husbandry and fishing could between them have provided ample animal protein but, apart from the sorghum from Kilwa, the archaeological evidence can tell us nothing about the contribution that plant food must also have made to the diet. This is unfortunate, particularly because of the important role that may have been played by a number of plants originating in South-East Asia, that were introduced to East Africa possibly about the beginning of the first millennium. It is tempting to see the introduction of Asian rice, coconuts, bananas, sugar-cane and some other plants, as a direct result of the settlement of Madagascar by Indonesians about 2000 years ago (Shepherd 1982). In a paper that some regard as controversial, Shepherd has argued that the southern end of the East African coast, particularly the Comoro Islands, played an important early role in the development of the coastal culture. If this was so, then perhaps one may be justified in seeing the enhancement of the coastal subsistence economy by the South-East Asian food plants as a vital factor in the growth of the coastal settlements. Whether such a view is justified or not, however, it is clear that by the second half of the first millennium AD, the subsistence economy of the East African coast must have been able to produce a surplus adequate to support a growth in social complexity. In particular, the environmental diversity of the coast and its hinterland probably allowed, and even encouraged, great flexibility in the subsistence economy. Thus, the camel bones that have been recovered from some coastal sites might be an indication of resource exchange with nomadic pastoralists of the dry interior.

Technology

Archaeological evidence from the East African coastal sites clearly indicates considerable technological sophistication. The main problem in interpreting that evidence is to determine how much of it originated from overseas trade, rather than from local expertise. Nevertheless, indigenous technology seems to have attained a remarkably high level. As might be expected, iron was both smelted and forged and evidence of this occurred in the earliest deposits at both Kilwa and Manda. In addition, at a somewhat later date these same sites produced evidence of working in copper-base alloy, in the form of crucibles occasionally containing traces of copper (Chittick 1974b; Chittick 1984). Perhaps most important of the uses to which this metal was put was the minting of coins, which were produced at Kilwa, at Zanzibar and at Mogadishu. Many of these have been recovered from coastal sites, along with rather less common coins from other parts of the world of Islam and even from China.

The most remarkable aspect of East African coastal technology, however, was undoubtedly seen in building craftsmanship. Coral was quarried, either on land or from the offshore reefs, and used both as dressed pieces and as rubble mixed with a lime-mortar that was obtained by burning coral. Plaster and concrete were also made with a similar lime base. Stone structures were built which were sometimes of considerable height and scaffolding, presumably with lashed mangrove poles, seems to have been well understood. Roofs consisted usually of a combination of mangrove rafters, stone and concrete but they could also be supported with columns and beams or could consist of vaults or domes (Fig. 7.8). Doors and windows usually had fitted woodwork, most houses possessed internal pit-toilets and washing places and drainage was provided both inside and outside of some buildings (Garlake 1966). All of this implies considerable craftsmanship: there must have been quarrymen, lime-burners, stone-masons, plasterers and carpenters, to name only the most obvious. In addition, some knowledge of architectural skills was obviously present. Whatever the contributions to this overall expertise from alien sources, the bulk of the actual work must have been done by local craftsmen and it is worth pointing out that the so-called 'pillar tomb' that is so common on the East African coast has no known parallels elsewhere.

A particularly important part of coastal technology must have been concerned with boat-building, although there is as yet no archaeological evidence to support this claim. Nevertheless, sewn-boats were recorded on this coast by the *Periplus of the Erythraean Sea*, nearly 2000 years ago (Freeman–Grenville 1975: 1–2) and the Portuguese (who knew as much about boats as anybody) noted them with interest at the end of the fifteenth century (Ravenstein 1898: 26). All the materials needed to construct these boats were available on the East African coast and it is likely that the *dau la mtepe* and the *mtepe*, with their sewn hulls and matting sails, were in fact often constructed on this coast. Although we now have very few details of how they were built (Chittick 1980; Prins 1982), the frequent graffiti of such boats, scratched into the wall plaster of houses and mosques up and down the coast, show how important they must have been to many people (Garlake and Garlake 1964; Chittick 1974b: Vol. 2, 266–7). It should be noted that boats constructed in the manner that these were, stand up particularly well to the rough treatment of the frequent strandings caused by the character of much of the eastern coast (Fig. 7.9).

Of the variety of other crafts practised on the coast, probably the most important was the spinning and weaving of cotton cloth, suggested by the number of spindle-whorls which occur in contexts dated to the first half of the second millennium. There was also the making of salt by evaporating sea water, for which there is some rather unsatisfactory ninth or tenth to late twelfth or thirteenth-century evidence at Mkadini on the Tanzanian coast (Chittick 1975). In addition, there was carving of ivory and bone, manufacture of shell beads and possibly of semi-precious stone beads, and the production of a range of pottery

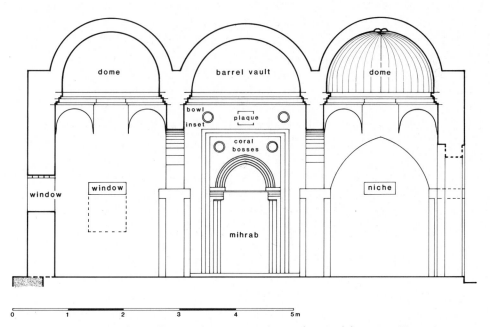

Fig. 7.8 Section through Small Domed Mosque, Kilwa. After Garlake (1966: Fig. 14).

including some with complex painted patterns and including lamps (Chittick 1974b).

It seems that by the end of the first millennium AD there was already a sound technological basis on the East African coast. In the centuries that followed, that foundation was able to support an increasing complexity of technological expertise and this in turn must have led to an increasing functional specialization within coastal society.

Social system

The archaeological evidence on the eastern coast is more explicit on the subject of social organization than is such evidence in some other parts of Africa. We are able to study the plans of a number of settlements, some of them walled, which

Fig. 7.9 Two *mitepe* used by David Livingstone in 1866. From Waller (1874: Vol. 1, 12).

range in size from small villages to large cities. The use of stone for some buildings has left us with clear evidence of the progress which urbanization had made in the area prior to Portuguese contact. Apparently, this was a society where many people lived in towns or cities but where many also remained in the rural areas. One suspects that the level of functional specialization was much higher in the larger settlements, with the bulk of the inhabitants of smaller settlements still engaged in primary production. In addition, the degree of social stratification seems to have been greater in the larger settlements. This is suggested by the range in quality and size of the houses, both within the settlements and between different settlements. At the bottom end of the scale were mud, wood and thatch buildings, about which little is known. Above these were small stone houses of one to three rooms only but with the larger houses provided with toilets, like those at Takwa (Wilson 1982: Figure 2). Higher again were multi-roomed houses with an enclosed courtyard, like some of those at Songo Mnara (Garlake 1966: Figure 74). At the top of the scale were large multi-roomed houses with multiple courtyards and monumental features, such as imposing entrances, like the so-called palace at Gedi (Kirkman 1963: Figure 2). Surely this is a classic example of social and economic stratification fossilized in archaeological evidence? The various houses suggest a society that ranged from slaves or lowly menials, to successful artisans, to wealthy merchants, to ruling merchant princes. There are also signs that social differentiation became more marked with time. For example, building in mud, wood and thatch was at first the most usual practice but building in stone gradually became more common. Also, the so-called palaces of Gedi and Songo Mnara probably originated as a group of interlocking houses belonging to one extended family. These could have been subsequently transformed into a 'palace', by the addition of monumental features, when the head of that family became the hereditary ruler of the settlement (Allen 1979: 24; also this book p. 163). An indication of the elevated status to which some of these rulers eventually aspired, is given by the coins bearing their names that were issued by various rulers, particularly during the thirteenth and fourteenth century. Indeed, at least one ruler seems to have been outstandingly ambitious, if the luxury of the 'palace' of Husuni Kubwa at Kilwa is considered. Perhaps of more general importance, however, is the indication, both from the number of medium-to-large stone houses and from the wide use of imported ceramics, that there came into existence a socially-superior merchant class comparable to the *wa-ungwana* class of recent Swahili towns and cities (Allen 1979; Donley 1982). Indeed, the many stone tombs that were constructed along the East African coast have been interpreted as providing additional evidence of the existence of such a class (Wilson 1979).

It remains to consider the extent to which these social developments along the coast led to state formation. Little or nothing has been said on this subject in the present chapter, largely because the available archaeological literature offers comparatively little relevant information. However, the existence of a few very much larger settlements, and their geographical relationships to neighbouring settlements of medium or small size, suggests that some cities, for example Mogadishu, Pate, Malindi, Mombasa and Kilwa, controlled the territory around them. Indeed, the considerable prosperity apparent in the early fourteenth century at Kilwa has been interpreted as evidence of a considerable extension of Kilwa's authority at that time, so that it included control of the gold trade from Sofala, far to the south in what is now Mozambique (Chittick 1977; on the archaeology of Sofala see Liesegang 1972). A coin minted in Kilwa even got as far as Great Zimbabwe (Huffman 1972: 362 and Plate 1). It seems most likely that some of the east coast cities did function as small city states from early in the present millennium and that, as time went on, some of these city states came to dominate others. Documentary sources since the sixteenth century suggest a political pattern of this sort, with Zanzibar, for instance, controlling much of the coast during the greater part of the nineteenth century.

Population pressures

The distribution and density of old settlements and of settlement sites along the East African coast, suggests that prior to Portuguese contact a long, narrow coastal strip supported a substantial population. Provided with both land and sea resources, and with fresh water available in many places, the coast must have contrasted strongly with the dry lands that characterized much of the interior. Thus the coast could well have provided a stimulus to population growth but with nowhere for excess population to go, other than further along the coast, for it is difficult to believe that coastal peoples would have been willing to adapt to the dry interior. In this way one can perhaps understand the long, narrow distribution of the East African coastal culture. However, the optimum coastal conditions, that must have been one factor in the development of this culture, were not limitless and to both the north and the south those conditions gradually petered out. In addition, even within the area of optimal attraction, soil character and water availability varied considerably, making some localities more attractive for settlement than others. In such circumstances, population pressure could well have been one of the factors that brought about the development of the coastal cities and city states.

However, the situation was probably more complex than this. The hinterland is not all dry, unattractive country. In some places, for instance, there are fertile areas and it is likely that, as research progresses, increasing evidence will be found of close contacts between the inhabitants of those areas and the peoples of the coast. For the moment, the similarity between some of the early indigenous pottery of the coast and that from Wenje, 100 kilometres up the Tana River, raises interesting possibilities, although the Wenje material still needs to be dated (p. 170). It is particularly interesting to learn, however, that the eighth and ninth centuries AD could have been a period of severe drought in the interlacustrine regions (Herring 1979: 48) and, if this were so, it is possible that the flow of several of the east coast rivers might have been reduced. It must be no coincidence that this was at the very time when the earliest of the settlements that grew into the coastal cities and towns were being established (Horton 1983).

Ideology

As with the cities and states of the West African savanna (Chapter 5), Islam was the major ideological factor in the cities and states of the East African coast. At every site there is at least one stone-built mosque and, significantly, the main congregational mosque usually occupies a central position within each settlement. In addition, the care and expense that was lavished on the building of mosques reinforces the impression that Islam filled an important role in coastal life. The adoption of Islamic beliefs by East African coastal communities was undoubtedly of great significance to those communities. Islam was the faith of urban, mercantile, literate South West Asia and its adoption brought East Africa into a huge common market; in particular it ensured commercial and cultural intercourse with the Arab lands to the north. It is surely significant that in Swahili the word for 'civilization' is *ustaarabu*, often understood to mean 'becoming like an Arab' (Chittick 1971: 112; Jahadhmy 1981: 10). On the East African coast, to become like an Arab meant to follow Islam, to live in a stone house in a city, and to be involved in trade.

It would be a mistake, however, to imagine that Islam was the primary cause of urbanization and state development on the East African coast, whatever the extent of its later influence on those developments. As in the West African savanna, Islam seems to have arrived after the initial changes had already taken place. Thus, in the fourteenth century when ibn Battuta visited Kilwa, Islam had already been accepted there but in the tenth century when al-Masudi visited the East African coast its occupants were clearly animists: 'Every man worships what he pleases, be it a plant, an animal or a mineral' (Freeman-Grenville 1975: 31–32, 16–17). The archaeological evidence now available from some sites confirms that Islam was usually adopted only some time after initial settlement. For example, before the building of the first congregational mosque at Shanga, which occurred in a period that ended about the middle of the thirteenth century, its site had been used for secular purposes, probably for housing (Horton 1980). At Gedi there was similar evidence of a 'pre-mosque period', with the site of the congregational mosque probably occupied by houses until as late as the middle of the fifteenth century (Kirkman 1954: 8–9, 14). At Kilwa its excavator thought that Islam began to arrive in the eleventh to twelfth centuries (Chittick 1974b) although, in contrast, it is thought probable that some of the inhabitants of Manda were Muslim from the time of its earliest settlement in the ninth century (Chittick 1984). Overall, we can conclude that although Islam played a very big part in the developments on the East African coast, it did not necessarily inaugurate them. So far as ideological input was concerned, unknown animistic beliefs probably contributed substantially. The strength of those beliefs may be judged from the fact that East African Islam has remained markedly syncretic until recent times.

External trade

So considerable is the archaeological evidence for long-distance external trade that has been found in the East African coastal sites, that it has often dominated discussion of those sites and greatly influenced interpretations. The cities and city states of the East African coast have been seen as a direct response to the growth of that trade. According to this view, the coastal cities grew up as the trading bases of agents for overseas mercantile interests. As such, they originated as colonial settlements of alien and sophisticated culture, clinging to the coast of a hostile continent, in which they had no interest other than the acquisition of primary products for export. In the long term, the settlements had little influence on the interior of the African continent and themselves were gradually Africanized as intermarriage took place between the colonists and the indigenes. In the process, however, African people adopted some aspects of the alien culture and there evolved that distinctive coastal culture which in recent times has come to be called Swahili.

The above picture might be a little overdrawn but will the available archaeological evidence support an interpretation along these general lines? Certainly, the evidence of long-distance, overseas trade is remarkable. The greater part of this consists of imported ceramics, material that is quite distinct from African potting traditions and can usually be assigned both to an area of origin and to an approximate date. At Kilwa, for example, the earliest deposits of the ninth and tenth centuries contained Islamic glazed wares that probably originated somewhere in the Persian Gulf area or were trans-shipped in that area. Although the types of ware changed with the passage of time, and the places from which they came also changed to some degree, such Islamic glazed wares continued to be imported till well after Portuguese contact. In addition, from about the thirteenth century Chinese porcelains began to arrive in Kilwa, indeed from about the fourteenth century onwards they equalled or exceeded the quantity of Islamic glazed wares. It is probably the occurrence of these Chinese porcelains, both at Kilwa and at other East African coastal sites, that has most profoundly convinced archaeologists of the extent of the long-distance trade of this coast. No doubt the porcelains were trans-shipped several times but the distance involved is still most impressive. However, imports other than ceramics have also been found in East African coastal sites. At Kilwa, for instance, glass vessels and beads of glass, carnelian and other semi-precious stones occurred widely distributed through time. Copper kohl sticks (metal rods for the application to the eyelids of antimony as a cosmetic) were probably also imported. The carnelian beads and perhaps the glass beads probably came from western India, the other items from various parts of the Islamic world (Chittick 1974b; Davison and Clark 1974). Furthermore, this whole collection of trade-goods consists only of those which happen to have survived in the archaeological record. As was the case with the trans-Saharan trade discussed in Chapter 5 (p. 117), one wonders about the imports that have left no trace. For instance, it is thought that cloth would have been one of the principal imports, particularly high quality cloth and coloured cloth (Chittick 1977: 216). Such a commodity could have been drawn from a very wide area indeed.

Why did overseas merchants supply such things to the East African coast? What did they get in return? Basically, they were tapping the natural resources of the African interior, as has already been discussed when examining the available resources of East Africa (p. 156). These primary products included ivory, rhinoceros horn, tortoise-shell, gold, copper, frankincense, myrrh, mangrove poles, ebony and other timbers, iron, ambergris, sandalwood and slaves, not to mention other commodities about which there is less certainty. Many of these exports would have come from deep in the African interior but the imported goods have not been found in the interior; with the notable exceptions of very small quantities of Chinese porcelain of the type known as 'celadon', which reached the site of Zimbabwe in the fourteenth century, and of some later Chinese wares which have been found at other sites on and south of the River Zambezi (Chittick 1977: 216).

What sort of a trade could this have been that gathered so many African resources but gave nothing in exchange? The answer lies partly in the differential preservation of the archaeological evidence, for not only would imported cloth not have survived but we would know very little at all about the exports without historical sources. Nevertheless, this does not explain why imports that do survive in the archaeological deposits of the coastal sites, are not in general found in the interior: after all, Chinese porcelains are tough material. The only explanation that seems possible, is that the pattern of trade was more complex than a direct, simple exchange of overseas goods for products of the African interior. Chittick has put his finger exactly on this problem, by distinguishing not two categories of goods that were traded, that is to say imports and exports, but four categories. These consist of: (1) the African goods sought for export; (2) the goods imported for trade with the interior; (3) the goods imported for use in the coastal towns; (4) the goods produced in those towns for trade with the interior (Chittick 1977: 215). Thus, the East African coastal settlements were acting as entrepôts: that is to say as commercial centres of import, export, collection and distribution, at a more complex level than might be expected in a simple coastal trading town. Two sorts of imports arrived from overseas: cloth that could be traded into the interior and luxury goods that were sought by the more successful occupants of the coastal cities and towns for prestige purposes. These exotic manufactures, of which the glazed earthenwares and the porcelains and some other items are all that has survived, were probably restricted by both economic and social factors to the coastal elite. To trade with the peoples of the interior, the merchants of the coastal settlements used much of the cloth that had been imported from overseas but they also transported into the interior considerable quantities of cotton cloth manufactured in the coastal settlements. In addition, before the thirteenth century, beads of marine shell were manufactured on the coast and large numbers of cowrie shells collected. Both of these were probably used for the inland trade, although imported glass beads seem to have taken the place of the shell beads in later times (Chittick 1977: 216).

It is also likely that the coastal communities traded some of their agricultural surplus into the interior. Nomadic pastoralists, residual groups of hunter gatherers and even the farmers of the drier areas would probably have welcomed such additions to their diet. Very likely they would also have welcomed salt that was probably produced in substantial quantities on the coast. In return for these various commodities, the inhabitants of the inland gave the primary products that the coastal merchants sought and which they, in turn, exported to the lands overseas.

It should be observed that a key factor in this somewhat complex pattern of trade was local input, of primary products and manufactures that originated from the coast itself. As has already been suggested (p. 156), environmental diversity and the consequent unevenness of resource distribution, must have necessitated the early development of local exchange systems on the East African coast and between it and its hinterland. In particular, coastal trading in small vessels could be expected to have developed early, on a coast so suited to inshore navigation. Some indication of this local trade network was found at Kilwa, where stone vessels made of a distinctive chlorite-schist appeared from about the eleventh to twelfth centuries onward. These are thought to have originated probably in Madagascar (Chittick 1974b: Vol. 1, 237). In addition, it was no doubt because of such a local, coastwise trading network that Kilwa was able to profit from the export of gold, from the Zimbabwe Plateau, by the southern Mozambique coastal settlement of Sofala (p. 176). Indeed, it seems that the more successful of the coastal cities, like Kilwa, were successful not only because of their location on trade-routes connecting the interior to overseas markets but also because of their location on coastal trade-routes which enabled them to act as collecting points where local products could be bulked and as distribution points from which prestigious imports could be dispensed.

Thus, it is probably not the case that the East African towns and cities resulted simply from the development of external trade with overseas markets. Certainly such trade had a substantial influence on their subsequent history but that trade was only part of a complex network involving local exchange systems that almost certainly pre-dated the overseas connections. As to the origins of these settlements, the situation was probably far more complex than has sometimes been claimed. Trade was obviously a factor of some importance but to treat the settlements as alien trading colonies is to ignore the existence of a number of other factors that, as we have seen, suggest a basically indigenous origin.

Conclusion

The processes of urbanization and state formation on the East African coast have sometimes been treated as though they resulted from a classic case of external stimulus. In particular, the larger settlements of this coast have been regarded as Islamic trading cities, founded by colonists who originated from the Persian Gulf area. Such a view has held that this coast was significant only as the edge of the wide Indian Ocean trading world, to which it supplied the products of the African interior and from which it received some of the products of the most sophisticated cultures of that time. Unfortunately, this interpretation has been arrived at by looking at the results rather than at the causes of the remarkable East African coastal developments.

Obviously external trade was extremely important to the settlements of this coast, no doubt there were some mercantile colonists from outside, but what was there that already existed on this coast to attract such attention? This question cannot be answered by excavating the more remarkable stone-built settlements of the thirteenth to fifteenth centuries, which is where so much of the archaeological field research on this coast has been concentrated. It is doubtful if it can even be answered by excavating the important settlement deposits of the ninth and tenth centuries, that have now begun to command more attention. The answer must lie in the investigation of coastal settlement archaeology during the last millennium BC and the first millennium AD, a task that, as yet, has scarcely been commenced. In addition, the large coastal settlements of the first half of the second millennium AD would undoubtedly be better understood if they could be viewed in the context of the whole settlement pattern of which they formed a part: in short, archaeologists have to look for and investigate the smaller settlements that were contemporary with such places as Kilwa, or Gedi, or Shanga. Already there are indications that, when these things are done, it will be found that the indigenous contribution to cultural development on the East African coast was more substantial than previously thought and that the origins of the East African coastal culture were African not Asiatic. We have seen that there probably existed a strong subsistence base, capable of producing a surplus, encouraging local exchange networks. There is also the possibility that the introduction of the South-East Asian food plants had a catalytic effect on coastal cultural evolution. To these things should be added the existence of a sophisticated technology, capable of encouraging functional specialization, and there should also be added the possibility of complex population pressures. As yet, there is little relevant evidence available from archaeological sources but surely it is significant that, at the end of the first millennium AD, similar pottery was in use both at widely separated coastal settlements and, apparently, inland?

It is also significant that such early coastal sites show a gradual change from construction in mud, wood and thatch to stone and that some of the later coastal sites remained substantially settlements of mud, wood and thatch buildings, some of the lesser important ones almost entirely so. In addition, so widespread were these coastal settlements that a really massive immigration would have to be invoked, if they are to be explained as alien foundations. It seems reasonable to conclude that the large settlements of the East African coast were not merely the edge of an outside world but the centre of remarkable cultural developments that were of African origin.

Chapter 8

A question of economic basis: Great Zimbabwe and related sites

Great Zimbabwe is one of the best-known and perhaps one of the most ill-used of the archaeological sites of Africa. Its fame is such that it has given its name to the country in which it is situated, the country formerly known as Rhodesia and before that as Southern Rhodesia. Its ill usage has had both intellectual and physical dimensions and started at the moment that it first became known to Europeans. The first such visitor was a German geologist, Carl Mauch, on the third of September 1871. After giving a careful account of the impressive stone ruins that he had seen, Mauch felt it necessary to explain their presence deep in the African interior and he did so in the following words:

> I do not think that I am far wrong if I suppose that the ruin on the hill is a copy of Solomon's Temple on Mount Moriah and the building in the plain a copy of the palace where the Queen of Sheba lived during her visit to Solomon. (Mauch, quoted by Summers 1963: 19)

Perhaps it is understandable that a nineteenth-century European, flushed with the excitement of something new and unexplained, should grasp at such an unlikely but respectable biblical explanation. Unfortunately, however, the myth of alien origin for the Great Zimbabwe buildings was to survive for a century, even surfacing as a political issue in the troubled times of the 1960s and 1970s (Garlake 1973: 209–10). This was probably because it became psychologically essential for some of the European colonial settlers of this part of Africa. Perhaps the most damaging aspect of the whole African colonial experience was the attempted denial to African peoples of their own cultural heritage, of which the attribution of Great Zimbabwe to outside influence, without a shred of evidence, must be the classic example.

This is not the place to discuss the long controversy about whether the origins of Great Zimbabwe were exotic or indigenous. There was never any doubt about its African origins in the minds of those who really understood the archaeological evidence and the whole subject has, in any case, been discussed extensively by others (for example Summers 1963; Garlake 1973; Garlake 1978a). The controversy has been mentioned here because it has influenced most of the research that has been conducted at this famous site. Intellectually, it has dictated the questions that have been asked by researchers; physically, it has sometimes occasioned both excavations and restoration work that were conducted in such a way as to destroy much of the archaeological evidence, without allowing it to yield the information that it must have contained. Excavations by Theodore Bent in 1891, by Richard Hall in 1902–4, by David Randall-MacIver in 1905 and by Gertrude Caton-Thompson in 1929 were all directed principally at the problem of who built the ruins and when (Bent 1896; Hall 1905; Randall-MacIver 1971; Caton-Thompson 1971). Even the more recent excavations and survey work of 1958 were mainly concerned with the chronological sequence of occupation within the stone ruins (Robinson, Summers and Whitty 1961).

It is only in the last decade or so that archaeologists have begun to ask themselves what the stone ruins of Great Zimbabwe and similar sites represent in social, economic and political terms. In particular, it has been realized that the stone wall enclosures of at least some of these sites are merely the central and most important features of quite large former settlements. At Great Zimbabwe, the recognition of extensive areas of huts densely-packed together outside the perimeter wall, has led to the revision of a population estimate put forward by Peter Garlake in 1973. Instead of an estimated 1000–2500 adults (Garlake 1973: 195), at the time of writing the latest estimate is a total of 18 000 (Huffman 1985a). It is most unfortunate, therefore, that archaeologists have been so obsessed by the stone structures at Great Zimbabwe and related sites that they have virtually ignored other parts of these sites. To demonstrate this point, Sinclair has calculated that of the estimated 600 square metres excavated and published from zimbabwe-tradition sites since the time of Randall-MacIver, all except about 20 square metres have been excavated in and immediately outside stone wall enclosures (Sinclair 1984). Translated into human terms this could mean that 'at least at Great Zimbabwe over 90 per cent of archaeological effort has been focused upon 2 per cent of the population' (Morais and Sinclair 1980: 351). In short, attention has concentrated on the elite and the commoners have been ignored. However, some idea of recent changes in research orientation may be gained from the fact that Huffman's excavations of the early 1970s (p. 197) will, when fully published, provide information about 1200 square metres of commoner areas (Huffman 1985a).

Great Zimbabwe has indeed been ill-used. The only 'mystery' or 'riddle' connected with this site is why it should have taken archaeologists so long to recognize it for what it is. In recent years Huffman has called it 'southern Africa's first town' (Huffman 1977) and others have seen it as the capital of the earliest state in its area (for example, Randles 1972). Far more archaeological evidence will be needed before such interpretations can be more than interesting hypotheses, because we have very little documentary or oral traditional evidence that can inform us directly about sites of the Great Zimbabwe-type. Nevertheless, it would seem likely that these sites on the Zimbabwe Plateau do indicate the presence of both urbanization and state formation during the first half of the second millennium AD. The real 'problem' of zimbabwe-type sites is to explain why and how these developments took place. In particular, there is the problem of the economic basis involved. What economic factors led to a growth in the size of some settlements and to increased centralization of authority? Indeed, how did those factors change so that by the time of late nineteenth-century European penetration there were merely ruins scattered through a rural landscape?

Geographical location and environmental factors

Most known sites of zimbabwe-type are located on the Zimbabwe Plateau, an area of high land much of which is over 1000 metres above sea-level. Situated between about 16° South and about 22° South, this plateau is bounded on the north by the valley of the Zambezi River, on the south by the valley of the Limpopo River, and on the east by an escarpment that runs down to the wide coastal plain of the Indian Ocean. To the west there is no clear boundary but the plateau merges gradually with the Kalahari Desert (Fig. 8.1). Described in this way, it might seem that the area consisted of a high inland plateau isolated from

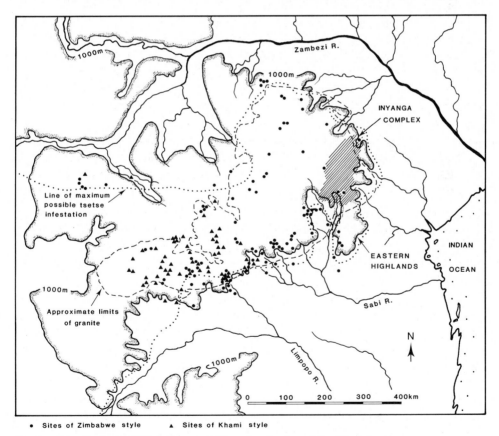

• Sites of Zimbabwe style ▲ Sites of Khami style

Fig. 8.1 Distribution of Zimbabwe and Khami style sites. After Garlake (1973: Figs 25 & 26).

the rest of the world and, indeed, from the rest of Africa. From what we know of its past, however, this was not the case and the people of the Zimbabwe Plateau seem to have had contact, from time to time, with Zambia and southern Zaïre, with the Transvaal and with the Indian Ocean coast. Via this latter contact there were even remote connections with other parts of the world; in earlier times with the Persian Gulf and China, in later times with Western Europe. Contacts outside the plateau were made easier by the many river valleys which dissect its sides, particularly those of the various tributaries of the Sabi and Mazoe Rivers, and by the relatively open character of much of the upland country.

The Zimbabwe Plateau has a wet season from about November to about March and a dry season from about April to about October, although there can be a little winter drizzle during the dry season. Temperatures are highest late in the dry season, slightly lower during the wet season and can fall below freezing-point during the winter months of the dry season. Rainfall tends in general to be heavier in the north and east of the plateau than in the south and west. Geologically, the plateau consists mainly of igneous and metamorphic rocks, particularly of granites and schists, amongst some of which there has been extensive mineralization (Collins 1965: 40–1). As a result of its overall geology, much of the landscape comprises gently rolling plains broken by granite inselbergs and by smooth, bare, rounded hills of granite. Parts of the plateau are deeply dissected by river valleys, however, leaving rugged ranges of hills between them. In addition, there are the mountains of the Eastern Highlands which contrast with much of the rest of the plateau. Variations in the detailed geology of the plateau have resulted in a variety of soil conditions, some soils being remarkably fertile, for instance, while others are very poor. Natural vegetation on the plateau varies a little with both altitude and soil but generally consists of savanna-woodland, the trees being scattered among wide grassy spaces. The trees tend to be more numerous in lower areas but some of the highest parts of the plateau consist of almost treeless grassy plains. The Eastern Highlands, on the other hand, have a variety of mountain trees as well as grassland, while the lowlands off the edge of the plateau are usually thickly wooded, mostly by *mopane* trees (Phimister 1976; Beach 1980).

Much of the Zimbabwe Plateau would have been undoubtedly attractive to early human settlement. Its relatively cool, well-watered and usually lightly wooded plains provided a generally healthy human environment. The plateau also possessed a variety of resources, of which its agricultural and pastoral potential was probably the most important. Extensive pasturage made this into classic livestock country for cattle, sheep and goats, but particularly for cattle. The considerable range in altitude between the plateau and the coastal plain, offered the possibility of transhumant pastoralism for overcoming seasonal variations in pasture and other conditions. Suitable climate and soils also made cultivation important, however, and provided the staple foods of sorghum, millet, beans and squashes (Garlake 1978a: 73). The overall significance of food production amongst the plateau's resources was very clearly indicated by a Portuguese, Antonio Bocarro, writing in the seventeenth century about the Mwene Mutapa state, that seems to have been one of the successors of Great Zimbabwe even though it was situated on the northern not the southern fringes of the plateau. According to Bocarro the land 'abounds with ... millet, some rice, many vegetables, large and small cattle, and many hens ... and the greater number of the Kaffirs are inclined to agricultural and pastoral pursuits, in which their riches consist' (Theal 1964: Vol. 3, 355).

There were, however, other riches amongst the resources of the plateau, of which gold was perhaps the most important and has certainly been the most discussed. This could be obtained both from alluvial deposits and from quartz reefs and became the basis of the long-distance trade of the Zimbabwe Plateau during the first half of the second millennium AD. In addition to gold, other metals could be obtained, including iron, copper and tin. Another resource of some importance was the granite, of which much of the plateau was made. This had the characteristic of continually exfoliating in thin layers from the many rock surfaces exposed to the marked daily changes of temperature. The thin, parallel-sided slabs of granite produced in this way collected as a scree around granite domes and inselbergs and could be readily broken up into rectangular blocks of uniform size. These provided an abundant building material that needed little or no further preparation. Indeed, supplies were virtually inexhaustible because exfoliation could be produced artificially by lighting fires on the rock surfaces and then quenching them with water (Garlake 1973). It was the ready availability of building stone in such a standard size and shape that gave many of the walls of Great Zimbabwe and of some other sites, their unusually regular appearance. For though drystone building was widely practised in prehistoric Africa, at least from Nigeria to the Transvaal, the neat, horizontal coursework of some of the zimbabwe-type ruins is unusual, if not unique. However, the resources of the plateau included other building materials as well as stone. Wood and grass were readily available for house construction and so were clays derived from decomposed granite, that formed the main ingredient of the 'mud' that was widely used in building. Known in this part of Africa as *daga*, this was sometimes of such high quality that it was used to produce free-standing structures that were able to survive considerable exposure. It is not surprising that some of the earlier excavators at Great Zimbabwe quite erroneously called this material 'cement' (Garlake 1973: 19). Also amongst the plateau's resources were clays suitable for potting and soapstone that could be carved. Finally, one should not overlook the importance of the wild fauna which not only provided ivory but could also supplement human food supplies.

Counterbalancing these various resources there were a number of environmental constraints that would have influenced the character of prehistoric settlement on the Zimbabwe Plateau. Probably most important of these was the tsetse fly, particularly *Glossina morsitans*, whose presence tended to discourage human settlement both because of its danger to human health and because it very rapidly killed the livestock on which so many human groups were dependent. Much of the plateau is free of tsetse fly, as Garlake has shown (Garlake 1978b: Figure 1). However, Summers has shown how tsetse distribution could have expanded during the last two millennia, given slightly warmer and wetter conditions (Summers 1967). Although Garlake doubts the evidence for such climatic changes, he has shown nevertheless how the very location of zimbabwe-type sites might have been influenced by the practice of transhumant pastoralism, on the seasonally-fluctuating boundaries of tsetse fly infestation (Garlake 1978b). At best it would seem that the plateau was a peninsula in a sea of tsetse, the limits of which constantly changed in response to a variety of ecological factors. Such circumstances were bound to affect the character of human settlement on the plateau itself.

Another constraint of importance was climatic variability, which often led to what the Shona (the principal inhabitants of the Zimbabwe Plateau) called *shangwa* (Beach 1980: 28–9). This was drought or some other comparable natural disaster. Thus the rains might arrive too late or fail completely or even be so abundant as to destroy the crops. Alternatively, locusts or other pests, whose appearance was climatically linked, might be similarly destructive. The result, according to Beach, was that although four years out of five might have normal rainfall, it was probable that the fifth would see some such disaster. The keeping of livestock (of which goats were the most numerous) was a major part of the strategy for surviving years of that sort, for not only could the animals be eaten during a famine but they could be exchanged for grain with neighbours who had not suffered so badly.

Variable soil fertility was also a constraining factor for plateau settlement. There were undoubtedly some areas of fertile red clay soil and some areas of fertile alluvial soil but large expanses of the plateau were covered by poor sandy soils developed on the granite. Thus it is probable that good land was limited and control of such land may have been one of the means by which rulers exerted economic control over their people (Sinclair 1984). Soil conditions affected not only cultivated crops, of course, but also the nutritional value of the pastures available for livestock. In addition, some parts of the land were agriculturally useless because they consisted of bare rock surfaces or because they were too steep to exploit. In the latter connection, however, the obvious solution was terracing and this was extensively employed in the Inyanga area of the Eastern Highlands during the second half of the present millennium. In that area not only cultivation terraces were constructed on hillsides but also stone-lined pits to house livestock, platforms for dwellings and channels to distribute water (Summers 1958).

Sources of information

Our knowledge of Great Zimbabwe and of comparable sites in the same area is heavily dependent on archaeological evidence. However, there is also both historical documentation and oral tradition that throw some light on the subject. Stone buildings on the Zimbabwe Plateau were certainly known to the Portuguese, who in the sixteenth and seventeenth centuries AD had trading posts along the Zambezi River and on adjacent parts of the plateau. The Portuguese were interested in controlling the gold trade from this part of Africa and sought to do so by exerting their influence on the Mwene Mutapa, a ruler of part of an area of similar culture that covered most of the country from the Zambezi to the Limpopo and from the Kalahari to the Indian Ocean. Unfortunately, the Portuguese had little direct knowledge beyond the area of the Mwene Mutapa's own Karanga kingdom, on the northern end of the Zimbabwe Plateau. Nevertheless, it is thought probable that this kingdom was one of the successor states to the one which had been centred on Great Zimbabwe, on the southern part of the plateau. If this was the case, then the Portuguese descriptions of what they observed in the territories of the Mwene Mutapa must have some relevence for our understanding of Great Zimbabwe itself. In addition, the Portuguese actually seem to have been told about Great Zimbabwe, although they never visited the place themselves. Their secondhand account was originally published in 1552 and provides an important if somewhat confused description, which is worth quoting in part:

> There are other mines in a district called Toróa, which by another name is known as the kingdom of Butua, which is ruled by a prince called Burrom, a vassal of Benomotapa, which land adjoins that aforesaid consisting of vast plains, and these mines are the most ancient known in the country, and they are all in the plain, in the midst of which there is a square fortress, of masonry within and without, built of stones of marvellous size, and there appears to be no mortar joining them. The wall is more than twenty-five spans in width, and the height is not so great considering the width. Above the door of this edifice is an inscription, which some Moorish merchants, learned men, who went thither, could not read, neither could they tell what the character might be. This edifice is almost surrounded by hills, upon which are others resembling it in the fashioning of the stone and the absence of mortar, and one of them is a tower more than twelve fathoms high.
>
> The natives of the country call all these edifices Symbaoe, which according to their language signifies court, for every place where Benomotapa may be is so called; and they say that being royal property all the king's other dwellings have this name ... When, and by whom, these edifices were raised, as the people of the land are ignorant of the art of writing, there is no record, but they say they are the work of the devil, for in comparison with their power and

knowledge it does not seem possible to them that they should be the work of man ... The distance of this edifice from Sofala in a direct line to the west is a hundred and seventy leagues, or thereabouts, and it is between 20° and 21° south latitude ...

In the opinion of the Moors who saw it, it is very ancient, and was built there to keep possession of the mines, which are very old, and no gold has been extracted from them for years, because of the wars. (João de Barros, as translated by Theal 1964: Vol. 6, 267–8)

Garlake is of the opinion that the place being described was Great Zimbabwe and, allowing for the fact that the information was already some years old when de Barros published it, this description suggests that this important urban site was already a ruin by the end of the fifteenth century (Garlake 1973: 53).

The de Barros description is the nearest that historical documentation comes to providing us with details of any value about Great Zimbabwe but it was based on information obtained at a time that was already too late to record the place as a functioning settlement. To understand the economic, social and political organization of this place, it is necessary to draw heavily on later Portuguese accounts of the Mwene Mutapa and other states, none of which were centred on exactly the same area as that on which Great Zimbabwe was situated. Also it is necessary to turn to oral tradition but here again there are problems. Great Zimbabwe was at its most prosperous about 600 years ago, which is a long time for oral traditions to have any real value. In addition, it is probable that the Ngoni invasions of the 1830s, and other tribal movements during the nineteenth century, caused something of a break in those traditions. Thus when Carl Mauch reached the site in 1871 he found people living there who seemed to know little about its history, significance and purpose. Nevertheless, sufficient oral traditions exist to demonstrate that Great Zimbabwe was built by the ancestors of the present Shona people, for whom it apparently formed an important political and religious centre. From these traditions it has been possible to reconstruct something of its religious significance (Garlake 1973), its social organization (Huffman 1981) and its position in Shona history as a whole (Beach 1980).

It is archaeological evidence, however, that has the greatest potential for informing us about Great Zimbabwe and similar sites (Fig. 8.2). Great Zimbabwe is the largest of an extensive group of stone ruins situated on the high granite country of the Zimbabwe Plateau. It has been estimated that about 150 ruins built in the Great Zimbabwe style, or in the later Khami style, survive in this area (Fig. 8.1) and that perhaps as many as another 50 have been destroyed since the 1890s (Garlake 1970a: 497; Garlake 1973: 162). Outside of the area, many more such sites have been located by fieldwork in Botswana and northern Transvaal (Huffman 1985a). The characteristic feature of the zimbabwe-style sites is the presence of single or multiple enclosures of drystone walls, which are

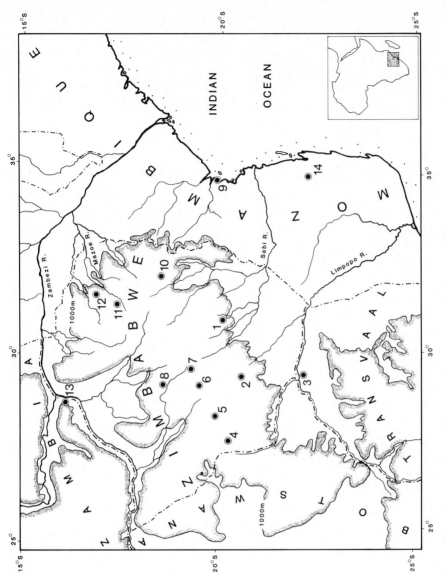

Fig. 8.2 Principal sites in the Zimbabwe region.
1: Great Zimbabwe. *2*: Chumnungwa. *3*: Mapungubwe. *4*: Leopard's Kopje. *5*: Khami. *6*: Dhlo Dhlo.
7: Naletale. *8*: Mtelegwa. *9*: Sofala. *10*: Chipadze's Ruin (Harleigh Farm). *11*: Nhunguza. *12*: Ruanga.
13: Ingombe Ilede. *14*: Manekweni.

usually free-standing and broad-based relative to their height. These walls are either constructed of regularly coursed, dressed masonry or of poorly coursed masonry and both types of walling are often found on the same site. Occasionally the walls are decorated with courses of stonework set in a chevron or herring-bone pattern, or (in the case of Great Zimbabwe) with courses of darker stone. Other typical architectural features are also to be found, including rounded bastions, stepped platforms and upright monoliths. The walls are usually built of granite blocks but on sites where granite was not available they are constructed of whatever stone was to hand. These stone-walled enclosures were evidently intended as 'containers', for apparently they usually sheltered small groups of circular huts with solid *daga* walls and thatched roofs. Alternatively on occasions they may have sheltered granaries (Huffman 1981: 6) or even groups of religious emblems (for example the Eastern Enclosure of the Hill Ruin at Great Zimbabwe).

Sites of this type have come to be called 'zimbabwe' (*madzimbabwe* is the more correct plural form) because this is what the Shona themselves called them. This word has been said to be a contraction of *dzimba dza mabwe*, meaning 'houses of stone' and has also been claimed to be derived from *dzimba woye*, meaning 'venerated houses', a phrase usually used to describe chiefs' houses or graves (Garlake 1978b: 479; Garlake 1973: 11). Shona linguists, however, regard both these interpretations as erroneous and point out that *dzimbahwe* itself means court, home or grave of a chief (Huffman 1985a). Most of these sites are situated on the Zimbabwe Plateau and within the modern state of Zimbabwe, which takes its name from the most famous of them. To avoid confusion, it has become customary amongst archaeologists and others to refer to this, the largest and most researched of these sites, as 'Great Zimbabwe'. However, sites of the same type do occur in more distant locations and there may well be more examples of this sort than have yet been reported. The most notable of such sites is Manekweni (or Manyikeni) situated on the coastal plain of Mozambique, only 50 kilometres from the Indian Ocean and some 270 kilometres from the nearest other known zimbabwe. This site consists of a single stone enclosure built of poorly coursed limestone blocks. The enclosure is subdivided by internal walls and contains traces of occupation in the form of an eroding hut floor of *daga* and two middens. Outside of the stone ruin there is extensive evidence of habitation in the form of low mounds, most of which are middens (Garlake 1976a). Another outlying site of zimbabwe-type has been found on the Songo Plateau, near the Cabora-Bassa Dam in central Mozambique (Ramos 1980).

Great Zimbabwe is by far the most outstanding of these sites. It consists of two main areas of stone ruins: a group of enclosures clustered around the boulders at the top of a precipitous granite hill and another group of enclosures on the far slope of an adjacent valley. Much of the 'Hill Ruin', as it has been called, consists of small enclosures separated by narrow twisting passages but at one end is the large 'Western Enclosure', which is bounded by walls over 9 metres high, that are capped by turrets and monoliths. This enclosure contained deposits over 4 metres in depth, made up of the remains of a succession of *daga* structures, and had room for about fourteen dwelling huts. At the other end of the Hill Ruin is the 'Eastern Enclosure', which is much smaller than the Western Enclosure, and is bounded on one side by a high stone wall that was originally capped by two courses of decorative stonework. The ground inside this enclosure slopes steeply upwards, it was originally terraced and supported groups of stone platforms in which were set some of the large number of monoliths that have been found in this enclosure, including some of soapstone which were surmounted by carved birds (on the soapstone birds from Great Zimbabwe, see Huffman 1985b). The most remarkable of the ruins in the valley, is a large stone enclosure with a maximum diameter of 89 metres, which has been variously called the 'Temple', the 'Circular Ruin', the 'Great Enclosure' and the 'Elliptical Building' (Fig. 8.3). Garlake, who prefers the last of these names, has described its outer wall as 'by far the largest single prehistoric structure in sub-Saharan Africa' (Garlake 1973: 27). This wall is 244 metres long and, at its greatest, 5 metres thick and 10 metres high. It has been estimated to contain 5151 cubic metres of stonework. Parts of the wall consist of exceptionally sophisticated drystone masonry, comprising the most regular coursing achieved at Great

Fig. 8.3 Great Zimbabwe at the beginning of this century. The Great Enclosure is at right centre and Zimbabwe Hill is in the background.

Zimbabwe and with the top of the wall capped by monoliths and a decorative frieze. Within this enclosure, the space is subdivided by other walls, many of which appear to belong to an earlier period than the outer wall. There is also a large conical tower, about 5.5 metres in diameter and over 9 metres high, built of solid drystone masonry and in itself constituting one of Africa's most remarkable prehistoric structures. Spreads of *daga* within the enclosure suggest that parts of its interior were originally occupied by *daga* structures, most of them probably huts. The remainder of the ruins in the valley at Great Zimbabwe consists of a series of small enclosures, a number of which were formerly named after early European visitors. Thus there was the 'Mauch Ruin', the 'Renders Ruin', the 'Posselt Ruin', the 'Philips Ruin' and the 'Maund Ruin'. Others had names such as the 'East Ruin', the 'No.1 Ruin', the 'Ridge Ruins', the 'Camp Ruin' and the 'Outspan Ruin' (Garlake 1973: 25–30). Although these have recently been renamed the 'valley homesteads' (Huffman 1985a), their former names are common in the literature.

Investigations at Great Zimbabwe and at other zimbabwe sites have been both architectural and archaeological. Architecturally, it has been possible to demonstrate an indigenous evolution of masonry techniques, at Great Zimbabwe, from poorly coursed to regularly coursed stonework, which finally devolved into uncoursed, loosely piled walling (Robinson, Summers and Whitty 1961). Architectural studies at Great Zimbabwe have also identified a number of distinctive features in the zimbabwe style of building. Thus the poorly coursed, early walls were frequently built among and over boulders, which were incorporated into their fabric. Regularly coursed, later walls, on the other hand, were usually built on level ground free of boulders. Doorways in these later walls were particularly distinctive, having rounded sides and high thresholds that frequently had curved steps, each successive one of which curved more sharply into the doorway, so that its greatest width was at the centre of the doorway and it gradually merged into the walls at the sides. Pairs of semi-circular projections, often called 'bastions', are to be found inside most doorways and passages in later walls and these have the effect of making entrances narrower and longer. Slots in the sides of many of these bastions seem originally to have held upright stone slabs (but see Huffman 1984: 597–8) and similar slabs were also set upright as monoliths: either in the ground, or grouped on low *daga* platforms, or along the tops of some of the walls. Other features associated with the regularly coursed later walling are stepped, curved platforms, perhaps intended either as seats or as display stands for ceremonial objects, and small stone 'turrets', either on the ground within enclosures or on the tops of the walls (Garlake 1973: 21–5).

Archaeological investigations of Great Zimbabwe and at related sites have tended to concentrate on the questions of the date of the stone structures and of the identity of their builders. A considerable amount of attention has also been given to the question of why these structures were built. It now appears that building in stone at Great Zimbabwe belongs approximately to the period from

AD 1250 to AD 1450 (Huffman 1981: 1). The builders were almost certainly descendants of people who had occupied the site since the end of the first millennium AD, a people whose culture was related to that known as the Leopard's Kopje culture, a cattle-oriented culture that possibly originated from south of the River Limpopo (Huffman 1978; Huffman 1982). In particular, Great Zimbabwe seems eventually to have inherited the role of Mapungubwe, a hilltop settlement on the south side of the Limpopo valley, which has been described as 'the first Zimbabwe Culture capital' (Huffman 1982: 146) and seems to have been at its most important in the twelfth century AD. However, the earliest certain evidence of occupation at Great Zimbabwe has been dated to about the fourth century AD (Garlake 1973: 102) and it would appear that the site may have already had a considerable history of occupation before the earliest stone walls were constructed. Why were they constructed? Archaeological opinion seems agreed that all zimbabwe-type stone structures were intended to be indicators of status for the dwelling places of the elite. In short, their first appearance may be regarded as a sign of considerable social and political change. That being the case, it is unfortunate that so much archaeological attention has been given to the stone ruins and so little to the rest of the settlement of which each ruin must have formed a part. As a result, not only has most attention been concentrated on a very small part of the population of these settlements, as Morais and Sinclair have claimed (p. 184), but the impressive character of the stone ruins at Great Zimbabwe has led to a concentration of work on that site while inadequate attention has been given to other zimbabwe sites. Indeed, so single-minded were the earliest excavators, that between them they virtually destroyed the archaeological deposits within the main stone-walled enclosures at Great Zimbabwe. However, both Randall-MacIver (1971) and Caton-Thompson (1971) recognized the necessity to excavate at other sites also, if they were ever to understand Great Zimbabwe itself. In addition, both of these excavators realized that the stone structures at Great Zimbabwe and similar sites were only part of the story. Thus Randall-MacIver wrote in 1906 that: 'It is, properly speaking, the huts which constitute the really essential part of the ruin in every case; the stone wall which the visitor so much admires is only the skin, the huts are the flesh and bone' (Randall-MacIver 1971: 84). Caton-Thompson went further by demonstrating, with her excavations in 1929 at the Maund Ruin at Great Zimbabwe (Fig. 8.4), how an incomprehensible jumble of stone walls made sense when one included in their plan the *daga* huts, of which they were the courtyard walls (Caton-Thompson 1971: Plate 57; Garlake 1973: Figure 3). Even as late as 1973, Garlake remarked of the Maund Ruin excavation that 'this was the first and only time that area excavation was to be undertaken at Great Zimbabwe and it promised an insight into the function of the enclosures and the social organization of their inhabitants' (Garlake 1973: 81). It is only in more recent years at Great Zimbabwe that attention has once again turned to area excavation and that interest has at long last focused on the whole

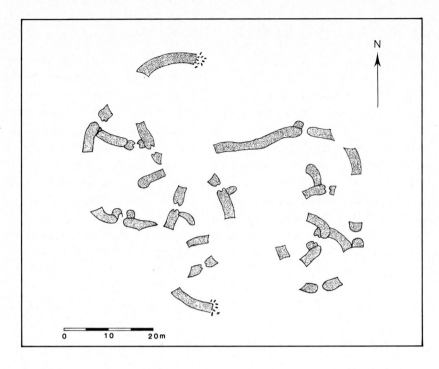

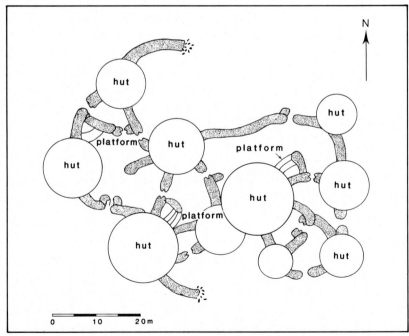

Fig. 8.4 Great Zimbabwe: the Maund Ruin. Above, plan of stone walls only. Below, plan of stone walls and *daga* huts as revealed by excavation. After Garlake (1973: Fig. 3).

settlement, of which the enclosures and their inhabitants formed only a part.

As a result of field surveys and excavation conducted during the 1970s by Thomas Huffman, it now appears that the stone enclosures at Great Zimbabwe were only the central structures within an extensive settlement of *daga* huts. This work has not yet been published in detail but for the first time we do have a plan (Fig. 8.5) of the entire settlement (Huffman 1981: Figure 1) and there has been some preliminary discussion of this work (Huffman 1977). Indeed Beach (1980: 86) has published an oblique aerial photograph of Huffman's that shows an area excavation of densely packed round huts at Great Zimbabwe. These are described in the caption as 'urban housing sites' and readers should note that the photograph has been printed upside-down! As mentioned in the introduction to the present chapter (p. 184), this new work has led to a revision of the population estimate of Great Zimbabwe made by Garlake in 1973. Instead of a population of 1000–2500 adults (Garlake 1973: 195), it is now suggested that the population may have numbered perhaps 5000 adults (Sinclair 1984) and it has been

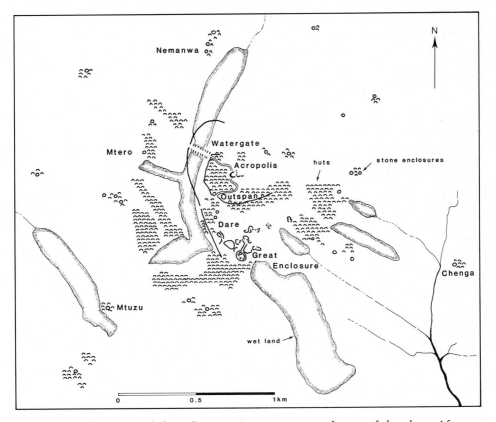

Fig. 8.5 Plan of Great Zimbabwe showing stone structures and areas of *daga* huts. After Huffman (1981: Fig. 1).

suggested that the total population was 10 000 (Morais and Sinclair 1980: 351) and may have been as high as 11 000 (Huffman 1977: 13) or even 18 000 (Huffman 1985a). The conclusion is inescapable: Great Zimbabwe had a concentration of population sufficient for it to be called a town or even a city. Beach has provided us with a description of what it must have been like:

> The effect of having so many people on a single site may easily be imagined: this was urban living. Inside the wall that enclosed the main site, the huts were so close together that their eaves must have been nearly touching. Judging from more modern settlements of the Shona, Zimbabwe must have had an appearance and atmosphere far different from that of today. A great deal of the valley, now green, must have been trampled bare by the passage of feet. From cockcrow to evening, the noise must have been tremendous. In certain weather conditions the smoke from hundreds if not thousands of cooking fires would have created conditions approaching that of smog. And, since so far there is no evidence for more elaborate arrangements, the people cannot have gone very far to defecate, with the result that disease may have been as much a factor at Zimbabwe as in some of its European counterparts. Zimbabwe has often been viewed through an aura of romance, but perhaps a cloud of smoke and flies would be more appropriate from a standpoint of archaeological accuracy. The contrast between the ruler and the ruled must have been quite striking. (Beach 1980: 46)

If Great Zimbabwe was the scene of an urban development on the scale which is now suggested, then the question arises of how it related to the other, smaller zimbabwe sites. Insufficient attention has as yet been given to these sites by archaeologists but, in the last few decades, general fieldwork and the excavation of a small number of sites has begun to throw some light on this problem. Chipadze's Ruin at Harleigh Farm near Rusape, for instance, seems to have been the earlier of two ruins at this site and it has been shown by excavation that it comprised a small settlement with cultural affinities to Great Zimbabwe. Occupied from about AD 1300 to some time after AD 1500, and with an apparent emphasis on cattle-keeping, this settlement consisted of stone screening walls enclosing areas within which were massive *daga* huts (Robins and Whitty 1966). It is difficult to avoid the conclusion that what the excavators investigated were the dwellings of a small political or religious elite and that somewhere nearby must have been the rest of the settlement in which lived the ordinary people who supported that elite.

A similar impression is gained from the most extensively published of the few other zimbabwe sites that have been excavated. Thus both Nhunguza Ruin and Ruanga Ruin are small sites, dated to about the fifteenth century AD, where stone screening walls enclosed only a small number of *daga* huts. Garlake is of the opinion that the adult population of such enclosures could never have been more than thirty and was probably more often nearer ten (Garlake 1973: 164). Several

pieces of evidence at the Nhunguza and Ruanga sites reinforce the impression
that the occupants of the stone-walled enclosures were merely an elite section of
a larger settlement. First, at Nhunguza the largest hut seems to have been
designed as a place for a person of authority to sit in audience, backed by the
symbols of that authority which were housed in an adjacent, secluded room.
Second, at both Nhunguza and Ruanga the pottery consisted of a limited range
of vessels and excluded cooking-vessels and bowls for eating and serving. This
characteristic, which has also been observed at other zimbabwe sites, is
interpreted as indicating that food was prepared outside the stone enclosures,
then brought into them and the vessels later removed. Third, at both these sites
there is a suggestion that there were other habitations outside of the stone
enclosures. At Ruanga it is possible that people of a lesser status than the
inhabitants of the enclosure were living on the Lower Platform, while at
Nhunguza the remains of at least six small huts were found outside of the
enclosure but were not investigated (Garlake 1972). It is from the zimbabwe site
of Manekweni, however, that has come some of the best evidence for social
differentiation in sites of this type. Here there is extensive surface evidence for
occupation outside of the stone enclosure (Garlake 1976a: 29) and excavation
has confirmed the presence of huts in this peripheral area (Morais and Sinclair
1980: 352). In addition, analysis of the faunal remains from this site has indicated
that whereas cattle dominated the meat diet of the people living in the central
enclosure and immediately around it, sheep or goat and game dominated that of
the people living on the periphery of the site (Barker 1978).

It is also becoming apparent that on the Zimbabwe Plateau itself there are
some sites that are culturally and chronologically related to the zimbabwe sites
but which do not have any zimbabwe-type stone structures. It is possible that
such sites are numerous but few have as yet been identified or investigated. Two
that have been excavated are Chivowa Hill and Montevideo Ranch, which have
yielded evidence of communities that engaged in both pastoralism and
(probably) sorghum and millet cultivation and for whom cattle seem to have
been particularly important. These would appear to have been rural peasant
communities that were contemporary with the various zimbabwe sites (Sinclair
1984). Indeed, the overall evidence from the various sites that are thought to be
culturally related to Great Zimbabwe would suggest that there existed a graded
series of settlements, from capital city to regional centre to rural village. If this
was the case, then it seems likely that a formally organized state existed on the
Zimbabwe Plateau during the second quarter of the present millennium. By one
means or another a small elite had acquired power over the rest of the
population.

Radiocarbon dating and imports from the East African coast, of which
ceramics are the most significant, have enabled archaeologists to piece together a
reasonably consistent chronology for the zimbabwe sites. This indicates that
they had ceased to be important by the end of the fifteenth century and indeed

that Great Zimbabwe itself came to a rather abrupt end by the middle of that century (Garlake 1968; Garlake 1970b).

Documentary and oral sources indicate the kingdom of the Mwene Mutapa, on the northern end of the Zimbabwe Plateau, as the immediate successor of the state that had been centred on Great Zimbabwe but it was in the south-western part of the plateau that the zimbabwe tradition of building in stone was to survive and indeed develop. The sites of Khami, Dhlo Dhlo and Naletale are particularly remarkable examples of this phenomenon. These and a number of less well-known, similar sites belong to the period from the late fifteenth to the eighteenth century AD. The stone structures typical of this later period consist mainly of revetment walls for building-platforms, on which *daga* huts were erected. These walls made considerable use of decorative features (Garlake 1973: 166–7). The most extensively investigated of these sites is Khami, where Keith Robinson (1959) excavated parts of a group of elite buildings, some of which were approached by underground passages and many were provided with 'drains of a rather advanced type' (Robinson 1959: 105). Khami is thought to have been the capital of the Torwa state, where many people moved when Great Zimbabwe was abandoned. For this reason, Huffman (1981: 15–16) has used the settlement pattern at Khami to throw light on the earlier one at Great Zimbabwe and in doing so has provided us with a plan of the Khami site (Fig. 8.6). This demonstrates that Khami, like Great Zimbabwe, consisted in the main of peasant housing, with the buildings of the elite occupying only a small part of the total area of the settlement.

The practice of building in stone also continued in the Inyanga area of the Eastern Highlands, where the majority of the numerous structures seem to belong to the second half of the second millennium AD (Summers 1958: 312–3). The Inyanga stone-building tradition differs in a number of ways from that of the zimbabwe sites, however, and it has been claimed that it has little or no relevance for the understanding of the latter (Garlake 1973: 172).

There is one other important source of archaeological evidence that must be mentioned. This consists of the traces of prehistoric mining, particularly for gold, which from time to time have been found on the Zimbabwe Plateau. These 'ancient workings', as they have often been called, have been associated with the builders of the zimbabwe sites and it has been suggested that the distribution of workings and ruins is similar (Summers 1969: 137–41). Summers (1969: 105) was able to list 1267 ancient workings, most of which resulted from gold mining. Both alluvial and quartz reef gold was mined; stopes, shafts and sometimes adits being used to exploit the latter. The miners rarely penetrated deeper than about 25 metres, because of the harder rocks met at depth, as well as ventilation or drainage problems (Phimister 1976). Nevertheless, it has been claimed that of the 3041 kilometres of gold reef pegged by European miners by August 1894, some 611 kilometres were covered by 'ancient workings' (Mennell and Summers 1955). The mining of placer deposits, both alluvial and eluvial, seems also to

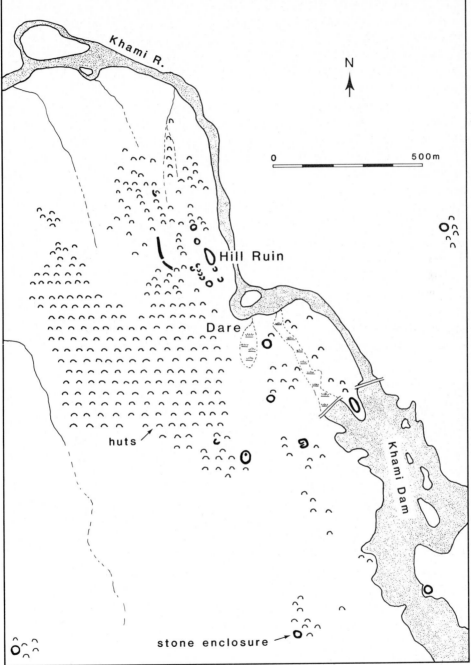
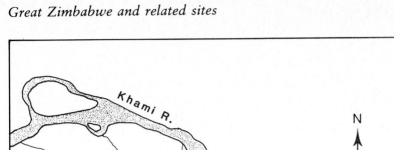

Fig. 8.6 Plan of Khami showing stone structures and areas of *daga* huts. After Huffman (1981: Fig. 13).

have been important and they were comparatively easy to exploit. It has, indeed, been suggested that the location of Great Zimbabwe was influenced by the presence of placer deposits in the vicinity (Phimister 1974). However, the main difficulty in discussing the archaeological evidence for prehistoric mining on the Zimbabwe Plateau, which included mining for copper and iron as well as gold, is that so many of the old workings were destroyed by modern mining early in the present century. Because of this, we know nothing like enough about the way that mining was organized, or about the chronology of its development and eventual decline. Nevertheless, Huffman (1974a) has argued that gold mining, at least, did not develop on the plateau until the eleventh century AD at the earliest and that the rise of the Great Zimbabwe state was a direct consequence of that mining and of the gold trade with the East African coast that it supported.

Subsistence economy

The archaeological evidence that has been reviewed above is deficient in many respects but it does provide us with some idea of how urbanization originated on the Zimbabwe Plateau and how states developed there. For instance, we have relatively little information about the all-important subsistence base but it is nevertheless possible to outline in general terms the nature of the economy that supported these developments. The archaeological evidence indicates that livestock husbandry was particularly important and that cattle dominated this husbandry. Consider, for example, the remarkable results of an analysis of a large quantity of animal bones excavated from a midden on the lower slopes of the hill at Great Zimbabwe, on the top of which is located the so-called Hill Ruin. It was estimated that this collection consisted of about 140 000 pieces of bone. Of these, 15 298 were selected as easily recognizable and on examination it was found that all except 218 pieces came from cattle. The bones remaining after this selection consisted of fragmentary material but a random sample of 5061 fragments showed that only 45 of them came from animals other than cattle. Amongst the other animals represented in the more recognizable material, domesticated sheep or goat was the most common but domesticated dog and a limited range of wild animals were also represented. The more recognizable material was also analysed for skeletal part, bone treatment and fragmentation, and minimum number of individuals. It was concluded that the food remains of the occupants of the Hill Ruin were dominated by cattle and that more than 75 per cent of the 1330 animals represented were immature when killed. It was also concluded that the cattle had been butchered on the hilltop rather than elsewhere (Brain 1974).

Evidence of a similar emphasis on cattle has also been found at other sites. Thus at Ruanga Ruin the animal bones excavated by Garlake indicated that mature domestic cattle were the main source of meat, although smaller bovids, either domestic sheep, goats or small buck, were also eaten (Garlake 1972: 134).

Cattle were also the most common animal at Harleigh Farm (Robins and Whitty 1966), Sinclair found the same thing at Chivowa Hill and Montevideo Ranch (Sinclair 1984) and Turner the same thing at Lekkerwater (Turner 1984). At all these sites sheep or goat and wild animals were also present but of considerably less importance. So far as it is possible to tell, the cattle seem to have been of the Sanga type, which are still kept by the Shona people of the area today. In an important and stimulating paper, Garlake has suggested that transhumant pastoralism for the intensive production of beef was a major factor in the location of zimbabwe-type settlements, many of which were situated on the edge of the tsetse-free highlands so as to be able to exploit lowland grazing when it was relatively tsetse-free during the dry seasons. Indeed, Garlake has argued that such specialist pastoralism is as likely to have formed part of the basis for the rise of Great Zimbabwe and its associated sites as gold mining and long-distance trade, to which the development has most commonly been solely attributed (Garlake 1978b).

Perhaps those immature cattle bones at the base of the hill at Great Zimbabwe should make us pause, however. If the Hill Ruin was occupied by an elite group, or if the ethnohistorical evidence for cattle sacrifice collected by Carl Mauch in 1871 has any bearing on the practices of 400–600 years earlier (Brain 1974: 308–9), then the bones from the hill midden may not constitute reliable evidence for the role of cattle in the overall subsistence economy. Indeed, there is a general danger that faunal evidence from zimbabwe sites will only throw light on the diet or rituals of the elite. This suspicion is reinforced by the discovery at Manekweni (p. 199), that whilst those people within and near the stone enclosure mainly ate beef, those living on the edge of the site ate mainly sheep or goat and game (Barker 1978). It is further supported by a sample of faunal material from Khami, which contains not only a preponderance of cattle but also a wide variety of other species, some of which are not likely to have been used as food; Thorp (1984) interpreted this as evidence of the activities of a traditional healer. Nevertheless, at the rural villages of Chivowa Hill and Montevideo Ranch cattle were still the most common animals (Sinclair 1984) and it is difficult to avoid the conclusion that cattle were at least a very important element of the pastoralism practised by the occupants of zimbabwe and related sites.

Both the location and the apparently continuous occupation of the zimbabwe sites suggest that pastoralism was only a part of the subsistence economy and perhaps not the most important part. Direct archaeological evidence is limited but ethnohistorical evidence (p. 186) suggests that it was grain cultivation, particularly of sorghum and millet, that provided the basic staple foods. In addition, there was probably a wide range of vegetables cultivated. Carbonized seeds from Great Zimbabwe and from related sites of the Leopard's Kopje Tradition (Robinson, Summers and Whitty 1961: 170; Huffman 1974b: 120; Huffman 1977: 13) confirm that sorghum was grown as well as finger millet (*Eleusine corocana*), pearl millet (*Pennisetum americanum*) and a variety of beans (*Voandzeia subterranea*) and peas (*Vigna* sp.). The role of livestock in this mixed economy was largely to cushion the effect of crop failure in bad years (p. 188) and, particularly in the case of cattle, to provide a means of amassing wealth in a negotiable form. Overall, the strength of the subsistence economy of the Zimbabwe Plateau during the first half of the present millennium was probably substantial. It seems likely that Bocarro (p. 187) was not exaggerating in the seventeenth century when he claimed that most of the people in this area were 'inclined to agricultural and pastoral pursuits, *in which their riches consist*' (my emphasis).

Technology

Archaeological evidence from zimbabwe and related sites indicates the existence of considerable technological expertise. The aspect of this that remains most obvious is the practice of building in stone. The construction of free-standing, drystone walls, especially on the scale and of the quality of some of those at Great Zimbabwe, requires great skill, as those of us who have tried our hand at even quite modest drystone work have quickly realised. Admittedly the tabular nature of the exfoliated granite provided an almost limitless supply of superb building material but the builders also knew how best to use it within their own technological limitations. Although they never seem to have grasped fully the importance of bonding, either between courses or between separate walls, their building technique, at its best, exhibited remarkable sophistication. Walls were broad-based to spread their load and tapered to their tops. They were rubble-filled, to economize on labour but the faces of the walls, so vital to the success of such a technique, were constructed with great care. Sharp corners and rectangular layouts were avoided and plans consisted of random curved forms. This emphasis on curves is also evident in the distinctive architectural features that were constructed. Overall, the stone structures of the zimbabwe sites, and of Great Zimbabwe particularly, imply remarkable technological skill; anyone doubting that should look closely at the details of the conical tower at Great Zimbabwe (p. 194). These structures also indicate the development, from an indigenous drystone walling tradition, of what Garlake has called 'an architecture that is unparalleled elsewhere in Africa or beyond' (Garlake 1973: 50).

However, the stone walls of the zimbabwe sites were merely one component of a building technology, a component for which evidence happens to have survived. Somewhat fragmentary evidence from a number of sites suggests that building in *daga* was just as important as building in stone, if not more so. Indeed, it seems that originally much of the impressive stonework at Great Zimbabwe that we so much admire, would have been plastered with *daga* up to a height of some 2 metres above the ground (Garlake 1973: 20). This highly plastic material was used for a variety of constructional purposes and was skilfully moulded into decorative patterns, as well as being beautifully finished to a hard, smooth, almost polished surface. The craftsmanship suggested by the remnants of *daga* that have survived, should also serve to remind us of other building skills of which we have no direct evidence, such as woodworking and thatching.

Another important aspect of the technology of the Zimbabwe Plateau during the first half of the present millennium comprised the related fields of mining and metallurgy. Archaeological evidence (p. 200) indicates that mining was a widespread activity conducted on a considerable scale, although in the case of gold mining at least it was very limited in depth, and recovery methods were inefficient (Phimister 1976: 15). The complete range of metals that were produced probably consisted of iron, copper, gold and tin, and Great Zimbabwe has yielded evidence of metalworking in all of these. Iron-working seems to have been particularly well developed, producing a range of hoes, axes, spearheads, arrowheads, knives and other things. Copper, bronze and gold, on the other hand, were used mainly for decorative purposes; often in the form of wire made with the assistance of iron tongs and drawplates but also as sheet or cast metal (Garlake 1973: 113–16).

Other crafts indicated by the archaeological evidence from the zimbabwe sites included the manufacture of pottery, much of which had polished and graphited exteriors. In addition, spinning, presumably of cotton, is suggested by the large number of perforated discs of potsherd which have been found, although there are other uses to which these might have been put (Garlake 1973: 116–17). If they were spindle-whorls, which is quite likely, then the presence of spinning would presumably suggest that weaving was also taking place and we could assume that textile manufacture was of some significance (Davison and Harries 1980). Finally amongst local crafts, it is worth noting the carving of soapstone, most of the evidence for which has come from Great Zimbabwe itself. Ritual bird figures, monoliths, flat-bottomed dishes, figurines and open moulds for casting cross-shaped ingots of copper, were all carved from this soft, easily worked and locally available stone. The manner in which the soapstone has been carved suggests a familiarity with wood-carving and serves to remind us of the many crafts in perishable materials that must have existed also at the zimbabwe settlements, but for which we have no evidence (Garlake 1973: 119–23, 130–1).

From what is known of the technology associated with the zimbabwe settlements, it would seem that there existed a varied range of caftsmanship. It is quite likely that by the second quarter of the second millennium AD there had, as a result, already developed a degree of functional specialization within the society to which these settlements belonged.

Social system

Great Zimbabwe and its associated sites provide many indications of social and economic stratification. The very stone structures that characterize most of these sites are symbols of privilege and power. They have no obvious practical role, such as defence. Rather, they seem to have been intended as containers, behind whose high walls could be hidden away both the living and the ceremonial areas of a ruling elite. Indeed, the walls themselves demonstrate the power of such a ruling group, able to spend its surplus wealth on such items of conspicuous consumption and able to exert the necessary control over substantial bodies of skilled and unskilled labour. Furthermore, some of the items recovered from within these stone-walled compounds seem to confirm the elevated status of their occupants. Thus there are objects of gold, of copper or bronze and of soapstone; there are also exotic objects such as glass beads and, at Great Zimbabwe itself, glass vessels and Islamic and Chinese ceramics: all these the products of long-distance trade via the East African coast. Moreover, there are some significant absences from the artefacts found in zimbabwe-type stone enclosures. Garlake has remarked on the 'extraordinarily limited range' of pottery, for instance, comprising, it would seem, drinking and brewing/storage vessels but lacking open bowls for cooking, serving and eating, and lacking pots suitable for fetching water. Garlake sees this evidence as suggesting that only a limited range of domestic activities took place within the enclosures and points out there is also an almost complete absence of grindstones from the enclosures (Garlake 1973: 112–13). Add to all this the impression that many of the stone enclosures contained huts with finely finished solid *daga* walls, at least one of which (at Nhunguza) seems to have been an 'audience hut', and the elite nature of the occupants of these enclosures is almost certainly established. If a clincher is needed, then perhaps it can be found in the remarkably small populations that the enclosures are thought to have housed. Garlake estimated the total population of the enclosures at Great Zimbabwe as between 100 and 200 adults and the population of all the other known zimbabwes at any one time as about 750 adults (Garlake 1973: 195–6).

Only in recent years have archaeologists begun to ask questions about the rest of the population of these settlements. As has already been discussed (pp. 197–8), evidence is now available that the stone enclosures were only central structures within more extensive settlements, which in the case of Great Zimbabwe may have had a total population of 18 000 people. With some justification, Huffman has referred to Great Zimbabwe as 'southern Africa's first town' (Huffman 1977). The ordinary townspeople lived in cramped conditions (Fig. 8.7), at a density of about three times that of the elite (Huffman 1977: 12) and, judging from the evidence at Manekweni (p. 199), they did not eat well. However, there was probably already social differentiation amongst the townspeople themselves, with functional specialization giving a special status to craftsmen such as blacksmiths and builders in stone.

At Great Zimbabwe, at least, urbanization was already in progress. Furthermore, if this site is examined in the context of all the other zimbabwe sites and all the other sites that are culturally and chronologically related, then it is possible to discern a graded series of settlements that suggests the existence of a formally organized state (p. 199). At one end of the scale was the capital at Great Zimbabwe, with its large population controlled by a powerful elite; at the other end were the rural villages with their peasant communities. In between were regional centres: smaller towns, each of which was controlled by its own elite group which probably owed some sort of allegiance to that of the capital.

Population pressures

A spatial analysis (Fig. 8.8) of the distribution of relevant archaeological sites on the Zimbabwe Plateau (bearing in mind that this may reflect the distribution of research rather than of sites), has demonstrated the existence of a settlement pattern in which the population showed a marked tendency to cluster (Sinclair and Lundmark 1984). Presumably this resulted from the operation of those environmental constraints which have already been discussed (pp. 187–8). Tsetse fly, climatic variability, and differences in soil fertility must all have played a part in making some areas more attractive to human settlement than others. Thus there was a marked preference for settlement on the southern edge of the plateau, which was high enough to be tsetse-free, within easy reach of lowland grazing that could only be exploited during its relatively tsetse-free dry season, had local areas with a higher rainfall than much of the rest of the plateau and possessed some areas of high soil fertility. Although this picture was

Fig. 8.7 Remains of commoner's hut excavated at Great Zimbabwe. Scale in feet.

somewhat complicated by settlement clusters of lesser importance in the mining areas of the central plateau, it would appear that the places most attractive to human settlement were relatively limited. This could well have occasioned local population pressures sufficient to give rise to the social changes inherent in the processes of urbanization and state formation. As Sinclair has written: 'Contrary to some widely held ideas, land does not appear to have been an unlimited resource in the region around Great Zimbabwe. Control of access to productive areas could well have been an important factor in the relations between elite and peasantry' (Sinclair 1981: 65).

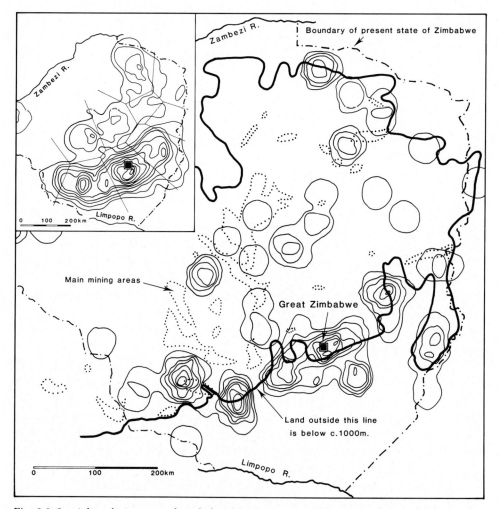

Fig. 8.8 Spatial analysis maps of zimbabwe sites. Large map: 50km clustering level; inset map: 155km clustering level and Garlake's (1978b) Thiessen polygon study. After Sinclair and Lundmark (1984: Fig. 5).

Some confirmation of the existence of local population pressures may, indeed, be provided by the eventual abandonment of Great Zimbabwe itself. Both Garlake (1973: 198) and Huffman (1972: 365) are of the opinion that abandonment resulted from environmental deterioration brought on by the large population. Certainly the large number of people that is now thought to have lived in Great Zimbabwe must have placed a tremendous demand on the available natural resources of the surrounding area. Firewood would soon have become locally scarce, necessitating its transport from ever-increasing distances (Huffman 1977: 13), wildlife to serve as a supplement to the human diet would have become virtually unobtainable (Brain 1974: 309), and the relatively limited areas of better soils must have been gradually exhausted by too frequent a cultivation and by overgrazing (Huffman 1972: 365). Thus, as may have been the case with Axum, it is possible that one of the very factors that gave rise to Great Zimbabwe also brought about its destruction. Without fundamental changes in technology and agricultural system, it was fated to destroy itself.

Ideology

It is probable that Shona religion was a contributory factor in the rise of Great Zimbabwe and of the state which it seems to have controlled. Indeed, one of the two main schools of thought concerning the origins of these developments sees religion as the *major* factor in their initiation (Huffman 1972: 353). The problem is that our knowledge of Shona religion is drawn from oral tradition and ethnography and from such sources it is difficult to estimate the exact role of religion in changes that took place some seven centuries ago. According to Garlake (1973: 184), 'Great Zimbabwe was very probably always a major religious centre', where *Mwari*, the Shona supreme god, was particularly reverenced and where cults of the *mhondoro*, spirits associated with the ruling dynasties, also flourished (1973: 174). Certainly there are archaeological features and artefacts at Great Zimbabwe that suggest religious and ancestral associations; particularly the monoliths, some surmounted by carved birds, that originally stood in the Eastern Enclosure of the Hill Ruin. However, there is no archaeological evidence to support Garlake's assumption that religion was 'probably the most important single factor in bringing about the first steps towards the cohesion, organization and stratification of the society', and Garlake himself recognizes this (1973: 184). Indeed, although Shona religion may have been very important as a means of reinforcing the authority of a ruling elite, the hypothesis that the rise of Great Zimbabwe and its associated sites was due to a religious minority, either of migrant or local origin, is unconvincing. The alternative school of thought to this religious hypothesis is the trade hypothesis, which 'maintains that Zimbabwe was a result of surplus wealth from the East African gold trade' (Huffman 1972: 353). This, at least, is an hypothesis that is susceptible to archaeological evaluation.

External trade

Both Arabic and early Portuguese documentary sources mention the existence of trade between Sofala, on what is now the southern coast of Mozambique, and the interior. Sofala (pp. 176 and 180) seems only to have been a clearing-house, where trade goods from the Islamic world and from India and China were imported for onward transmission to the interior, which in turn exported primary products via Sofala. Most sought-after of those products was gold, although at the time of the first Portuguese contact ivory was another important export and it is probable that other commodities, including copper, were also handled. The imports, according to the Portuguese, were principally cloth, beads and glazed ceramics. The source of the gold that passed through Sofala was said by ibn Battuta, early in the fourteenth century, to be Yufi in the land of the Limiin, one month's march from Sofala (Freeman–Grenville 1975: 31), and it has been suggested that the land of the Limiin was the Zimbabwe Plateau and that Yufi was Great Zimbabwe itself (Huffman 1972: 361–2). A number of questions arise from this. First: does the archaeological evidence at the various zimbabwe sites throw any light on this trade? Second: to what extent was this trade unusual and to what extent was it merely part of a complex network of external trade that involved both long-distance and inter-regional exchange? Third and most important: what role, if any, did this trade play in the rise of Great Zimbabwe and its associated sites? Is it really possible to claim, as has been done, that: 'The Zimbabwe Culture can be described as an indigenous reaction to an external stimulus – the East Coast gold trade' (Huffman 1977: 9)?

Without doubt there is archaeological evidence for the existence of trade between the Zimbabwe Plateau and the East African coast. This evidence is particularly abundant for the sixteenth and seventeenth centuries AD, when the Portuguese had trading posts in the Zambezi Valley and on the northern part of the plateau. For the earlier periods, of more relevance to the present discussion, there is much less evidence but it is nonetheless remarkable. The most important of it comes from the so-called 'Renders Ruin' at Great Zimbabwe itself, where a hoard of material included a glazed Persian bowl of thirteenth or fourteenth-century date. With it were a number of Chinese celadon dishes, some sherds of a Chinese stoneware vessel, another glazed Persian bowl and fragments of engraved and painted Near Eastern glass, all of about the same date. In addition there was a piece of coral, an iron spoon, an iron lamp holder with a copper suspension chain, a copper box, two copper finger rings and (nearby) two small bronze bells. There were also several tens of thousands of glass beads, some brass wire and a quantity of cowrie shells. This hoard was excavated by Hall in 1903 but in 1941 a further collection of some 30 000 beads was found in another part of the same ruin by E. Goodall (Garlake 1973: 131–3). This extraordinary assortment of exotic objects demonstrates that about the fourteenth century Great Zimbabwe was probably in direct contact with the trading cities of the

East African coast. These objects from the Renders Ruin have often been interpreted as part of the stock of a visiting Arab trader but the diverse nature of the goods and their location within what has been thought to be part of the royal wives' living area, makes it more likely that they were part of the contents of a royal repository (Huffman 1981: 6). In addition, the unique character of this collection suggests that it must have had considerable prestige value to its owner.

Another remarkable piece of archaeological evidence for trading contacts between the Zimbabwe Plateau and the coast, consists of a coin minted in Kilwa probably in the early fourteenth century. This coin was excavated at Great Zimbabwe itself and appears to be the only one ever recovered from a scientific context at that site (Huffman 1972: 362 and Plate 1). Of more use as evidence for trade with the coast, because they are more common, are the large numbers of glass beads recovered both from Great Zimbabwe and from many other zimbabwe sites. The ultimate origin of these beads is still unknown but they are similar to beads found in the East Coast cities and like them they came from the Indian Ocean trade. Cowries are also very occasionally found at other zimbabwe sites, as well as at Great Zimbabwe. Otherwise, evidence of imports from the coast is lacking, although the appearance at zimbabwe sites of spindle-whorls, that are absent from earlier sites, has been interpreted as an indication that the craft of spinning spread from the coast as a result of trading contacts (Huffman 1971: Garlake 1973: 117). It should perhaps be no surprise, that a trade in which textiles and gold were the most important commodities has left so little archaeological evidence. Nevertheless, there is strong circumstantial evidence for the importance of trading between the Zimbabwe Plateau and the coast. There was a sudden and considerable increase in building activity at Great Zimbabwe during the fourteenth century, at precisely the same time that equally sudden and considerable expansion was taking place in the cities of the East African coast, particularly in Kilwa in the south. Equally, the fortunes of both Great Zimbabwe and the coastal cities declined at the same time during the fifteenth century. The most likely explanation for such a coincidence of prosperity must be that there was a 'close economic connection' (Garlake 1976b: 224).

The second question that was asked, concerned the extent to which this trade was part of a more general network of long-distance and inter-regional exchange. In addition to items that must have derived from the East Coast trade, the Renders Ruin hoard contained a large quantity of material that suggests the existence of a substantial internal African trade. Thus there were about 30 kilograms of iron wire and about 100 kilograms of iron hoes, axes and chisels. With them were 'cakes of copper', ivory, two unusual spearheads, three iron gongs and three iron rods that were probably strikers for the gongs. There were also a soapstone dish, twenty small pieces of perforated gold sheathing, some gold wire and a handful of gold beads (Garlake 1973: 133). The gongs are bell-shaped and were made of two sheets of iron welded together round the flanges, although neither sheet metal-work nor welding seem to have been local techniques. Seven other similar gongs have been found at Great Zimbabwe and single examples have been found at Chumnungwa Ruins and Dhlo Dhlo Ruins. Such gongs are characteristic of parts of Zambia, the Congo Basin and West Africa but two of the burials at the remarkable Zambezi Valley site of Ingombe Ilede were accompanied by gongs of this type (Fagan and others 1969: 92–4) and their presence at Great Zimbabwe would presumably indicate trading connections in the Ingombe Ilede area. This probability is reinforced by the discovery of single examples of cross-shaped copper ingots, of a characteristic Ingombe Ilede form, at the zimbabwe-type site of Chumnungwa and at another ruin site in the Great Zimbabwe area. Three similar ingots have also been found in the Mtelegwa Ruin. It seems that during the fourteenth and fifteenth centuries the Ingombe Ilede people were mining copper on some scale and as there are salt deposits in their area and a lack of such deposits on the Zimbabwe Plateau, it is likely that they traded salt as well as copper in that direction. In exchange they probably took gold beads and ornaments, and iron tools and weapons. The comparatively few glass beads at Ingombe Ilede sites suggests that their trade was with other internal African communities rather than with the East Coast (Garlake 1976b: 224). Furthermore, this Ingombe Ilede–Zimbabwe Plateau trade was probably just one small part of a complex internal trading network, of which the rest has left little evidence that has yet been identified. As Brian Fagan has demonstrated for the region north of the Zimbabwe Plateau, the demand for raw materials, particularly iron, copper and salt, ensured the growth of such networks (Fagan 1969). As in other parts of Africa, it is likely that internal trading of this sort substantially pre-dated long-distance external trade. If this was the case, then the East Coast gold trade quite probably took advantage of an existing trading network, rather than creating something new.

The third and final question concerned the role of the East Coast trade in the rise of Great Zimbabwe and the other zimbabwe sites. The quick answer is that it was probably very important, but that its role in the social and economic changes that led to urbanization and state formation was to facilitate rather than to originate. The cause of these developments was deeper and more complex than a mere trade in luxuries but without doubt that trade provided the elite with prestige goods and with a form of wealth that could be used to enhance their authority.

Conclusion

Great Zimbabwe and its related sites comprise the archaeological evidence for social and political developments that took place on the Zimbabwe Plateau during the first half of the present millennium. The stone structures that have so dominated archaeological research housed a small ruling elite, who governed settlements varying in size from the capital city of Great Zimbabwe itself, with a population of perhaps 18 000 people, to smaller regional towns. The authority of this elite probably extended also to rural villages that were too small and too unimportant to justify their own elite residences. The size of Great Zimbabwe would suggest that urbanization was already in process, at the very least at this place. The presence of comparable elite structures in so many of the other settlements would suggest that some progress had also been made towards the formation of a state. Why and how had all this happened?

The most basic reason was almost certainly the successful subsistence agriculture of this area. A generally healthy environment that was tsetse-free and with access to other areas that were seasonally tsetse-free, it supported a mixed farming economy in which grain, vegetables and livestock – particularly cattle – all played a part. This combination of cultivation and livestock would have helped to even out the effects of bad years and must inevitably have led to an increase in the population. However, good soils were limited and it is very probable that the tsetse boundaries fluctuated. Thus some areas must have been more productive than others and those who controlled such areas, or could gain control of them, must in time have come to control the less fortunate members of an expanding population.

However, there were some alternatives to agriculture: mining, trade and crafts of various sorts. The development of these activities provided some escape from the problem of limited productive land. They also provided the emerging elite with further sources of wealth that could be controlled. In particular, it is likely that a far-reaching and complex network of inter-regional trade in raw materials had developed within south central Africa, before Indian Ocean merchants were able to benefit from it. How could the latter have known that there was gold to be had from the Zimbabwe Plateau, unless it was already reaching the coast? Nevertheless, the gold trade with the East Coast must in time have become extremely important in creating surplus wealth, that further enhanced the power of the Zimbabwe Plateau elite. Even the most conservative estimate suggests that between seven and nine million ounces of gold was made available for trade and internal consumption before 1890 (Phimister 1976: 17). It is not difficult to imagine the impact on Plateau society of the volume of goods (particularly cloth and beads) that must have been obtained in exchange for the portion of this quantity that was traded prior to the middle of the present millennium. It seems unlikely that the gold trade 'caused' the rise of Great Zimbabwe but nevertheless it must have had a great effect on it.

The apparent reasons for the decline and abandonment of Great Zimbabwe and its associated sites consist of a reversal of the factors that gave rise to their growth. The gold trade declined, probably because of falling world prices and the depletion of the more easily worked deposits on the Zimbabwe Plateau. More important, however, the environment around Great Zimbabwe collapsed: overcropped, overgrazed, overhunted, overexploited in every essential aspect of subsistence agriculture, it ceased to be able to carry the very concentration of people that it had given rise to.

Chapter 9

The problem of archaeological visibility: other precolonial cities and states in tropical Africa

The previous six chapters have presented a series of case-studies of archaeological evidence for urbanization and state formation in precolonial, tropical Africa. It is important to realize that the choice of the areas which have been discussed in some detail has been mainly dictated by the character of the archaeological evidence and by the extent of archaeological research. As a result, the picture that is provided is an incomplete one: a series of islands of information projecting from a sea of uncertainty and ignorance. Not only have the individual case-studies given somewhat lopsided impressions of developments in the selected areas, but also there were numerous precolonial cities and states in tropical Africa that are known to us from the evidence of ethnohistory or oral tradition, that have not been included at all. The main reason for this omission is that archaeological evidence for such entities is either totally absent or so limited that its detailed discussion is hardly possible at the present time.

The basic problem is one of archaeological visibility. Some manifestations of early urbanization and state formation in Africa are of such a character that their archaeological investigation is peculiarly difficult. For instance, the capital city of Buganda (Gutkind 1963), a state near Lake Victoria, was described in 1889 as 'one of the great capitals of Africa' (Ashe 1889: 52), but it was constructed totally of grass, wood and other organic materials and it moved frequently, particularly on the death of the *Kabaka*, the ruler of Buganda (Gutkind 1960: 29). The sites of these large settlements are, therefore, unlikely to have much depth of deposit or structural remains and no archaeological investigation of them seems ever to have been attempted. Thus there appears to be no archaeological information about a settlement that John Hanning Speke, its first European visitor, described as ' . . . a magnificent sight. A whole hill was covered with gigantic huts such as I had never seen in Africa before' (Speke 1863: 283). It is indeed fortunate that such travellers left us both descriptions and illustrations of what they saw, and Henry Morton Stanley's picture of the capital of Buganda in 1875, when it was at Rubaga, is reproduced here as an indication of how much archaeology may be missing (Fig. 9.1).

There is, however, no theoretical reason why archaeology should not be able to investigate such short-lived settlements of ephemeral materials. Provided that erosion has not destroyed the inevitably shallow evidence, survey and excavation techniques do now exist that would enable information to be obtained from sites of this type. Nevertheless, they have been seldom applied to this particular problem in Africa. A lack of sophistication in research design has led to the excavation of many a larger African settlement site for much the same reason that George Leigh Mallory gave for wanting to climb Mount Everest: 'Because it is there' (Bartlett 1980: 710). In such circumstances it is hardly surprising that it is the sites with solid remains of stone, fired brick, or mud that have attracted attention and that sites with less substantial structural remnants have often been ignored. In recent years there has been something of a change in the objectives of archaeological fieldwork in this respect but in much of tropical Africa the period since the early 1970s has seen a diminution in archaeological field research, for both political and economic reasons, so that there has not yet been sufficient opportunity to demonstrate what could be done with sites of supposed low archaeological visibility. To some degree, the whole history of archaeology can be seen as an ever-widening realization of what constitutes data and of how such data can be obtained and analysed. In short, it is quite likely that the low archaeological visibility of the sites in question is to some extent more apparent than real.

In spite of the inadequacies of the archaeological evidence for early cities and states of Africa, the case studies in the previous six chapters do provide, with one major exception, some general indication of the geographical distribution of

Fig. 9.1 Rubaga, the capital of Buganda in 1875. From Stanley (1878: Vol. 1).

these developments. The major exception is, indeed, of the greatest importance, because it consists of a huge area of the continent extending across the modern states of the Congo Republic, Zaïre, Angola, Zambia, Rwanda, Burundi and Uganda. Most of this area lies south of the Equator. Ethnohistorical and oral traditional evidence indicate that it was the location of a succession of cities and states from at least the sixteenth century AD onwards. Some of these, like the Kingdom of Kongo in the sixteenth century, or the state of Buganda in the nineteenth century, clearly impressed early European visitors. They were often particularly interested in the cities that they came across and Dapper (1686) has left us a remarkable illustration of a seventeenth-century Equatorial African city (Fig. 9.2). Even making allowance for considerable artistic licence, this appears to have been a settlement of both considerable size and organization. Nevertheless, archaeology has contributed relatively little to our knowledge of precolonial cities and states in this part of Africa. The Lozi Kingdom, for instance, is known from oral history not archaeology (Prins 1980). Such evidence as does exist from this whole area is hardly enough to support the sort of detailed discussion that has been attempted in the series of case studies presented in this book. Because of the importance of the area, however, it is worth reviewing the

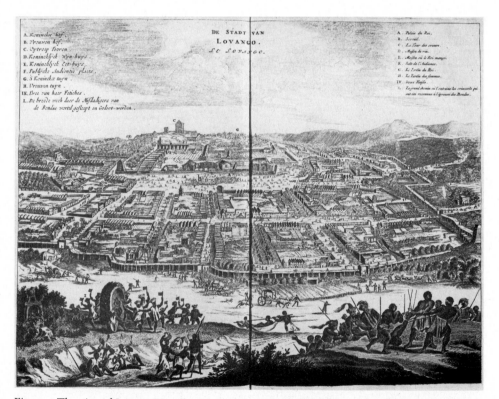

Fig. 9.2 The city of Loango (in what is now the Congo Republic) in the seventeenth century. From Dapper (1686: 320–1).

little evidence that is available, to see what light it can throw on the origins of social complexity in the Equatorial region.

To begin with the Kingdom of Kongo itself, the site of the capital city, Mbanza Kongo (São Salvador), is known but has never been excavated (Maret 1982: 80). Situated in northern Angola (Fig. 9.3), it is now planned to do some work there (p. 18) but at the time of writing the only archaeological evidence relevant to the Kongo state is a cemetery excavated at Mbanza Mbata, where elite graves produced clear evidence of European trading contacts during the seventeenth and eighteenth centuries (Maret 1982: 82). This is not very much for a state for which we have both contemporary accounts (e.g. Pigafetta 1591) and modern historical studies (e.g. Randles 1968).

The situation is very much better for the Luba state, which is known to have existed in the savanna of south-east Zaïre during the eighteenth and nineteenth centuries (Reefe 1981). In this case, archaeological evidence provides a complete cultural sequence from the fifth century AD to the beginning of the nineteenth century and indicates the emergence of an hierarchical society by the end of the

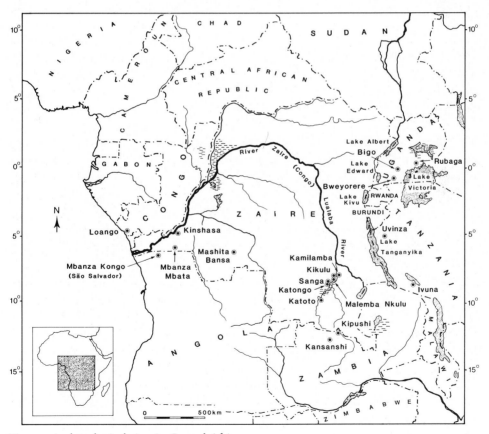

Fig. 9.3 Archaeological sites in Central Africa.

first millennium (Maret 1979). The sequence is supported by more than forty radiocarbon dates and constitutes the most successful piece of archaeological research concerning the later prehistory of Central Africa. Unfortunately, however, the available evidence consists entirely of burials; clustered in cemeteries in the Upemba Depression, particularly on the banks of Lake Kisale on the upper Lualaba River (Fig. 9.3). Settlement sites are known but appear to have only shallow deposits that have been extensively disturbed by continuous occupation. As a result, they have not been excavated but a total of over 265 graves have been. These were situated at the sites of Sanga, Katongo, Kamilamba, Kikulu and Malemba Nkulu (Maret 1982: 89).

The Upemba Depression sequence can, therefore, tell us nothing about early urbanization in this area but it is quite informative on the subject of social evolution and early state emergence. This first became apparent after the excavations of Jacques Nenquin at Sanga in 1957 and Jean Hiernaux in 1958, which produced evidence of a remarkably sophisticated material culture during a period dated from the seventh to ninth century AD. Called by Nenquin the 'Kisalian', this culture was characterized by finely made and distinctive pottery, by skilful metal-working in both iron and copper and by graves containing evidence of accumulated wealth (Nenquin 1963; Hiernaux et al. 1971). More recent excavations at Sanga by Pierre de Maret (Maret 1977) and at other sites by the same researcher (Maret 1979; Maret 1982) have revised Nenquin's dating and placed the Kisalian in its chronological context. The sequence thus established commenced in the fifth century AD with the Kamilambian tradition, which was replaced by the Early Kisalian tradition at the end of the eighth century. This, in turn, was succeeded by the Classic Kisalian tradition in the eleventh century, that was followed by the Kabambian tradition that appeared at the end of the fourteenth century. The Kabambian has been divided into Kabambian A and B, the latter ending at the beginning of the nineteenth century. The latest of the archaeological evidence is, indeed, comparable with the material culture of the Luba as studied in recent times. Thus, as Maret had claimed, 'It becomes apparent that in establishing an Iron Age sequence in the Upemba rift one is actually studying the emergence of the Luba Kingdom' (Maret 1979: 234).

Anthropometric studies of the Sanga skeletons and of the present-day Luba, which are said to show strong affinities between the two, would seem to support this idea. In addition, the archaeological evidence suggests the gradual development of social stratification, political organization and functional specialization. For example, as far back as the Early Kisalian, ceremonial iron axes were placed in graves. These had handles decorated with nails, and were much like those later used by the Luba as symbols of authority. In one such Early Kisalian grave, the deceased had also been buried with an iron anvil, another symbol of power among Bantu-speaking peoples (Figs. 9.4 & 9.5). Iron bells found in graves of this period may have been indicative of authority. At Katoto, a

Fig. 9.4 Early Kisalian burial at Kamilamba, Zaïre. Note ceremonial iron axe at left centre and iron anvil to left of skull.

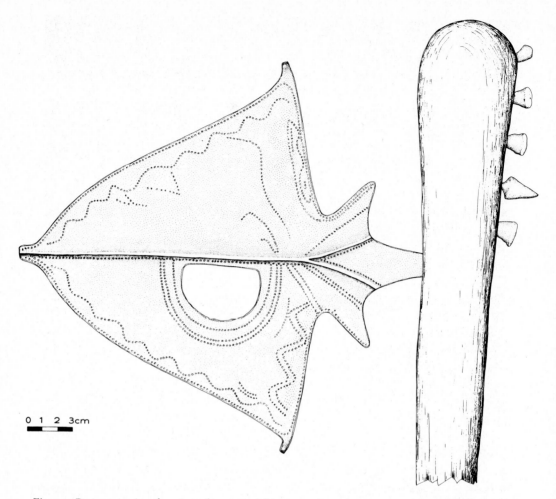

Fig. 9.5 Reconstruction drawing of ceremonial iron axe from burial at Kamilamba (Fig. 9.4).

cemetery in the southern part of the Upemba Rift belonging to a tradition approximately contemporaneous with the Kisalian, the richest graves included not only ceremonial axes and anvils but also evidence of child sacrifices. Social stratification was further indicated in the Classic Kisalian by the unequal distribution of grave-goods between the various burials. It was observed that the few graves that contained an unusually large number of pots also contained uncommon things like cowries and ivory pendants. Furthermore, such wealth appeared to be partly hereditary, since some children's graves were among the wealthiest. (Maret 1979; Maret 1982)

Following Bisson (1975), it seems possible that the development of political organization in the Luba area can be inferred from the archaeological evidence for the use of copper. This metal was particularly valued in much of Africa during later prehistoric times, being variously used as a medium of exchange, for personal adornment, for status symbols and for cult objects (Herbert 1984). In the Upemba Depression sequence (Maret 1979) there is no evidence of copper in the Kamilambian and its first appearance is in the Early Kisalian when there were a few copper objects, mainly in the form of hammered bangles. It is very common, however, in the Classic Kisalian, when it was used for both a wide range of personal ornaments and for some functional objects. Thus far it would appear that the role of copper was principally as an indicator of wealth, prestige and status. With the Kabambian came a marked change; distinctive copper *croisettes* (little crosses) appeared, probably originally as ingots but later used as currency. As time went by, these crosses grew smaller and more uniform in shape (Maret 1981), and it is thought that they may have first been used as a special-purpose currency (for buying wives for instance) but gradually evolved into a general-purpose unit of exchange. Thus the smaller, later crosses could have been used for a variety of small purchases. The use of these crosses as a form of money is further suggested by the fact that at Sanga they were often found in or near the hands of the deceased and that one grave that contained 140 of the smallest crosses had them tied up into groups of five (Bisson 1975: 287). The use of such a currency would imply the existence of a certain level of political sophistication.

The level of craftsmanship, indicated by the archaeological evidence for the Kisalian, suggests the attainment of some degree of functional specialization by the early part of the present millennium. The skilful handling of iron, copper, ivory, bone and pottery hints at the presence of professional artisans. The range of metalwork alone is one of the most impressive in tropical Africa: including (for the Kisalian) iron hoes, knives, axes, spears, arrows, harpoon heads, fish-hooks, necklaces, pendants and chain; together with copper belts, necklaces, bangles, bracelets, small knives, spearheads and fish-hooks. Basket-weaving was also practised and there may well have been specialist traders bringing copper from the Copperbelt, some 200 kilometres to the south (Maret 1979).

The relative proximity of one of the richest sources of copper in Africa must, indeed, have played a part in the developments in south-east Zaïre. From Kansanshi and Kipushi, in northern Zambia, Bisson (1976) obtained prehistoric evidence for both the mining and smelting of copper. It is apparent that exploitation of the Kansanshi deposits commenced possibly as early as the fourth century AD and there is also now evidence that copper was being smelted at a similar date in the Lubumbashi region of south-east Zaïre (Anciaux de Faveaux and Maret 1984). The Kansanshi evidence led Bisson to reject the hypothesis sometimes advanced, that Arab or Swahili traders were responsible for both the origin of states and the start of large-scale copper mining in this part of Africa. Similarly, Maret has argued that the Kisalian evidence for an hierarchical society as early as the end of the first millennium AD, rules out long-distance trade as a possible cause of this development. Rather, he sees a combination of fishing, hunting and agriculture as permitting a high population density that 'led to a need for political integration' (Maret 1979: 234). Certainly, the evidence for the Classic Kisalian is suggestive of some form of early state, and this at a time when the only indication of any contact with the outside world consists of a few cowrie shells from the Indian Ocean coast. Nevertheless, the possible role of internal trading networks should not be forgotten, and local exchanges of copper, iron and salt were probably particularly important (Fagan 1969). The people of the Classic Kisalian may well have participated in such networks by trading dried fish from the lakes and rivers of the Upemba Depression. When Europeans first entered the area, fish was the main export (Maret 1982: 90).

Apart from this remarkable evidence from south-east Zaïre, there is relatively little archaeological data from Equatorial Africa that is informative on the subject of early cities and states. The city of Concobela (Ngombela), for instance, has been identified with the site of Kingabwa, near Kinshasa, but has now been destroyed by clay digging and covered by a garbage dump (Maret 1982: 83). Similarly, the mounds of Mashita Bansa (meaning 'the city of the heaps'), a site situated in south-central Zaïre, can tell us little as yet although test excavations were carried out there in 1984 (Maret 1982: 84; Maret 1985). Even the excavation of some of the royal tombs of Rwanda was of rather limited value, as the three graves investigated contained burials of the late nineteenth and early twentieth centuries. One of these, however, was of a king who had been dead since the seventeenth or eighteenth century and was only buried in 1930 or 1931! This burial was accompanied by numerous grave-goods which had also remained unburied until this century and these are of some interest because they included items symbolic of royalty (Van Noten 1972). A similar problem of limited time-depth exists for the site of Ryamurari, the old capital of the Ndorwa Kingdom in Rwanda. Remains of circular mud walls indicate the king's enclosure, and there are also cattle kraals built of cattle dung and garbage, but excavation has produced radiocarbon dates of the eighteenth and twentieth centuries (Van Noten 1982: 75).

However, Rwanda is part of what is sometimes called the 'interlacustrine' area, where a number of states are known from oral tradition to have developed by about the middle of the present millennium (Webster 1979). As the name implies, this area is situated between Lake Victoria on the east and Lakes Albert, Edward, Kivu, and Tanganyika on the west. The environment is one of cool highlands with montane forests and grasslands: generally good cattle country. One of the states in this area was Buganda and although there is no archaeological evidence to throw light on the development of Bugandan urbanization (p. 214), Oliver (1959a) was able to make a preliminary study of the royal tombs and of their associated jaw-bone temples. Nevertheless, rather more archaeological work has been carried out on Ankole, another one of the interlacustrine states. As with that of Buganda, the capital of Ankole moved many times, but careful use of oral tradition enabled Oliver (1959b) to identify a number of capital sites in the field. Subsequently, one of these, Bweyorere, was excavated by Posnansky (1968), demonstrating the difficulties of extracting useful information from this type of site. Bweyorere consists of a series of low banks on the top of a hill, forming irregular, incomplete enclosures. Posnansky excavated 31 interrupted, staggered trenches into the site and was able to identify the remains of the palace, a circular building of organic material over 15 metres in diameter, that had been destroyed by fire. The deposit was shallow, however, and no other habitation structures were found, although pottery and bones were generally distributed. Oral tradition indicated occupation of this site at three different periods: in the seventeenth century, in the eighteenth century and in the nineteenth century respectively. Radiocarbon dating was in general agreement with this overall time-span. Animal bones from the site indicated the importance of cattle to its occupants but also suggested that hunting was common. Posnansky concluded that:

> Bweyorere represents a large pastoral settlement with evidence of a palace site far larger than those encountered by the nineteenth century European travellers to Ankole and with the earliest trade goods yet known from the lacustrine region. (Posnansky 1968: 165)

It is interesting to note, however, that Posnansky thought that the site had a population of 'probably no more than a few hundred people' and that it 'was not a town and there is no trace of the practice of any crafts' (Posnansky 1968: 173).

The earliest site in the interlacustrine area relevant to the present discussion, and the one that has been most investigated, is Bigo, some way to the north of Ankole. This site consists of some 10 kilometres of ditches and banks, enclosing an area of about 5 square kilometres (Fig. 9.6). The earthworks form two main enclosures, within the larger of which is a central group of smaller enclosures. The height and width of bank and ditch vary greatly, the greatest height from the bottom of the ditch to the top of the bank being over 7 metres. Situated within and around the central enclosures are three large mounds. Bigo was first

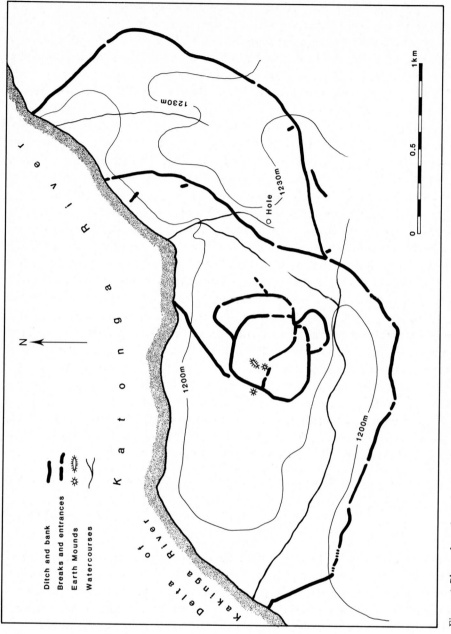

Fig. 9.6 Plan of earthworks at Bigo, Uganda. After Wayland (1934).

224

described in 1909, first mapped properly in 1921, and has been the subject of considerable published discussion. Oral tradition ascribes the site to the Bacwezi dynasty, whose state seems to have been the forerunner of others in the interlacustrine area. The site is associated with two smaller earthwork enclosures, Kagogo to its north-west and Kasonko to its north-east, and with a large earthen dam, presumably for irrigation, at Ntusi. All four of these sites are situated within an area less than 20 kilometres across (Wayland 1934; Shinnie 1960; Posnansky 1969).

Bigo itself has been excavated on two occasions; once by Shinnie in 1957 (Shinnie 1960) and once by Posnansky in 1960 (Posnansky 1969). These excavations indicated that there was settlement at Bigo prior to the construction of the bank and ditch system and radiocarbon dates suggested an overall occupation date in the fifteenth and sixteenth centuries AD. Although very few traces of timber structures were found, Posnansky was able to identify the location of the royal enclosure by other means (Posnansky 1969: 135) and Shinnie was of the opinion that 'there was considerable human occupation at the centre of the complex' (Shinnie 1960: 27). The excavated animal bones, however, revealed an emphasis on cattle and it seems likely that the outer enclosures were intended for penning cattle rather than for defence. Some support for this idea is gained from the fact that more attention seems to have been given to the digging of the ditch than to the construction of the bank. Nevertheless, as Posnansky has suggested (1969: 145), it is also possible that the immensity of the earthworks was intended to bestow prestige on those who lived there. Certainly they may be regarded as a form of monumental construction: in one place Shinnie found the rock-cut ditch to be nearly 4 metres deep, when he excavated a section across it (Shinnie 1960: 17), and Posnansky (1969: 144) estimated that more than 200 000 cubic metres of earth and rock had been removed in making the ditches as a whole. The size and direction of the labour force necessary to accomplish such work, together with the presence at this site of a royal enclosure, would imply the existence of some degree of political centralization. It would appear that Bigo was the pastoral equivalent of a city, the capital, indeed, of the earliest known state in the interlacustrine area.

In spite of the problem of archaeological visibility in the Equatorial region of Africa, the little evidence that exists relevant to the origins of social complexity is of the greatest importance. In both south-east Zaïre and in the interlacustrine area, there are indications that political integration and centralization were already in progress at a sufficiently early date for there to be no question of them resulting from external influences. Until the second half of the present millennium, these areas remained so remote from the world outside of the African continent, that external long-distance trade cannot have played a part in state formation as has been so often suggested elsewhere. One must look for purely indigenous factors. Here the evidence does not serve us well but, as with other areas discussed in this book, the existence of a sound subsistence base and of an adequate technology were of primary importance. Added to these is the likelihood of localized population pressures resulting from competition for some particularly important but limited part of the resource base: fish, perhaps, in the case of the Kisalian, grazing rights, maybe, in the case of Bigo. It seems possible that such pressures resulted in the emergence of an elite, whose presence is suggested by the archaeological evidence at these sites. It also seems likely that local trading networks, particularly in copper, iron and salt, contributed to these developments. Salt, for instance, is known to have been produced in east Central Africa at Uvinza, from the middle of the first millennium AD (Sutton and Roberts 1968) and at Ivuna, from early in the second millennium AD (Fagan and Yellen 1968).

Thus, the question of archaeological visibility in Central Africa is one to which fieldworkers and excavators would do well to address themselves. Not only may the sites of this area be capable of making a significant contribution to our understanding of the emergence of social complexity in this part of Africa but also what we learn here may help to explain developments in other parts of the continent. In addition, any broadening in our concept of archaeological visibility could well have notable repercussions in the other areas studied in this book. Archaeologists engaged in the investigation of the later prehistory of tropical Africa have to learn to see better.

Chapter 10
What are the common denominators?

The examples of African precolonial urbanization and state formation that have been discussed in Chapters 3–9 come from a wide range of environments. In general terms these include: river valley, in such cases as Kerma on the Nile or Jenne on the Niger; mountain plateau, for example Axum in Ethiopia or Great Zimbabwe in the country now called after it; savanna plain, for instance Koumbi Saleh or Kano in West Africa; rainforest, such as Ife or Benin in Nigeria; and coastal fringe as with Kilwa or Gedi in East Africa. The geographical locations of these developments within the continent are equally diverse. The middle Nile was so positioned that it had substantial and long-standing contacts with Egypt and the eastern Mediterranean. Axum was situated beside a major trade route between the Mediterranean world and the lands of the Indian Ocean and directly on a trade route from the Red Sea to the Nile Valley near Meroë. The West African savanna, on the other hand, was separated from the outside world by one of the greatest deserts on earth, the repeated traversal of which necessarily attenuated the influence of external factors. This was even more the case for the West African forest, situated far to the south of the desert margins and backed by the empty Atlantic Ocean that for long centuries was a far more effective barrier than the Sahara. Different again were the cities and towns of the East African coast, which looked out on the Indian Ocean that itself provided links with a number of distant cultures of some technological sophistication. More remote from such contacts but still in touch with them was the Zimbabwe Plateau, for even it was far from being isolated in the African interior, as were the Kisalian people of south-east Zaïre or the occupants of Bigo in the central African interlacustrine area. Such environmental and geographical diversity would suggest that we must look elsewhere for any common factors that might explain the appearance of social complexity in some parts of the African continent and, equally, its failure to appear in other parts.

Nevertheless, when considering the details of each of the environments that have been discussed, it is apparent that each relevant area had its own characteristic environmental advantages. True, these were limited in every case by the existence of environmental constraints but the ingenuity of human culture served to mitigate their impact to some extent. Nowhere is this more starkly illustrated than on the middle Nile; on the one hand the river offered life but on the other hand much of the surrounding environment was so harsh that life could not be supported. Yet, by means of irrigation, human populations were able to exploit the river and to overcome the environmental constraints so successfully that this area was the scene of some of tropical Africa's earliest states and cities and of the longest succession of such developments. A similar interplay of environmental advantage, environmental constraint and human culture can be discerned (to varying extents) in each of the cases that have been considered, although never with quite the same ease as in the case of the middle Nile. This interplay was a dynamic one and clearly its outcome in each case was normally very much in favour of the human inhabitants, except when episodic imbalance threatened collapse of the often delicately balanced system. However, this does not go very far in explaining the emergence of social complexity in Africa; clearly, human beings thrive better in some places than in some others, but this is no reason why they should build cities or create states.

In the cases under review, however, it is the numbers of people who thrived that may be significant. The population densities of such areas seem to have been rather higher than was usual in the rest of this generally thinly populated continent. It is apparent that all of the areas discussed had a strong subsistence base with a potential for producing a storable, transportable surplus. All the people concerned were agriculturalists, growing a range of food plants suited to the local environments and in all cases keeping livestock, even though this was severely limited by trypanosomiasis in the case of the West African forest. Of course, the farmers and the pastoralists were often different groups of people, interacting one upon the other; but from this very symbiosis came strength, just as weakness resulted from their periodic conflicts. In addition, there are signs that in some areas there was an intensification of agricultural strategy and this in a continent where agricultural systems have traditionally tended to be extensive rather than intensive. Thus, on the middle Nile more efficient irrigation was achieved by introducing the ox-driven waterwheel; in the Inland Niger Delta of Mali recessional cultivation of rice was developed to a sophisticated level; in the Ethiopian Highlands slopes were terraced and water-storage dams constructed. Developments of this sort would suggest that populations in such areas were indeed increasing, that they had in fact reached the impasse faced by many agricultural societies of the ancient world: more food meant more people and more people required more food. It is surely significant that one of the most persistent exports from the African continent was human beings. True, it was typically one's neighbours who were enslaved not one's own people, but the overall pressure on limited resources was lessened.

In each of the cases considered, the exploitation of those resources was accomplished not only by means of a mixed agricultural strategy but also by the application of a varied and sometimes sophisticated metallurgically-based technology. Most of the societies with which we are concerned seem to have been particularly proficient in the working of iron and the importance of iron technology as an enabling and intensifying agent in later African prehistory can hardly be exaggerated. Without iron, the farmers of the West African forest could not have exploited their heavily vegetated environment as successfully as they did, nor could the pastoralists of Bigo in Uganda have dug such impressive rock-cut ditches. Iron provided both the tools to exploit available resources and the weapons to discourage others who coveted them. In addition to iron-working and other metallurgical skills, the technological grasp of the various groups of people discussed in this book covered a varying range of abilities. Although engineering knowledge of the sort indicated by the Axumite stelae seems to have been unusual, there was, nevertheless, a widespread understanding of building techniques, in stone, in fired brick, in mud-brick, in coursed mud, in wood, in grass, and in other organic materials. Building technology was both accomplished and diverse. Furthermore, there appear to have been other crafts, usually including such things as pottery making, woodworking, textile production, and leather working. In some instances, however, there must have been people with technological skills specific to the region: such as boatbuilders and sailors on the middle Nile or on the East African coast, and scribes in Meroë or in Axum where indigenous alphabets were developed. One is led to the conclusion that specialist artisans were involved in at least some of these activities. When it is considered that a number of the cases studied also have evidence suggesting the existence of religious functionaries, government officials and specialist traders, it becomes apparent that some degree of functional specialization was probably present in all of the areas examined.

Inevitably, some resources were more limited than others and, as Haas (1982: 151) has claimed, it is '*control over the production or procurement* of the resources in question', that gives rulers their power (p. 10). Certainly, all of the case studies examined in this book show unmistakable signs of the emergence of an elite who told other people what to do. The question is, what were the vital resources that they controlled? Most commonly this is answered by pointing to the existence of raw materials such as gold, ivory and other things which commanded a high price on the world market. Control of these meant control of long-distance trade and control of long-distance trade provided prestige and wealth. Thus appeared the African elites, thus developed the cities and the states. The problem with this explanation is not that it is basically incorrect but that it is wrongly timed. Looking at the archaeological evidence on the middle Nile, in the Ethiopian Highlands, or along the East African coast, it is obvious that external long-distance trade did sometimes play a major role in African urbanization and state formation, but it seems increasingly likely that this was as an intensifier rather than as an originator. Thus we now have evidence that hints at an indigenous origin for the development of social complexity on the East African coast; the earliest urbanization in the West African savanna pre-dates the growth of large-scale trans-Saharan trade; and in central Africa there are signs of increasing social complexity at a time before there was any substantial long-distance trade with the outside world. In addition, neither Zimbabwe nor the West African forest contain sufficient evidence to indicate long-distance trade on any large scale at an early date. Even in the case of the middle Nile and the Ethiopian Highlands, one suspects that there was a strong local input at an early stage.

If external long-distance trade was merely an intensifier or a catalyst of changes that had already commenced, then the question remains of what started them. There seem to be two possibilities. The first is that extensive *internal* trading networks pre-existed external trading contacts and that African elites first gained power by controlling resources that were important in such internal exchange systems. The three commodities copper, iron and salt are likely to have been amongst these resources but there could have been many more, including the gold and the ivory that subsequently became so vital to the overseas trade. Indeed, the earliest commodities to be exchanged by internal trade were probably foodstuffs and other plant and animal resources. The very ecological diversity of much of Africa makes this likely and, in fact, the movement of such commodities has remained significant down to modern times. Thus shea-butter is still exported today from northern Nigeria to the south of that country, whilst kola nuts travel in the opposite direction (Shaw 1984: 156) and Africa has many similar examples of resource exchange. Although archaeology tends to be silent on perishable goods of this sort, there is some indication that early internal trading networks really did exist, particularly in Central Africa, West Africa and Ethiopia. This being the case, it seems likely that external long-distance trade merely plugged into the extant circuitry of the internal networks.

A second possible explanation is that elite power was first acquired by the control of land, not of any land but of land with an unusually high production potential. The role of this factor is, indeed, seen as possibly complementary to that of internal trade, rather than as alternative to it. Given the relatively poor quality of many African soils, together with their often moisture-stressed condition, and given situations of apparently expanding populations, the greatest area of competition was very likely to be around land which was more highly productive than was usual. In all of the case-studies examined, it is possible to find indications that such land may have existed. Thus, in the middle Nile area, fertile silts which could be reached by the available irrigation technology were limited and the proportion of each year for which they could be watered varied with position. As a result, some areas of land must have been more productive than others. On the north-eastern Ethiopian plateau, periodic drought must have given irrigated land a particularly significant role during the resultant episodes of famine. The generally water-stressed environment of the West African savanna was bound to give the limited areas available for recessional cultivation, such as the Inland Niger Delta, a particular importance. In the West African forest, it seems to have been the upper interfluves and the forest-savanna ecotonal areas that provided the best farmlands and again these were limited. For the East African coast it was a matter of fertile soils and water availability, some areas being better provided for than others. On the Zimbabwe Plateau, it was again a matter of soils, where some soils were particularly fertile in an otherwise rather rocky area with granite soils of indifferent or poor fertility. For Central Africa there is not enough evidence to do much more than guess at what the situation might have been. Nevertheless, it seems likely that the Upemba Depression of south-east Zaïre offered a well-watered area where both aquatic and agricultural resources would have been superior to much of the surrounding savanna, and it seems likely that Bigo in western Uganda was sitting in the middle of prime montane grazing lands for cattle.

In this way, it appears possible that the crucial common factor underlying the emergence of African elites was access to and control of land that was more highly productive than was usual. If this was the case, then we have a purely indigenous explanation for the origin of social complexity in some parts of tropical Africa. Doubtless, local trading networks also played an important role, both economically and symbolically, and clearly, external long-distance trade eventually came to act as an intensifying agent of considerable significance. Nevertheless, this 'productive land hypothesis', as it might be called, does provide an originating agent, within each locality, of the developments that we are seeking to understand. It also provides an hypothesis that is testable, as field research progresses.

With the emergence of an elite in the societies that have been discussed, social stratification became inevitable. All of the archaeological examples that have been examined show signs of such social differentiation to a greater or lesser degree. There were clearly those few who were in charge and those masses who did what they were told. Less easy to recognize are the people in the middle, who acted on behalf of the elite but were neither of their ranks nor of those of the labouring class. Whatever the details of the hierarchy, however, in each of the cases reviewed in this book it was legitimized and reinforced by one form or another of religious ideology. In all instances, the earliest manifestations of this were indigenous, presumably animistic, religions but in cases where there was prolonged contact with the outside world these were eventually replaced or overlaid by Christianity or Islam. Whatever its form, however, it does seem that in each case the spiritual came to the aid of the material. That is, perhaps, to understate the case. Some scholars would think that such a view underrates the importance of African indigenous religions, particularly during the earlier phases of the processes with which this book has been concerned. They would point out that such religions were a means of manipulating the forces believed to control fertility, in all senses of that word, and therefore gave power to those who were believed to be able to do this. In that case, the role of religion could have been much more than merely validating the authority of those who had acquired power by other means: African power-holders were nearly always priests *themselves*. As such, they could indeed have claimed control of the best land or of the internal exchange systems or even, eventually, of their end of external long-distance trade networks, and who would have been prepared to deny them?

This book has been more concerned with archaeological evidence than with theoretical matters: it has attempted to keep its feet on the ground. However, any attempt to identify some of the main factors that gave rise to the cities and states of precolonial Africa has theoretical implications. Turning back to some of the discussion of Chapter 2, it would appear that the power theory of state formation advocated by Haas (p. 10) does indeed help to understand the African situation and therefore does have some explanatory value. Furthermore, it does seem that Lonsdale (p. 14) is correct in concluding that state formation in Africa was a very slow process, involving the coercive centralization of power, and resulting from local politics not from external ideas. This being the case, one is inclined to agree with Renfrew (p. 11) that the division into 'pristine' and 'secondary' states, which has so often been made, is a meaningless exercise.

The question remains, however, as to whether one *should* mix up the development of cities and the formation of states, as has been done here. It seems difficult to avoid this: centralization of power, social stratification, functional specialization, these and other related developments, together with population growth, produced not only the authority structure that we call the state but also the urban unit or units on which it was so often centred. This is not to say that all states had static cities: medieval Ethiopia is an example of how this need not be so. Nevertheless, most did have settlements in which relatively large groups of people were congregated: whether they are called large villages, towns or even cities hardly matters, the important point is that they were relatively dense aggregations of population. In this respect one recalls Mabogunje's straight-forward definition of urbanization (p. 12). Indeed, in the minds of the people involved, it seems that the ideas of state and city may well have been inextricably associated. Thus, in 1893, Lugard found it necessary to emphasize the close association of state, ruler and city in the case of Buganda: 'The Waganda consider their country to be where the King is, and if no Kabaka of the Royal blood is installed in Mengo, the result would be a break-up of the people' (Lugard 1893: 36). It is with the overall process of the coming-together of people in tropical Africa that this book has been concerned.

Bibliography

Adams, W.Y. 1961. The Christian potteries at Faras. *Kush* 9, 30–43.

Adams, W.Y. 1965. Sudan Antiquities Service excavations at Meinarti, 1963–64. *Kush* 13. 148–76.

Adams, W.Y. 1966. Post-Pharaonic Nubia in the light of archaeology, Part III. *Journal of Egyptian Archaeology* 52, 147–62.

Adams, W.Y. 1974. Sacred and secular polities in ancient Nubia. *World Archaeology* 6(1), 39–51.

Adams, W.Y. 1976. Meroitic north and south. A study in cultural contrasts. *Meroitica* 2, 11–26.

Adams, W.Y. 1977. *Nubia: Corridor to Africa*, Allen Lane, London. (Reprinted in 1984 without revision but with a new preface reporting on recent developments.)

Adams, W.Y. 1981. Ecology and economy in the Empire of Kush. *Zeitschrift für Ägyptische Sprache* 108, 1–12.

Adams, W.Y. 1982. Qasr Ibrim: an archaeological conspectus. In *Nubian studies: proceedings of the Symposium for Nubian Studies, Selwyn College, Cambridge, 1978*, ed. J.M. Plumley, 25–33. International Society for Nubian Studies, Aris & Phillips, Warminster, England.

Adams, W.Y. 1984. The first colonial empire: Egypt in Nubia, 3200–1200 BC. *Comparative Studies in Society and History* 26(1), 36–71.

Adams, W.Y. in press. The Nubian town from ancient to modern times. In *The indigenous African town* ed. M. Posnansky. University of California Press.

Adams, W.Y., Alexander, J.A. and Allen, R. 1983. Qasr Ibrim 1980 and 1982. *Journal of Egyptian Archaeology* 69, 43–60.

Addo-Fening, R. 1976. The gold mining industry in Akyem Abuakwa c.1850–1910. *Sankofa* 2, 33–9.

Africanus, Leo. 1896. *The history and description of Africa*, 3 vols, ed. R. Brown. Hakluyt Society, London.

Ajayi, J.F.A. and Smith, R. 1971. *Yoruba warfare in the nineteenth century*, 2nd edn. Cambridge University Press, Cambridge.

Alagoa, E.J. 1970. Long-distance trade and states in the Niger Delta. *Journal of African History* 11(3), 319–29.

Alexander, J. 1972. The beginnings of urban life in Europe. In *Man, settlement and urbanism*, eds. P.J. Ucko, R. Tringham and G.W. Dimbleby, 843–50. Duckworth, London.

Bibliography

Ali, A.M. 1972. Meroitic settlement of the Butana (central Sudan). In *Man, settlement and urbanism*, eds. P.J. Ucko, R. Tringham and G.W. Dimbleby, 639–46. Duckworth, London.

Allen, J. de V. 1974. Swahili culture reconsidered: Some historical implications of the material culture of the northern Kenya coast in the eighteenth and nineteenth centuries. *Azania* 9, 105–38.

Allen, J. de V. 1979. The Swahili house: Cultural and ritual concepts underlying its plan and structure. In *Swahili houses and tombs of the coast of Kenya*, eds. J. de V. Allen and T.H. Wilson. Art and Archaeology Research Papers, London.

Allen, J. de V. 1980. Settlement patterns on the East African coast, c. AD 800–1900. In *Proceedings of the 8th Panafrican Congress of Prehistory and Quaternary Studies, Nairobi, 5 to 10 September 1977*. eds. R.E. Leakey and B.A. Ogot, 361–3. The International Louis Leakey Memorial Institute for African Prehistory, Nairobi.

Allen, J. de V. 1982. The 'Shirazi' problem in East African coastal history. In *From Zinj to Zanzibar: Studies in history, trade and society on the eastern coast of Africa, (Paideuma 28)*, eds. J. de V. Allen and T.H. Wilson, 9–27.

Allen, J. de V. 1983. Shungwaya, the Mijikenda, and the traditions. *International Journal of African Historical Studies* 16(3), 455–85.

Allison, P.A. 1962. Historical inferences to be drawn from the effect of human settlement on the vegetation of Africa. *Journal of African History* 3(2), 241–9.

al-Sa'di. 1964. *Tarikh es-Soudan*, texte Arabe édité et traduit par O. Houdas, Adrien-Maisonneuve, Paris.

Anciaux de Faveaux, E. and Maret, P. de, 1984. Premières datations pour la fonte du cuivre au Shaba (Zaïre). *Bulletin de la Société Royale Belge d'Anthropologie et de Préhistoire* 95, 5–20.

Andah, B.W. 1976. An archaeological view of the urbanization process in the earliest West African states. *Journal of the Historical Society of Nigeria* 8(3), 1–20.

Andrews, F.W. 1948. The vegetation of the Sudan. In *Agriculture in the Sudan*, ed. J.D. Tothill, 32–61. Oxford University Press, London.

Anfray, F. 1963. La première campagne de fouilles à Matarā, près de Sénafé (Novembre 1959 – Janvier 1960), *Annales d'Ethiopie* 5, 87–166.

Anfray, F. 1967. Matarā, *Annales d'Ethiopie* 7, 33–88.

Anfray, F. 1968. Aspects de l'archéologie éthiopienne. *Journal of African History* 9(3), 345–66.

Anfray, F. 1972a. Fouilles de Yeha. *Annales d'Ethiopie* 9, 45–64.

Anfray, F. 1972b. L'archéologie d'Axoum en 1972. *Paideuma* 18, 60–78.

Anfray, F. 1973. Nouveaux sites antiques. *Journal of Ethiopian Studies* 11(2), 13–27.

Anfray, F. 1981. The civilization of Aksum from the first to the seventh century. In *General History of Africa*, Vol. 2, *Ancient civilizations of Africa*, ed. G. Mokhtar, 362–80. Heinemann, University of California, Unesco; London, Berkeley, Paris.

Anfray, F. and Annequin, G. 1965. Matarā, deuxième, troisième et quatrième campagnes de fouilles. *Annales d'Ethiopie* 6, 49–85.

Annequin, G. 1965. Château de Gouzara. *Annales d'Ethiopie* 6, 22–5.

Anquandah, J. 1982. *Rediscovering Ghana's past*. Longman, Harlow; Sedco, Accra.

Arkell, A.J. 1961. *A history of the Sudan from the earliest times to 1821*, 2nd edn. University of London Press, London.

Ashe, R.P. 1889. *Two Kings of Uganda*. Sampson Low etc., London.

Babayemi, S.O. 1974. The Upper Ogun and Old Oyo Game Reserve. *Nigerian Field* 39(1), 4–12.

Barker, G. 1978. Economic models for the Manekweni Zimbabwe, Mozambique. *Azania* 13, 71–100.

Bartlett, J. 1980. *Familiar quotations*, 15th edn. Macmillan, London.

Bascom, W. 1955. Urbanization among the Yoruba. *The American Journal of Sociology* 60(5), 446–54.

Bascom, W. 1959. Urbanism as a traditional African pattern. *Sociological Review* (N.S.) 7, 29–43.

Beach, D.N. 1980. *The Shona and Zimbabwe 900–1850*. Heinemann, London.

Beaujeu-Garnier, J. and Chabot, G. 1967. (Translated by Yglesias, G.M. and Beaver, S.H.) *Urban geography*. Longmans, London.

Bedaux, R.M.A., Constandse-Westermann, T.S., Hacquebord, L., Lange, A.G. and van der Waals, J.D. 1978. Recherches archéologiques dans le Delta Intérieur du Niger (Mali). *Palaeohistoria* 20, 19–220.

Beek, G.W. van, 1967. Monuments of Axum in the light of South Arabian archeology. *Journal of the American Oriental Society* 87(2), 113–22.

Bellamy, C.V. 1904. A West African smelting house. *Journal of the Iron and Steel Institute* 66, 99–126.

Bent, J.T. 1893. *The sacred city of the Ethiopians*. Longmans, Green, and Co., London.

Bent, J.T. 1896. *The ruined cities of Mashonaland*, New edition (Reissue). Longmans, London.

Binger, Capitaine. 1892. *Du Niger au Golfe de Guinée*. 2 vols. Hachette, Paris.

Bisson, M.S. 1975. Copper currency in central Africa: the archaeological evidence. *World Archaeology* 6(3), 276–92.

Bisson, M.S. 1976. The prehistoric coppermines of Zambia. Ph.D. thesis, University of California, Santa Barbara. University Microfilms International.

Bivar, A.D.H. and Shinnie, P.L. 1962. Old Kanuri capitals. *Journal of African History* 3(1), 1–10.

Blake, J.W. 1942. *Europeans in West Africa, 1450–1560*, 2 vols. Hakluyt, London.

Bloch, M.R. 1963. The social influence of salt. *Scientific American* 209, 88–98.

Boisragon, A. 1897. *The Benin Massacre*. Methuen, London.

Bonnet, C. 1982a. Les fouilles archéologiques de Kerma (Soudan). *Genava* 30, 29–70.

Bonnet, C. 1982b. La ville de Kerma. In *Nubian studies: proceedings of the Symposium for Nubian Studies, Selwyn College, Cambridge, 1978*, ed. J.M. Plumley, 45–56. International Society for Nubian Studies, Aris & Phillips, Warminster, England.

Bonnet, C. 1984. Archaeological mission of the University of Geneva to Kerma, 1983–1984 season. *Nyame Akuma* 24/25, 18–19.

Bosman, W. 1967. *A new and accurate description of the coast of Guinea*, 4th edn. Cass, London (1st English edn. 1705).

Bovill, E.W. 1968. *The golden trade of the Moors*, 2nd edn. Oxford University Press, London.

Bowdich, T.E. 1966. *Mission from Cape Coast Castle to Ashantee*, 3rd edn. Cass, London, (1st edn. 1819).

Bradbury, R.E. 1959. Chronological problems in the study of Benin history. *Journal of the Historical Society of Nigeria* 1(4), 263–87.

Bradley, R.J. 1982. Varia from the city of Meroë. *Meroitica* 6, 163–70.

Brain, C.K. 1974. Human food remains from the Iron Age at Zimbabwe. *South African Journal of Science* 70, 303–9.

Budge, E.A.W. 1907. *The Egyptian Sudan: its history and monuments*. Vol. 2. Kegan Paul, Trench, Trübner & Co., London.

Bulliet, R.W. 1975. *The camel and the wheel*. Harvard University Press, Cambridge, Massachusetts.

Butzer, K.W. 1976. *Early hydraulic civilization in Egypt: a study in cultural ecology*. Chicago University Press, Chicago.

Butzer, K.W. 1981. Rise and fall of Axum, Ethiopia: a geo-archaeological interpretation. *American Antiquity* 46(3), 471–95.

Buxton, D.R. 1947. The Christian antiquities of Northern Ethiopia. *Archaeologia* 92, 1–42.

Buxton, D.R. 1970. *The Abyssinians*. Thames & Hudson, London.

Buxton, D.R. 1971. The rock-hewn and other medieval churches of Tigré Province, Ethiopia. *Archaeologia* 103, 33–100.

Calvocoressi, D. and David, N. 1979. A new survey of radiocarbon and thermoluminescence dates for West Africa. *Journal of African History* 20(1), 1–29.

Camps, G. 1982. Le cheval et le char dans la préhistoire Nord-Africaine et Saharienne. In *Les chars préhistoriques du Sahara*, eds. G. Camps and M. Gast, 9–22. Université de Provence, Aix-en-Provence.

Caney, R.W. and Reynolds, J.E. 1976. *Reed's marine distance tables*, 3rd edn. Reed, London.

Carneiro, R.L. 1970. A theory of the origin of the state. *Science* 169, 733–8.

Carter, P.L. and Flight, C. 1972. A report on the fauna from the sites of Ntereso and Kintampo Rock Shelter Six in Ghana: with evidence for the practice of animal husbandry during the second millennium BC *Man* 7(2), 277–82.

Caton-Thompson, G. 1971. *The Zimbabwe culture: ruins and reactions*, 2nd edn. Cass, London, (1st edn. 1931).

Chandler, T. and Fox, G. 1974. *3000 years of urban growth*. Academic Press, New York and London.

Childe, V.G. 1950. The urban revolution. *The Town Planning Review* 21, 3–17.

Childe, V.G. 1951. *Social evolution*. Watts, London.

Childe, V.G. 1957. Civilization, cities and towns. *Antiquity* 31, 36–8.

Chittick, N. 1965. The 'Shirazi' colonization of East Africa. *Journal of African History* 6(3), 275–94.

Chittick, N. 1966. Six early coins from near Tanga. *Azania* 1, 156–7.

Chittick, N. 1967. Discoveries in the Lamu Archipelago. *Azania* 2, 37–67.

Chittick, N. 1971. The coast of East Africa. In *The African Iron Age*, ed. P.L. Shinnie, 108–41. Clarendon Press, Oxford.

Chittick, N. 1974a. Excavations at Aksum, 1973–4: a preliminary report. *Azania* 9, 159–205.

Chittick, N. 1974b. *Kilwa: An Islamic trading city on the East African coast*, 2 vols. Memoir No.5 of the British Institute in Eastern Africa, Nairobi.

Chittick, N. 1975. An early salt-working site on the Tanzanian coast. *Azania* 10, 151–3.

Chittick, N. 1977. The East Coast, Madagascar and the Indian Ocean. In *The Cambridge history of Africa*, ed. R. Oliver, Vol. 3, 183–231. Cambridge University Press, Cambridge.

Chittick, N. 1980. Sewn boats in the western Indian Ocean, and a survival in Somalia. *International Journal of Nautical Archaeology and Underwater Exploration* 9(4), 297–309.

Chittick, N. 1981. The *Periplus* and the spice trade. *Azania* 16, 185–90.

Chittick, N. 1984. *Manda: Excavations at an island port on the Kenya coast.* Memoir No. 9 of the British Institute in Eastern Africa, Nairobi.

Claessen, H.J.M. and Skalník, P. (eds.) 1978. *The early state*. Mouton, The Hague.

Clarke, S. 1912. *Christian antiquities in the Nile Valley: a contribution towards the study of the ancient churches*. Clarendon Press, Oxford.

Cohen, R. and Service, E.R. (eds.) 1978. *Origins of the state: the anthropology of political evolution*. Institute for the study of human issues, Philadelphia.

Collins, M.O. (ed.) 1965. *Rhodesia: its natural resources and economic development*. M.O. Collins, Salisbury, Rhodesia.

Connah, G. 1972. Archaeology in Benin. *Journal of African History* 13(1), 25–38.

Connah, G. 1975. *The archaeology of Benin*. Oxford University Press, Oxford.

Connah, G. 1981. *Three thousand years in Africa: man and his environment in the Lake Chad region of Nigeria*. Cambridge University Press, Cambridge.

Connah, G. 1985. Agricultural intensification and sedentism in the firki of N.E. Nigeria. In *Prehistoric intensive agriculture in the tropics*, ed. I.S. Farrington, 765–85. BAR International Series 232, Oxford.

Contenson, H. de, 1962. Les monuments d'art Sud-Arabe découverts sur le site de Haoulti (Ethiopie) en 1959. *Syria: Revue d'art oriental et d'archéologie* 39, 64–87.

Contenson, H. de, 1963a. Les fouilles de Haoulti en 1959: rapport préliminaire. *Annales d'Ethiopie* 5, 41–86.

Contenson, H. de, 1963b. Les fouilles à Axoum en 1958: rapport préliminaire. *Annales d'Ethiopie* 5, 1–40.

Contenson, H. de, 1981. Pre-Aksumite culture. In *General history of Africa*, Vol. 2, *Ancient civilizations of Africa*, ed. G. Mokhtar, 341–61. Heinemann, University of California, Unesco; London, Berkeley, Paris.

Cotterell, A. (ed.) 1983. *The encyclopedia of ancient civilizations*. Macmillan, London.

Coursey, D.G. 1980. The origins and domestication of yams in Africa. In *West African culture dynamics: Archaeological and historical perspectives*, eds. B.K. Swartz, and R.E. Dumett, 67–90. Mouton, The Hague.

Crawford, O.G.S. 1951. *The Fung kingdom of Sennar*. John Bellows, Gloucester.

Crawford, O.G.S. 1956. Editorial notes. *Antiquity* 30, 129–31.

Crossland, L.B. 1976. Excavations at Nyarko and Dwinfuor sites of Begho – 1975. *Sankofa* 2, 86–7.

Curtin, P.D. 1973. The lure of Bambuk gold. *Journal of African History* 14(4), 623–31.

Daniel, G. 1968. *The first civilizations: The archaeology of their origins*. Thames and Hudson, London.

Dapper, O. 1686. *Description de l'Afrique ... Traduite du Flamand*, Chez Wolfgang, Waesberge, Boom & van Someren, Amsterdam.

Dark, P.J.C. 1973. *An introduction to Benin art and technology*. Clarendon Press, Oxford.

Darling, P.J. 1974. The earthworks of Benin. *Nigerian Field* 39(3), 128–37.

Darling, P.J. 1976. Notes on the earthworks of the Benin Empire. *West African Journal of Archaeology* 6, 143–9.

Darling, P.J. 1982. Ancient linear earthworks of Benin and Ishan, Southern Nigeria, 2 vols. Unpublished Ph.D. thesis, University of Birmingham.

Darling, P.J. 1984. *Archaeology and history in southern Nigeria*, 2 vols. Cambridge Monographs in African Archaeology 11, BAR International Series 215(i) & (ii), Oxford.

Datoo, B.A. 1970. Rhapta: the location and importance of East Africa's first port. *Azania* 5, 65–75.

Davidson, B. 1959. *Old Africa rediscovered*. Gollancz, London.

Davidson, B. 1970. *The lost cities of Africa*. Little, Brown & Co., Boston. (Originally published 1959 as *Old Africa rediscovered*, Gollancz, London.)

Davison, C.C. and Clark, J.D. 1974. Trade wind beads: An interim report of chemical studies. *Azania* 9, 75–86.

Davison, P. and Harries, P. 1980. Cotton weaving in south-east Africa: its history and technology. *Textile History* 11, 175–92.

Denyer, S. 1978. *African traditional architecture*. Heinemann, London.

Desplagnes, L. 1903. Etude sur les Tumuli du Killi, dans la région de Goundam. *L'Anthropologie* 14, 151–72.

Desplagnes, L. 1951. Fouilles du tumulus d'El Oualedji (Soudan); annoté par R. Mauny. *Bulletin de l'IFAN*. Dakar, 13(4), 1159–73.

Devisse, J. et al. (eds.) 1983. *Tegdaoust III: Recherches sur Aoudaghost (Campagnes 1960–1965)*. A.D.P.F., Paris.

Donley, L.W. 1982. House power: Swahili space and symbolic markers. In *Symbolic and structural archaeology*, ed. I. Hodder, 63–73. Cambridge University Press, Cambridge.

Doresse, J. (trans. E. Coult) 1959. *Ethiopia*. Elek Books, London.

Dummett, R.E. 1979. Precolonial gold mining and the state in the Akan region: with a critique of the Terray Hypothesis. *Research in economic anthropology* 2, 37–68.

Dunham, D. 1950. *The royal cemeteries of Kush, Vol. 1: El Kurru*. Harvard University Press, Cambridge, Massachusetts.

Dunham, D. 1955. *The royal cemeteries of Kush, Vol. 2: Nuri*. Museum of Fine Arts, Boston, Massachusetts.

Dunham, D. and Macadam, M.F.L. 1949. Names and relationships of the royal family of Napata. *Journal of Egyptian Archaeology* 35, 139–49.

Eades, J.S. 1980. *The Yoruba today*. Cambridge University Press, Cambridge.

Egharevba, J. 1968. *A short history of Benin*, 4th edn. Ibadan University Press, Ibadan.

Ehret, C. 1979. On the antiquity of agriculture in Ethiopia. *Journal of African History* 20, 161–77.

Emery, W.B. 1938. *The royal tombs of Ballana and Qustul*, 2 vols. Government Press, Cairo.

Emery, W.B. 1948. *Nubian treasure: an account of the discoveries at Ballana and Qustul*. Methuen, London.

Emery, W.B. 1965. *Egypt in Nubia*. Hutchinson, London.

Endt, D.W. von, 1978. Was civet used as a perfume in Aksum? *Azania* 13, 186–8.

Eyo, E. 1974. Odo Ogbe Street and Lafogido: contrasting archaeological sites in Ile-Ife, Western Nigeria. *West African Journal of Archaeology* 4, 99–109.

Fagan, B.M. 1969. Early trade and raw materials in south central Africa. *Journal of African History* 10(1), 1–13.

Fagan, B.M., Phillipson, D.W. and Daniels, S.G.H. 1969. *Iron Age cultures in Zambia (Dambwa, Ingombe Ilede and the Tonga)*, Vol. 2. Chatto and Windus, London.

Fagan, B.M. and Yellen, J.E. 1968. Ivuna: ancient salt-working in southern Tanzania. *Azania* 3, 1–43.

Fage, J.D. and Verity, M. 1978. *An atlas of African history*, 2nd edn. Edward Arnold, London.

Fairman, H.W. 1938. Preliminary report on the excavations at Sesebi (Sudla) and ʾAmārah West, Anglo-Egyptian Sudan, 1937–8. *Journal of Egyptian Archaeology* 24, 151–6.

Filipowiak, W. 1966. Expédition archéologique Polono-Guinéenne à Niani (Guinée). *Africana Bulletin* 4, 116–27.

Filipowiak, W. 1969. L'expédition archéologique Polono-Guinéenne à Niani, en 1968. *Africana Bulletin* 11, 107–17.

Flight, C. 1975. Gao, 1972: First interim report: a preliminary investigation of the cemetery at Sané. *West African Journal of Archaeology* 5, 81–90.

Flight, C. 1976. The Kintampo Culture and its place in the economic prehistory of West Africa. In *Origins of African plant domestication*, eds. J.R. Harlan, J.M.J. de Wet and A.B.L. Stemler, 211–21. Mouton, The Hague.

Forman, W., Forman, B., and Dark, P. 1960. *Benin art*. Hamlyn, London.

Freeman-Grenville, G.S.P. 1960. East African coin finds and their historical significance. *Journal of African History* 1(1), 31–43.

Freeman-Grenville, G.S.P. 1975. *The East African coast: Select documents from the first to the earlier nineteenth century*, 2nd edn. Collings, London.

Fried, M.H. 1967. *The evolution of political society: an essay in political anthropology*. Random House, New York.

Gallay A. et al. 1982. Mbolop Tobé (Santhiou Kohel, Sénégal): Contribution à la connaissance du mégalithisme sénégambien. *Archives suisses d'anthropologie générale* (Genève) 46(2), 217–59.

Garlake, P.S. 1966. *The early Islamic architecture of the East African coast*. Oxford University Press, London.

Garlake, P.S. 1968. The value of imported ceramics in the dating and interpretation of the Rhodesian Iron Age. *Journal of African History* 9(1), 13–33.

Garlake, P.S. 1970a. Rhodesian ruins – a preliminary assessment of their styles and chronology. *Journal of African History* 11(4), 495–513.

Garlake, P.S. 1970b. The decline of Zimbabwe in the fifteenth century. *Rhodesian Prehistory* 5, 6–8.

Garlake, P.S. 1972. Excavations at the Nhunguza and Ruanga Ruins in northern Mashonaland. *South African Archaeological Bulletin* 27, 107–43.

Garlake, P.S. 1973. *Great Zimbabwe*. Thames and Hudson, London.

Garlake, P.S. 1974. Excavations at Obalara's Land, Ife: an interim report. *West African Journal of Archaeology* 4, 111–48.

Garlake, P.S. 1976a. An investigation of Manekweni, Mozambique. *Azania* 11, 25–47.

Garlake, P.S. 1976b. Great Zimbabwe: a reappraisal. In *Proceedings of the Panafrican Congress of Prehistory and Quaternary Studies: 7th Session, Addis Ababa, December 1971*, eds. B. Abebe, J. Chavaillon and J.E.G. Sutton, 221–26. Provisional Military Government of Socialist Ethiopia, Ministry of Culture, Addis Ababa.

Garlake, P.S. 1977. Excavations on the Woye Asiri Family Land in Ife, Western Nigeria. *West African Journal of Archaeology* 7, 57–96.

Garlake, P.S. 1978a. *The kingdoms of Africa*. Elsevier-Phaidon, Oxford.

Garlake, P.S. 1978b. Pastoralism and *Zimbabwe*. *Journal of African History* 19(4), 479–93.

Garlake, P.S. and Garlake M. 1964. Early ship engravings of the East African coast. *Tanganyika Notes and Records* 63, 197–206.

Garstang, J., Sayce, A.H., and Griffiths, F.W. 1911. *Meroë, the city of the Ethiopians*. Oxford University Press, Oxford.

Gerster, G. 1970. *Churches in rock: Early Christian art in Ethiopia*, translated by R. Hosking. Phaidon, London.

Gibbon, E. 1952. *The decline and fall of the Roman Empire*, 2 vols. Encyclopaedia Britannica, Inc., Chicago.

Goodwin, A.J.H. 1957. Archaeology and Benin architecture. *Journal of the Historical Society of Nigeria* 1(2), 65–85.

Goodwin, A.J.H. 1963. A bronze snake head and other recent finds in the old palace at Benin. *Man* 63, 142–5.

Goody, J. 1971. *Technology, tradition and the state in Africa*. Oxford University Press, London.

Griffith, F. Ll. 1922. Oxford excavations in Nubia. *Annals of Archaeology and Anthropology* 9, Liverpool Institute of Archaeology, Liverpool University Press, Liverpool.

Grove, A.T. 1978. *Africa*, 3rd edn. Oxford University Press, Oxford.

Gutkind, P.C.W. 1960. Notes on the kibuga of Buganda. *Uganda Journal* 24(1), 29–43.

Gutkind, P.C.W. 1963. *The royal capital of Buganda*. Mouton, The Hague.

Gwynne, M.D. 1975. The origin and spread of some domestic food plants of Eastern Africa. In *East Africa and the Orient: Cultural syntheses in pre-colonial times*, eds. N. Chittick and R.I. Rotberg, 248–71. Africana Publishing Company, New York and London.

Haas, J. 1982. *The evolution of the prehistoric state*. New York University Press.

Håland, R. 1980. Man's role in the changing habitat of Mema during the old kingdom of Ghana. *Norwegian Archaeological Review* 13, 31–46.

Hall, R.N. 1905. *Great Zimbabwe*. Methuen, London.

Harlan, J.R. and Pasquereau, J. 1969. Décrue agriculture in Mali. *Economic Botany* 23(1), 70–74.

Harris, D.R. 1976. Traditional systems of plant food production and the origins of agriculture in West Africa. In *Origins of African plant domestication*, eds. J.R. Harlan, J.M.J. de Wet and A.B.L. Stemler, 311–56. Mouton, The Hague.

Hawkes, C.F.C. 1951. British prehistory half-way through the century. *Proceedings of the Prehistoric Society* 17, 1–15.

Haycock, B.G. 1968. Towards a better understanding of the Kingdom of Cush (Napata-Meroë). *Sudan Notes and Records* 49, 1–16.

Herbert, E.W. 1973. Aspects of the use of copper in pre-colonial West Africa. *Journal of African History* 14(2), 179–94.

Herbert, E.W. 1984. *Red gold of Africa: Copper in precolonial history and culture.* University of Wisconsin Press, Madison.

Herring, R.S. 1979. Hydrology and chronology: The Rodah Nilometer as an aid in dating interlacustrine history. In *Chronology, migration and drought in interlacustrine Africa*, ed. J.B. Webster, 39–86. Longman, London.

Hiernaux, J. et al. 1971. *Fouilles archéologiques dans la vallée du Haut-Lualaba. I Sanga 1958.* Musée Royal de l'Afrique Centrale, Tervuren, Belgium.

Hintze, F. 1959. Preliminary report of the Butana Expedition 1958, made by the Institute for Egyptology of the Humboldt University, Berlin. *Kush* 7, 171–96.

Hodgkin, T. 1975. *Nigerian perspectives*, 2nd edn. Oxford University Press, Oxford.

Home, R. 1982. *City of Blood revisited: a new look at the Benin expedition of 1897.* Rex Collings, London.

Horton, M.C. 1980. *Shanga 1980: An interim report of the National Museums of Kenya archaeological project at Shanga, during the summer of 1980, as part of the work of Operation Drake.* Operation Drake, London.

Horton, M.C. 1983. Personal communication.

Huffman, T.N. 1971. Cloth from the Iron Age in Rhodesia. *Arnoldia* (Rhodesia) 5, 1–19.

Huffman, T.N. 1972. The rise and fall of Zimbabwe. *Journal of African History* 13(3), 353–66.

Huffman, T.N. 1974a. Ancient mining and Zimbabwe. *Journal of the South African Institute of Mining and Metallurgy* 74, 238–42.

Huffman, T.N. 1974b. *The Leopard's Kopje Tradition.* Museum Memoir No. 6, Trustees of the National Museums and Monuments of Rhodesia. Salisbury, Rhodesia.

Huffman, T.N. 1977. Zimbabwe: southern Africa's first town. *Rhodesian Prehistory* 7(15), 9–14.

Huffman, T.N. 1978. The origins of Leopard's Kopje: an 11th century Difaquane. *Arnoldia* (Rhodesia). Series of miscellaneous publications, National Museums and Monuments of Rhodesia, 8(23), 1–23.

Huffman, T.N. 1981. *Snakes and birds: Expressive space at Great Zimbabwe.* Inaugural lecture, University of Witwatersrand, Johannesburg. Witwatersrand

University Press, Johannesburg. (Also published in 1981 in *African Studies* 40(2), 131–50.)

Huffman, T.N. 1982. Archaeology and ethnohistory of the African Iron Age. *Annual Review of Anthropology* 11, 133–50.

Huffman, T.N. 1984. Expressive space in Zimbabwe culture. *Man* (N.S.) 19, 593–612.

Huffman, T.N. 1985a. Letter to author dated 5 September 1985.

Huffman, T.N. 1985b. The soapstone birds from Great Zimbabwe. *African Arts* 18(3), 68–73, 99–100.

Hull, R.W. 1976a. *African cities and towns before the European conquest*. Norton, New York.

Hull, R.W. 1976b. Urban design and architecture in precolonial Africa. *Journal of Urban History* 2(4), 387–414.

Hunwick, J. 1971. Songhay, Bornu and Hausaland in the sixteenth century. In *History of West Africa*, Vol. 1, eds. J.F.A. Ajayi and M. Crowder, 202–39. Longman, London.

Hunwick, J.O. 1973. The mid-fourteenth century capital of Mali. *Journal of African History* 14(2), 195–206.

Jahadhmy, A.A. 1981. *Learner's Swahili-English, English-Swahili Dictionary*. Evans, London.

Jakobielski, S. 1982. Polish excavations at Old Dongola in 1976 and 1978. In *Nubian studies: proceedings of the Symposium for Nubian Studies, Selwyn College, Cambridge 1978*, ed. J.M. Plumley, 116–26. International Society for Nubian Studies, Aris & Phillips, Warminster, England.

Johnson, M. 1970a. The cowrie currencies of West Africa, Part I. *Journal of African History* 11(1), 17–49.

Johnson, M. 1970b. The cowrie currencies of West Africa, Part II. *Journal of African History* 11(3), 331–53.

Johnson, S. 1921. *The history of the Yorubas*. Routledge, London.

Joire, J. 1943. Archaeological discoveries in Senegal. *Man* 43, 49–52.

Joire, J. 1955. Découvertes archéologiques dans la région de Rao (Bas-Sénégal). *Bulletin de l'IFAN*. Dakar, 17(B), 249–333.

Jones, E. 1966. *Towns and cities*. Oxford University Press, London.

Jones, E.W. 1956. Ecological studies on the rain forest of southern Nigeria, IV, part II. *Journal of Ecology* 44, 83–117.

Keay, R.W.J. 1959. *Vegetation map of Africa south of the Tropic of Cancer*. Oxford University Press, London.

Kenyon, K.M. 1956. Jericho and its setting in Near Eastern history. *Antiquity* 30, 184–97.

Kiéthéga, J.–B. 1983. *L'or de la Volta Noire: Archéologie et histoire de l'exploitation traditionnelle (Région de Poura, Haute-Volta)*. Karthala, Paris.

Kirkman, J.S. 1952. The excavations at Kilepwa. An introduction to the medieval archaeology of the Kenya coast. *The Antiquaries Journal* 32, 168–84.

Kirkman, J.S. 1954. *The Arab city of Gedi: excavations at the Great Mosque. Architecture and finds*. Oxford University Press, London.

Kirkman, J.S. 1959. Mnarani of Kilifi: The mosques and tombs. *Ars Orientalis* 3, 95–112.

Kirkman, J.S. 1960. *The tomb of the dated inscription at Gedi*. Occasional Paper No. 14, Royal Anthropological Institute of Great Britain and Ireland, London.

Kirkman, J.S. 1963. *Gedi: the Palace*. Mouton & Co., The Hague.

Kirkman, J.S. 1964. *Men and monuments on the East African coast*. Lutterworth Press, London.

Kirkman, J.S. 1966. *Ungwana on the Tana*. Mouton & Co., The Hague.

Kirkman, J.S. 1975. Some conclusions from archaeological excavations on the coast of Kenya, 1948–1966. In *East Africa and the Orient: Cultural syntheses in pre-colonial times*, eds. N. Chittick and R.I. Rotberg, 226–47. Africana Publishing Company, New York and London.

Kirwan, L.P. 1972. The Christian Topography and the Kingdom of Axum. *Geographical Journal* 138(2), 166–77.

Kluckhohn, C. 1960. The moral order in the expanding society. In *City invincible: a symposium on urbanization and cultural development in the ancient Near East*, eds. C.H. Kraeling and R.M. Adams, 391–404. Chicago University Press, Chicago.

Kobishchanov, Y.M. (trans. L.T. Kapitanoff) 1979. *Axum* (edited by J.W. Michels). Pennsylvania State University Press, University Park and London.

Kobish[ch]anov, Y.M. 1981. Aksum: political system, economics and culture, first to fourth century. In *General history of Africa*, Vol. 2, *Ancient civilizations of Africa*, ed. G. Mokhtar, 381–400. Heinemann, University of California, Unesco; London, Berkeley, Paris.

Köhler, O. 1953–4. Das 'Pferd' in den Gur-sprachen. *Afrika und Übersee* 38, 93–110.

Krapf-Askari, E. 1969. *Yoruba towns and cities*. Clarendon Press, Oxford.

Krencker, D. 1913. *Deutsche Aksum-Expedition*. Band II, Georg Reimer, Berlin.

Kuper, L. and Smith, M.G. (eds.) 1969. *Pluralism in Africa*. University of California Press, Berkeley and Los Angeles.

Law, R. 1978. Slaves, trade, and taxes: the material base of political power in pre-colonial West Africa. *Research in Economic Anthropology* 1, 37–52.

Law, R. 1980a. Wheeled transport in pre-colonial West Africa. *Africa* 50(3), 249–62.

Law, R. 1980b. *The horse in West African history*. Oxford University Press, Oxford.

Lawal, B. 1973. Dating problems at Igbo-Ukwu. *Journal of African History* 14(1), 1–8.

Leclant, J. 1973. Glass from the Meroitic necropolis of Sedeinga (Sudanese Nubia). *Journal of Glass Studies* 15, 52–68.

Levtzion, N. 1973. *Ancient Ghana and Mali*. Methuen, London.

Liesegang, G. 1972. Archaeological sites on the Bay of Sofala. *Azania* 7, 147–59.

Livingstone, F.B. 1967. The origin of the sickle-cell gene. In *Reconstructing African culture history*, eds. C. Gabel and N.R. Bennett, 139–66. Boston University Press, Boston.

Logan, P.N. 1929. The walled city of Kano. *Journal of the Royal Institute of British Architects* 36(10), 402–6.

Lonsdale, J. 1981. States and social processes in Africa: A historiographical survey. *African Studies Review* 24(2 & 3), 139–225.

Lugard, F.D. 1893. In British Parliamentary Papers. Africa. No. 2 (1893). C.–6848, 1–102.

Mabogunje, A.L. 1962. *Yoruba towns*. Ibadan University Press, Ibadan.

Mabogunje, A.L. 1968. *Urbanization in Nigeria*. University of London Press, London.

McIntosh, R.J. 1983. Floodplain geomorphology and human occupation of the upper Inland Delta of the Niger. *The Geographical Journal* 149(2), 182–201.

McIntosh, R.J. 1985. Letter to author dated 12 July 1985.

McIntosh, S.K. and McIntosh, R.J. 1979. Initial perspectives on prehistoric subsistence in the Inland Niger Delta (Mali). *World Archaeology* 11(2), 227–43.

McIntosh, S.K. and McIntosh, R.J. 1980. *Prehistoric investigations in the region of Jenne, Mali*, 2 vols. Cambridge Monographs in African Archaeology 2, BAR International Series 89(i) & (ii), Oxford.

McIntosh, R.J. and McIntosh, S.K. 1981a. The Inland Niger Delta before the Empire of Mali: evidence from Jenne-Jeno. *Journal of African History* 22, 1–22.

McIntosh, R.J. and McIntosh, S.K. 1981b. West African prehistory. *American Scientist* 69, 602–13.

McIntosh, R.J. and McIntosh, S.K. 1982. The 1981 field season at Jenne-Jeno: preliminary results. *Nyame Akuma* 20, 28–32.

McIntosh, R.J. and McIntosh, S.K. 1983a. Forgotten tells of Mali: New evidence of urban beginnings in West Africa. *Expedition* 25, 35–46.

McIntosh, S.K. and McIntosh, R.J. 1983b. Current directions in West African prehistory. *Annual Review of Anthropology* 12, 215–58.

McIntosh, S.K. and McIntosh, R.J. 1984. The early city in West Africa: towards an understanding. *African Archaeological Review*. 2, 73–98.

McLeod, M.D. 1981. *The Asante*. British Museum, London.

McWhirter, N. 1980. *Guinness book of records*. Guinness Superlatives Ltd., London.

Maliphant, G.K., Rees, A.R., and Roese, P.M. 1976. Defence systems of the Benin empire – Uwan. *West African Journal of Archaeology* 6, 121–30.

Manson-Bahr, P.E.C. and Apted, F.I.C. 1982. *Manson's tropical diseases*, 18th edn. Baillière Tindall, London.

Maret, P. de, 1977. Sanga: new excavations, more data, and some related problems. *Journal of African History* 18(3), 321-37.

Maret, P. de, 1979. Luba roots: the first complete Iron Age sequence in Zaïre. *Current Anthropology* 20(1), 233–5.

Maret, P. de, 1981. L'évolution monétaire du Shaba Central entre le 7ᵉ et le 18ᵉ siècle. *African Economic History* 10, 117–49.

Maret, P. de, 1982. The Iron Age in the west and south. In *The archaeology of Central Africa*, ed. F. Van Noten, 77–96. Akademische Druck – und Verlagsanstalt, Graz, Austria.

Maret, P. de, 1985. Letter to author, dated 20 May 1985.

Mathew, G. 1975. The dating and the significance of the *Periplus of the Erythraean Sea*. In *East Africa and the Orient: cultural syntheses in pre-colonial times*, eds. N. Chittick, and R.I. Rotberg, 147–63. Africana Publishing Company, New York and London.

Matthews, D. and Mordini, A. 1959. The monastery of Debra Damo, Ethiopia. *Archaeologia* 97, 1–58.

Mauny, R. 1961. *Tableau géographique de l'Ouest Africain au Moyen-Age d'après les sources écrites, la tradition et l'archéologie.* Mémoires de l'IFAN. 61, Dakar.

Mauny, R. 1978. Trans-Saharan contacts and the Iron Age in West Africa. In *The Cambridge history of Africa*, Vol. 2, ed. J.D. Fage, 272–341. Cambridge University Press, Cambridge.

Mennell, F.P. and Summers, R. 1955. The 'ancient workings' of Southern Rhodesia. *Occasional Papers of the National Museum of Southern Rhodesia*, No. 20, 765–78.

Monod, T. 1969. Le 'Ma'den Ijâfen': une épave caravanière ancienne dans la Majâbat Al-Koubrâ. In *Actes du Ier Colloque international d'Archéologie africaine, 1966.* Fort-Lamy, 286–320.

Moorey, P.R.S. (ed.) 1979. *The origins of civilization: Wolfson College Lectures 1978.* Clarendon Press, Oxford.

Morais, J. and Sinclair, P. 1980. Manyikeni, a Zimbabwe in Southern Mozambique. In *Proceedings of the 8th Panafrican Congress of Prehistory and Quaternary Studies, Nairobi, 5 to 10 September 1977*, eds. R.E. Leakey and B.A. Ogot, 351–4. The International Louis Leakey Memorial Institute for African Prehistory, Nairobi.

Morton-Williams, P. 1972. Some factors in the location, growth and survival of towns in West-Africa. In *Man, settlement and urbanism*, eds. P.J. Ucko, R. Tringham, and G.W. Dimbleby, 883–90. Duckworth, London.

Mumford, L. 1961. *The city in history: its origins, its transformations, and its prospects.* Secker and Warburg, London.

Munro-Hay, S. 1980. 'Ēzānā (Ezana/Ezanas): some numismatic comments. *Azania* 15, 109–119.

Munro-Hay, S. 1982. The foreign trade of the Aksumite port of Adulis. *Azania* 17, 107–25.

Munson, P.J. 1976. Archaeological data on the origins of cultivation in the southwestern Sahara and their implications for West Africa. In *Origins of African plant domestication*, eds. J.R. Harlan, J.M.J. de Wet and A.B.L. Stemler, 187–209. Mouton, The Hague.

Murdock, G.P. 1959. *Africa: its peoples and their culture history.* McGraw-Hill, New York.

Nenquin, J. 1961. *Salt: A study in economic prehistory.* Dissertationes Archaeologicae Gandenses, Vol. 6. De Tempel, Bruges, Belgium.

Nenquin, J. 1963. *Excavations at Sanga, 1957: the protohistoric necropolis.* Musée Royal de l'Afrique Centrale, Tervuren, Belgium.

Nzewunwa, N. 1980. *The Niger Delta: Aspects of its prehistoric economy and culture.* Cambridge Monographs in African Archaeology 1, BAR International Series 75, Oxford.

O'Connor, A.M. 1981. *Urbanization in tropical Africa, an annotated bibliography.* Hall, Boston.

Ojo, G.J.A. 1966a. *Yoruba culture.* University of London Press, London.

Ojo, G.J.A. 1966b. *Yoruba palaces.* University of London Press, London.

Oliver, P. (ed.) 1971. *Shelter in Africa*. Praeger, New York.

Oliver, R. 1959a. The royal tombs of Buganda. *Uganda Journal* 23(2), 124–33.

Oliver, R. 1959b. Ancient capital sites of Ankole. *Uganda Journal* 23(1), 51–63.

Oliver, R. and Fagan, B.M. 1975. *Africa in the Iron Age*. Cambridge University Press, Cambridge.

Oliver, R. and Fage, J.D. 1962. *A short history of Africa*. Penguin, Harmondsworth.

Oxford English Dictionary. 1933. Volume X, Clarendon Press, Oxford (1970 reprint).

Ozanne, P. 1969. A new archaeological survey of Ife. *Odu* (N.S.) 1, 28–45.

Pankhurst, R. 1961. *An introduction to the economic history of Ethiopia from early times to 1800*. Lalibela House, distributed by Sidgwick & Jackson, London.

Pankhurst, R. 1979. Ethiopian medieval and post-medieval capitals: their development and principal features. *Azania* 14, 1–19.

Phillipson, D.W. 1977a. *The later prehistory of eastern and southern Africa*. Heinemann, London.

Phillipson, D.W. 1977b. The excavation of Gobedra rock-shelter, Axum: an early occurrence of cultivated finger millet in northern Ethiopia. *Azania* 12, 53–82.

Phillipson, D.W. 1979. Some Iron Age sites in the lower Tana Valley. *Azania* 14, 155–60.

Phillipson, D.W. 1985. *African archaeology*. Cambridge University Press, Cambridge.

Phimister, I.R. 1974. 'Ancient' mining near Great Zimbabwe. *Journal of the South African Institute of Mining and Metallurgy* 74, 233–7.

Phimister, I.R. 1976. Pre-colonial gold mining in southern Zambezia: a reassessment. *African Social Research* 21, 1–30.

Pigafetta, F. 1591. *A report of the Kingdom of Congo*, translated by M. Hutchinson, 1881. Murray, London.

Pirenne, J. 1970. Haoulti, Gobochela (Melazo) et le site antique. *Annales d'Ethiopie* 8, 117–27.

Pitt Rivers, Lieutenant-General. 1900. *Antique works of art from Benin*. Printed privately, London.

Portères, R. 1970. Primary cradles of agriculture in the African continent, In *Papers in African prehistory*, eds. J.D. Fage and R.A. Oliver, 43–58. Cambridge University Press, Cambridge. (Originally published in 1962 in French in *Journal of African history* 3(2), 195–210.)

Posnansky, M. 1968. The excavation of an Ankole capital site at Bweyorere. *Uganda Journal* 32(2), 165–82.

Posnansky, M. 1969. Bigo bya Mugenyi. *Uganda Journal* 33(2), 125–50.

Posnansky, M. 1973. Aspects of early West African trade. *World Archaeology* 5(2), 149–62.

Posnansky, M. 1975. Connections between the lacustrine peoples and the coast. In *East Africa and the Orient: Cultural syntheses in pre-colonial times*, eds. N. Chittick and R.I. Rotberg, 216–25. Africana Publishing Company, New York and London.

Posnansky, M. 1976. Archaeology and the origins of the Akan society in Ghana. In

Problems in economic and social archaeology, eds. G. de G. Sieveking, et al., 49–59. Duckworth, London.

Posnansky, M. 1980. Trade and the development of the state and town in Iron Age West Africa. In *Proceedings of the 8th Panafrican Congress of Prehistory and Quaternary Studies, Nairobi, 5 to 10 September 1977.* eds. R.E. Leakey and B.A. Ogot, 373–5. The International Louis Leakey Memorial Institute for African Prehistory, Nairobi.

Posnansky, M. and McIntosh, R. 1976. New radiocarbon dates for Northern and Western Africa. *Journal of African History* 17(2), 161–95.

Powell, J.E. (trans.) 1949. *Herodotus*, 2 vols. Clarendon Press, Oxford.

Price, B.J. 1978. Secondary state formation: an explanatory model. In *Origins of the state: The anthropology of political evolution*, eds. R. Cohen and E.L. Service, 161–86. Institute for the Study of Human Issues, Philadelphia.

Prins, A.H.J. 1982. The *mtepe* of Lamu, Mombasa and the Zanzibar sea. In *From Zinj to Zanzibar: Studies in history, trade and society on the eastern coast of Africa*, (*Paideuma* 28), eds. J. de V. Allen and T.H. Wilson, 85–100.

Prins, G. 1980. *The hidden hippopotamus: Reappraisal in African history: the early colonial experience in western Zambia.* Cambridge University Press, Cambridge.

Ramos, M. 1980. Une enceinte (Monomotapa?) peu connue du plateau du Songo, Mozambique. In *Proceedings of the 8th Panafrican Congress of Prehistory and Quaternary Studies, Nairobi, 5 to 10 September 1977.* eds. R.E. Leakey and B.A. Ogot, 373–5. The International Louis Leakey Memorial Institute for African Prehistory, Nairobi.

Randall-MacIver, D. 1971. *Mediaeval Rhodesia*, reprint, Cass, London, (1st ed. 1906).

Randles, W.G.L. 1968. *L'ancien royaume du Congo.* Mouton, Paris.

Randles, W.G.L. 1972. Pre-colonial urbanization in Africa south of the Equator. In *Man, settlement and urbanism*, eds. P.J. Ucko, R. Tringham and G.W. Dimbleby, 891–7. Duckworth, London.

Rathje, W.L. 1971. The origin and development of lowland Maya classic civilization. *American Antiquity* 36, 275–85.

Rathje, W.L. 1972. Praise the gods and pass the metates: A hypothesis of the development of lowland rainforest civilizations in Mesoamerica. In *Contemporary archaeology*, ed. M.P. Leone, 365–92. Southern Illinois University Press, Carbondale.

Ravenstein, E.G. 1898. *A journal of the first voyage of Vasco da Gama, 1497–1499*, (translated and edited). Hakluyt Society, London.

Reefe, T.Q. 1981. *The rainbow and the kings: a history of the Luba Empire to 1891.* University of California Press, Berkeley.

Reisner, G.A. 1923. *Excavations at Kerma*, Parts I–III, Parts IV–V, Harvard African Studies Vol. V & VI. Peabody Museum of Harvard University, Cambridge, Massachusetts.

Renfrew, C. 1972. *The emergence of civilization: the Cyclades and the Aegean in the third millennium BC.* Methuen, London.

Renfrew, C. 1983. The emergence of civilization. In *The encyclopedia of ancient civilizations*, ed. A. Cotterell, 12–20. Macmillan, London.

Richards, P.W. 1952. *The tropical rain forest: an ecological study*. Cambridge University Press, Cambridge.

Ricks, T.M. 1970. Persian Gulf seafaring and East Africa: ninth–twelfth centuries. *African Historical Studies* 3(2), 339–57.

Robert, D. 1970. Les fouilles de Tegdaoust. *Journal of African History* 11, 471–93.

Robert, D., Robert, S. and Devisse, J. (eds.) 1970. *Tegdaoust: Recherches sur Aoudaghost*, Vol. 1. Arts et Métiers Graphiques, Paris.

Robert, S. and Robert, D. 1972. Douze années de recherches archéologiques en République Islamique de Mauritanie. *Annales de la Faculté des Lettres et Sciences Humaines, Université de Dakar* 2, 195–233.

Robins, P.A. and Whitty, A. 1966. Excavations at Harleigh Farm, near Rusape, Rhodesia. *South African Archaeological Bulletin* 21, 61–80.

Robinson, K.R. 1959. *Khami ruins: report on excavations undertaken for the Commission for the Preservation of Natural and Historical Monuments and Relics, Southern Rhodesia, 1947–1955*. Cambridge University Press, Cambridge.

Robinson, K.R., Summers, R. and Whitty, A. 1961. *Zimbabwe excavations 1958*. Occasional Papers. The National Museums of Southern Rhodesia, 3(23A), 157–332.

Roese, P.M. 1981. Erdwälle und Gräben im ehemaligen Königreich von Benin. *Anthropos* 76, 166–209.

Roth, H.L. 1903. *Great Benin: its customs, art and horrors*. King, Halifax.

Ryder, A.F.C. 1969. *Benin and the Europeans, 1485–1897*. Longmans, London.

Saliège, J.F. et al. 1980. Premières datations de tumulus pré-islamiques au Mali: site mégalithique de Tondidarou. *C.R. Acad. Sc. Paris Série D* 291, 981–4.

Sassoon, H. 1980. Excavations at the site of early Mombasa. *Azania* 15, 1–42.

Sayce, A.H. 1911. Part II – The historical results. Second interim report on the excavations at Meroë in Ethiopia. *Annals of Archaeology and Anthropology* 4, Liverpool Institute of Archaeology, Liverpool University Press, Liverpool.

Sergew, H.S. 1972. *Ancient and medieval Ethiopian history to 1270*. United Printers, Addis Ababa.

Service, E.R. 1975. *Origins of the state and civilization: the process of cultural evolution*. Norton, New York.

Shaw, T. 1970. *Igbo-Ukwu*, 2 vols. Faber and Faber, London.

Shaw, T. 1973. A note on trade and the Tsoede Bronzes. *West African Journal of Archaeology* 3, 233–8.

Shaw, T. 1975a. *Why 'darkest' Africa? Archaeological light on an old problem*. The University Lectures 1974, Ibadan University Press, Ibadan.

Shaw, T. 1975b. Those Igbo-Ukwu radiocarbon dates: facts, fictions and probabilities. *Journal of African History* 16(4), 503–17.

Shaw, T. 1977a. Hunters, gatherers and first farmers in West Africa. In *Hunters, gatherers and first farmers beyond Europe*, ed. J.V.S. Megaw, 69–125. Leicester University Press, Leicester.

Shaw, T. 1977b. *Unearthing Igbo-Ukwu*. Oxford University Press, Ibadan.

Shaw, T. 1978. *Nigeria: Its archaeology and early history*. Thames and Hudson, London.

Shaw, T. 1980. New data on the pre-European civilizations of southern Nigeria. In *Proceedings of the 8th Panafrican Congress of Prehistory and Quaternary Studies,*

Nairobi, 5 to 10 September 1977, eds. R.E. Leakey and B.A. Ogot, 376–8. The International Louis Leakey Memorial Institute for African Prehistory, Nairobi.

Shaw, T. 1984. Archaeological evidence and effects of food-producing in Nigeria. In *From hunters to farmers: the causes and consequences of food production in Africa*, eds. J.D. Clark and S.A. Brandt, 152–7. University of California Press, Berkeley.

Shepherd, G. 1982. The making of the Swahili: a view from the southern end of the East African coast. In *From Zinj to Zanzibar: Studies in history, trade and society on the eastern coast of Africa*, (*Paideuma* 28), eds. J. de V. Allen and T.H. Wilson, 129–47.

Shinnie, M. 1965. *Ancient African Kingdoms*. Arnold, London.

Shinnie, P.L. 1955. *Excavations at Soba*. Sudan Antiquities Service, Occasional Papers No. 3, Khartoum.

Shinnie, P.L. 1960. Excavations at Bigo, 1957. *Uganda Journal* 24(1), 16–28.

Shinnie, P.L. 1967. *Meroë: a civilization of the Sudan*. Thames and Hudson, London.

Shinnie, P.L. and Bradley, R.J. 1980. *The capital of Kush 1: Meroë excavations 1965–1972*, (*Meroitica* 4). Akademie-Verlag, Berlin.

Shinnie, P.L. and Kense, F.J. 1982. Meroitic iron working. *Meroitica* 6, 17–28, 43–9.

Shinnie, P.L. and Shinnie, M. 1978. *Debeira West: a mediaeval Nubian town*. Aris & Phillips, Warminster, England.

Siddle, D.J. 1968. War-towns in Sierra Leone: a study in social change. *Africa* 38(1), 47–56.

Simoons, F.J. 1965. Some questions on the economic prehistory of Ethiopia. *Journal of African History* 6(1), 1–12.

Sinclair, P. 1981. An archaeological outline of two social formations of the Late Iron Age in Zimbabwe and Mocambique. *Resumenes de Comunicaciones, Seccion VIII, Union Internacional de Ciencias Prehistoricas y Protohistoricas, X Congreso, Mexico*, 64–5.

Sinclair, P. 1982. Chibuene – An early trading site in southern Mozambique. In *From Zinj to Zanzibar: Studies in history, trade and society on the eastern coast of Africa* (*Paideuma* 28), eds. J. de V. Allen and T.H. Wilson, 149–64.

Sinclair, P. 1984. Some aspects of the economic level of the Zimbabwe state. In *Papers presented in honour of Miss G. Caton-Thompson*, (*Zimbabwea* 1), National Museums and Monuments of Zimbabwe, 48–53.

Sinclair, P. and Lundmark, H. 1984. A spatial analysis of archaeological sites from Zimbabwe. Paper read at the conference of the Southern African Association of Archaeologists, Gabarone, Botswana, 1983, In *Frontiers: Southern African archaeology today*, eds. M. Hall, et al., 277–88. Cambridge Monographs in African Archaeology, 10, BAR International Series 207, Oxford.

Sjoberg, G. 1960. *The preindustrial city*. Free Press of Glencoe, Illinois.

Smith, R. 1970. The canoe in West African history. *Journal of African History* 11(4), 515–33.

Spear, T.T. 1978. *The Kaya Complex: a history of the Mijikenda peoples of the Kenya coast to 1900*. Kenya Literature Bureau, Nairobi.

Speke, J.H. 1863. *Journal of the discovery of the source of the Nile.* Blackwood, London.

Stanley, H.M. 1878. *Through the Dark Continent,* 2 vols + maps. Sampson Low, Marston, Searle & Rivington, London.

Summers, R. 1958. *Inyanga: prehistoric settlements in Southern Rhodesia.* Cambridge University Press, Cambridge.

Summers, R. 1963. *Zimbabwe: a Rhodesian mystery.* Nelson, Johannesburg.

Summers, R. 1967. Archaeological distributions and a tentative history of tsetse infestation in Rhodesia and the Northern Transvaal. *Arnoldia* (Rhodesia). Series of miscellaneous publications, National Museums of Southern Rhodesia 3(13), 1–18.

Summers, R. 1969. *Ancient mining in Rhodesia and adjacent areas.* Museum Memoir No. 3, Trustees of the National Museums of Rhodesia. Salisbury, Rhodesia.

Sutton, J.E.G. 1982. Archaeology in West Africa: a review of recent work and a further list of radiocarbon dates. *Journal of African History* 23(3), 291–313.

Sutton, J.E.G. and Roberts, A.D. 1968. Uvinza and its salt industry. *Azania* 3, 45–86.

Szumowski, G. 1957. Fouilles au nord du Macina et dans la région de Ségou. *Bulletin de l'IFAN.* Dakar, 19(B), 224–58.

Tamrat, T. 1972. *Church and state in Ethiopia 1270–1527.* Clarendon Press, Oxford.

Theal, G.M. ed. 1964. *Records of south-eastern Africa,* 9 vols. Printed for the Government of the Cape Colony, 1898–1903, facsimile reprint, Struik, Cape Town.

Thilmans, G. and Descamps, C. 1974. Le site mégalithique de Tiékène-Boussoura (Sénégal): Fouilles de 1973–1974. *Bulletin de l'IFAN.* Dakar, 36(B), 447–96.

Thilmans, G. and Descamps, C. 1975. Le site mégalithique de Tiékène-Boussoura (Sénégal): Fouilles de 1974–1975. *Bulletin de l'IFAN.* Dakar, 37(B), 259–306.

Thomassey, P. and Mauny, R. 1951. Campagne de fouilles à Koumbi Saleh. *Bulletin de l'IFAN.* Dakar, 13(1), 438–62.

Thomassey, P. and Mauny, R. 1956. Campagne de fouilles de 1950 à Koumbi Saleh (Ghana?). *Bulletin de l'IFAN.* Dakar, 18(B), 117–40.

Thorp, C. 1984. A cultural interpretation of the faunal assemblage from Khami Hill Ruin. Paper read at the conference of the Southern African Association of Archaeologists, Gabarone, Botswana, 1983. In *Frontiers: Southern African archaeology today,* eds. M. Hall, et al., 266–76. Cambridge Monographs in African Archaeology 10, BAR International Series 207, Oxford.

Trigger, B.G. 1965. *History and settlement in Lower Nubia.* Yale University Publications in Anthropology Number 69, New Haven.

Trigger, B.G. 1969a. The myth of Meroë and the African Iron Age. *African Historical Studies* 2(1), 23–50.

Trigger, B.G. 1969b. The social significance of the diadems in the royal tombs at Ballana. *Journal of Near Eastern Studies* 28(4), 255–61.

Trigger, B.G. 1970. The cultural ecology of Christian Nubia. In *Kunst und Geschichte Nubiens in Christlicher Zeit,* ed. E. Dinkler, 347–79. Aurel Bongers, Recklinghausen.

Trigger, B.G. 1973. Meroitic language studies: strategies and goals. In *Sudan im Altertum*, ed. F. Hintze. Internationale Tagung für meroitische Forschungen in Berlin 1971. *Meroitica* 1, Akademie-Verlag, Berlin, 243–72.

Trigger, B.G. 1982. Reisner to Adams: paradigms of Nubian cultural history. In *Nubian studies: proceedings of the Symposium for Nubian Studies, Selwyn College, Cambridge, 1978*, ed. J.M. Plumley, 223–6. International Society for Nubian Studies, Aris & Phillips, Warminster, England.

Turner, G. 1984. Vertebrate remains from Lekkerwater. *South African Archaeological Bulletin* 39, 106–8.

Ullendorff, E. 1960. *The Ethiopians: an introduction to country and people*, Oxford University Press, London.

Vanacker, C. 1979. *Tegdaoust II: recherches sur Aoudaghost: fouille d'un quartier artisanal*. Institut Mauritanien de la Recherche Scientifique No. 2.

Van Noten, F.L. 1972. *Les tombes du Roi Cyirima Rujugira et de la Reine-Mère Nyirayuhi Kanjogera: description archéologique*. Musée Royal de l'Afrique Centrale, Tervuren, Belgium.

Van Noten, F.L. 1982. The Iron Age in the north and east. In *The archaeology of Central Africa*, ed. F.L. Van Noten, 69–76. Akademische Drück – und Verlagsanstalt, Graz, Austria.

Vantini, G. 1970. *The excavations at Faras, a contribution to the history of Christian Nubia*. Nigrizia, Bologna.

Vercoutter, J. 1962. Un palais des 'Candaces', contemporain d'Auguste (Fouilles à Wad-ban-Naga 1958–1960). *Syria: revue d'art oriental et d'archéologie* 39, 263–99.

Verin, P. 1976. The African element in Madagascar. *Azania* 11, 135–51.

Waller, H. 1874. *The last journals of David Livingstone, in Central Africa, from 1865 to his death ...*, 2 vols. Murray, London.

Wayland, E.J. 1934. Notes on the Biggo bya Mugenyi: some ancient earthworks in northern Buddu. *Uganda Journal* 2(1), 21–32.

Webster, J.B. ed. 1979. *Chronology, migration and drought in interlacustrine Africa*. Longman, London.

Weeks, K.R. 1967. *The Classic Christian townsite at Arminna West*. Publications of the Pennsylvania-Yale Expedition to Egypt, Number 3. New Haven and Philadelphia.

Welsby, D. 1984. Preliminary report on excavations at Soba East, 1983–84. *Nyame Akuma* 24/25, 35–6.

Wheeler, Sir M. 1956. The first towns? *Antiquity* 30, 132–6.

Wilks, I. 1962. A medieval trade-route from the Niger to the Gulf of Guinea. *Journal of African History* 3(2), 337–41.

Willett, F. 1967. *Ife in the history of West African sculpture*. Thames and Hudson, London.

Willett, F. 1977. *Baubles, bangles and beads; trade contacts of mediaeval Ife*. Thirteenth Melville J. Herskovits Memorial Lecture, Edinburgh University.

Willett, F. and Fleming, S.J. 1976. A catalogue of important Nigerian copper-alloy castings dated by their thermoluminescence. *Archaeometry* 18(2), 135–46.

Wilson, T.H. 1978. *The monumental architecture and archaeology north of the Tana River*. National Museums of Kenya, Xerox.

Bibliography

Wilson, T.H. 1979. Swahili funerary architecture of the north Kenya coast. In *Swahili houses and tombs of the coast of Kenya*, eds. J. de V. Allen and T.H. Wilson. Art and Archaeology Research Papers, London.

Wilson, T.H. 1980. *The monumental architecture and archaeology of the central and southern Kenya coast.* National Museums of Kenya, Xerox.

Wilson, T.H. 1982. Spatial analysis and settlement patterns on the East African coast. In *From Zinj to Zanzibar: Studies in history, trade and society on the eastern coast of Africa*, (*Paideuma* 28), eds. J. de V. Allen and T.H. Wilson, 201–19.

Wittfogel, K.A. 1957. *Oriental despotism.* Yale University Press, New Haven.

Wright, H.T. and Johnson, G.A. 1975. Population, exchange, and early state formation in southwestern Iran. *American Anthropologist* 77, 267–89.

York, R.N. 1973. Excavations at New Buipe. *West African Journal of Archaeology* 3, 1–189.

Zabkar, L.V. 1975. *Apedemak, lion god of Meroë: A study in Egyptian-Meroitic syncretism.* Aris & Phillips, Warminster, England.

Index

Index

Index